Contemporary Cases in Sales Management

Contemporary Cases in Sales Management

Charles M. Futrell
Texas A & M University

The Dryden Press
Hinsdale, Illinois

Acquisitions Editor: Anita Constant
Project Editor: Bernice Gordon
Production Manager: Peter Coveney
Art Director: Stephen Rapley
Cover design by Alan Wendt
Copy editing by Madelyn Roesch

Library of Congress Catalog Card Number: 80-65797
ISBN: 0-03-054736-9
Printed in the United States of America
1 2 3 4 5 6 7 8   090   9 8 7 6 5 4 3 2

The Dryden Press Series in Marketing

Contents

Preface

Contemporary Cases in Sales Management provides both the undergraduate and the graduate student with exposure to situations in
consumer and industrial markets, problems faced by sales managers in
these markets, and the opportunity to choose a course of action in the
relatively risk-free atmosphere of the classroom. Many of the cases
require the integration of information obtained in functional university
courses, e.g., marketing, finance, accounting, into a solution of the case.
The objective of the book is to present material that will assist the
student in making a transition from academic analysis to the practical
application of concepts in real business situations.

  All cases have been class tested over the past three years and deal
with actual industrial situations. The cases involve both large and small
companies and vary in length. They cover all issues basic to sales
management. The book is designed to be used by itself or with other
texts. It has taken almost five years to bring together a group of cases
that are readable, interesting, and challenging. I have not chosen to use
highly quantitative material because through my eight years of experience in sales and contact with sales managers in the U.S.A. and Canada,
I have not seen a necessity to use such material. However, several
cases can be subjected to sales forecasting, statistical, and sales and
marketing cost analysis at a level used by first- and middle-level sales
managers.

Sections of the Book

The book consists of the following six parts. Part One is an introduction to sales management and begins with a case students enjoy and relate to—that of a university newspaper. Part Two involves the importance of sales planning, forecasting, budgeting, and resource allocation. The SB&H case can be analyzed using a computer. The author should be contacted for the computer deck. The important topic of time and territory management is covered by a nice selection of cases. The Representative Rubber Company exercise is an excellent introduction to what is involved in TTM. The ChemGrow, Inc. case can also be analyzed using the computer.

Part Four includes a variety of cases involving sales force staffing and training of sales personnel. Part Five deals with motivation, compensation and leadership. Several general cases are included in Part Six. The David Namer case in this section can be used to indicate the various stages in a sales presentation and the ethical considerations involved. The Mermax Toy Company case can be used as a term project. As would be expected, much of the subject material in the cases does not relate to one specific area. For example, compensation often involves such things as performance appraisal, leadership, and motivation. A short, apparently simple case can be expanded to encompass many topics.

Accompanying the book is a complete, comprehensive *instructor's manual* containing case summaries, objectives, problems, alternative solutions, and for some cases a description of what actually happened in reality. Also included are answers to the questions at the end of the cases and several objective test questions that can be used with each case. I use these as "pop" tests to help keep students motivated to be prepared for class. The manual is designed to greatly reduce preparation time.

Acknowledgments

I have been fortunate to have many people contribute to this book. I am grateful for the guidance of Professor Charles H. Hindersman, Southern Illinois University, and Professor James L. Taylor, University of Alabama. Special thanks go to Professor Darrell Hankins, University of Alabama at Birmingham, for editing several cases for this text. Cases and exercises were contributed by people from all over, including: Professors M. J. S. Collins, Caulfield Institute of Technology (Australia); David Kurtz, Seattle University; Louis E. Boone, University of Central Florida; Conway Rucks and John E. Mertes, both of University of Arkansas at Little Rock; William D. Perreault, Jr., Kevin M. Lebensburger, Rollie Tillman, Jr., and James E. Littlefield all of the University of North Carolina at Chapel Hill; Lawson E. Barclay and Paul E. Thistlethwaite both of Western Illinois University; Barbara A. Pletcher, California State University at Sacramento; Edward A. Riordan, Wayne State University; Gerald Crawford, University of North Florida; James M. Clapper, Wake Forest University; Harry E. Allison, California State University at Hayward; Jeffrey A. Barach, Tulane University; Kendall A. Adams and Adam K. Gehr, Southern Illinois University; Zarrel V. Lambert, Auburn University; Fred Kniffin, University of Connecticut; Dale Varble, Western Michigan University; Subhash C. Jain, University of Connecticut; and James L. Taylor, University of Alabama.

Finally, I express great appreciation to my graduate assistant, Les Levitan, and my Ph.D., graduate, and undergraduate students for their comments on the cases and instructor's notes. Typing and preparation was done by Mrs. Dawn Barton and support given by Sam Gillespie, head of the marketing department. My sincere gratitude goes to The Dryden Press, especially Anita Constant, Bernice Gordon, and Alan Wendt for their expert help. And, a special word of thanks to Madelyn Roesch, my talented copy editor.

The project took my time and attention away from my wife Sue and children Amy and Greg. This book is for them.

Charles M. Futrell

Part 1

Introductory Cases in Sales Management

Case 1

The Battalion

It was a late October afternoon in 1979. Dave Jackson sat in front of a typewriter staring at the blank piece of paper in it.

Jackson was Director of Student Publications at Texas A&M University (TAMU) and was responsible for the university's newspaper, *The Battalion*. As director of the newspaper, he had been asked by his superiors to submit a report suggesting solutions to some of *The Battalion*'s problems. The blank page represented the report so far.

The History of TAMU TAMU was founded as Texas Agricultural and Mechanical College in 1876, and was one of the first land grant colleges founded under the Morrill Act. It is located in College Station in east central Texas, between Dallas and Houston, with experimental stations and research centers throughout Texas.

A&M College grew from its original four students in 1876 to 9,800 students in 1963. In 1963, the name was officially changed to Texas A&M University. TAMU was all male, all military until 1966 when mandatory ROTC enrollment was dropped. In 1967, women were allowed to enroll as full-time students. In 1979, TAMU had an enrollment of 32,000 students, a 100 per cent increase in six years. Growth

This case was prepared by W. Scott Sherman, graduate student, under the direction of Professor Charles M. Futrell. Names, data and events represented herein may be disguised, distorted, or otherwise non-factual. Copyright © 1980.

is slowing, but the enrollment is expected to continue to increase for some time.

TAMU awards undergraduate and graduate degrees in a wide number of disciplines including agriculture, science, engineering, liberal arts, education, and architecture. In addition, TAMU has both a veterinary and a medical school and is one of the largest research institutions in the nation.

The Battalion itself *The Battalion* is Texas A&M University's 22,500 circulation student-run newspaper, first published in 1878. During the academic year the paper is published five times a week, Monday through Friday. Between one and three issues a week are published during holidays and summer months. In a full calendar year, 195 issues are published.

The newspaper's market consists of College Station and the adjoining city of Bryan. Bryan and College Station were six miles apart when TAMU was founded, but, as the university has grown, the two cities grew together into one metropolitan area. Population for the combined cities is approximately 89,000. About 40,000 live in College Station, the remainder in Bryan and surrounding unincorporated areas.

The Battalion concentrates on the university and College Station markets, with marginal coverage of Bryan and other surrounding areas. The major competitor in the area is the Bryan *Eagle*, a daily newspaper with primary emphasis on the permanent, non-university populace of the area. The *Eagle* has attempted to improve student readership, but *The Battalion* still is the stronger force in the campus and university community markets. Exhibit 1 shows the Bryan-College Station area and the primary market areas of each paper.

The Battalion organization The three main departments within *The Battalion* are editorial, advertising, and production.

The editorial department consists solely of students. Jackson serves as an advisor to the editor and teaches an editing course in which students work with the independent staff to produce the paper. The budget for the newspaper is determined by the student publications board working with Jackson and the student editor.

The advertising department is headed by Dolly Dinarella, a professional member of the newspaper's staff. Dinarella has been with the newspaper for several years. The rapid growth in the university and the community have created many changes and problems for her and the advertising department.

In 1975, Dinarella ran the advertising department with the help of one student salesperson. In 1977, a second salesperson was hired, and in 1978, a third was added.

Exhibit 1
The Bryan-College Station area
Newspaper Markets

The Battalion

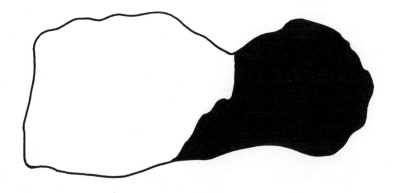

The Bryan *Eagle*

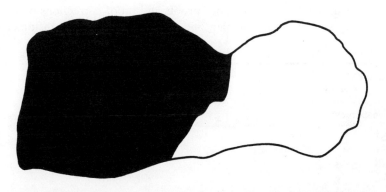

A fourth salesperson was recently hired, primarily to increase the chances that at least two experienced student salespersons would be available during the summer months. In previous summers, Dinarella has been left short-handed when students took off for the summer or graduated.

Dinarella is on salary while the student salespeople are on commission. In the past month, the commission schedule was changed. Previously, salespeople were paid on a commission basis of 15 per cent for the first 250 column inches a month, and 20 per cent on sales above that amount. The salespeople are now paid according to the commission schedule shown in Exhibit 2.

Exhibit 2
Commission Schedule

Inches[a]	Commission
less than 125 inches	.23
125 to 150 inches	.27
150 to 175 inches	.32
175 to 200 inches	.38
200 or more inches	.45

[a]Column inches are arrived at by multiplying the length of an ad in inches by its width in columns. An ad 5 inches in depth running over 2 columns is 10 column inches.

Dinarella is responsible for all major continuing advertisers such as grocery stores and discount houses, as well as national and agency business. Outside of these large accounts, each of the salespeople has an assigned sales territory. The students are responsible for soliciting and maintaining all accounts in their territories not covered by Dinarella. A map of the territories is shown in Exhibit 3.

Responsibilities of the student salespersons include helping the customer design the ad, "running" proofs and proof corrections between the customer and the newspaper, and making sure that the customer's

Exhibit 3
Sales Territories

Salesperson	Graduation date
TST	Dec. 1979
LSY	Aug. 1980
JUK	Dec. 1980
SL	Dec. 1980

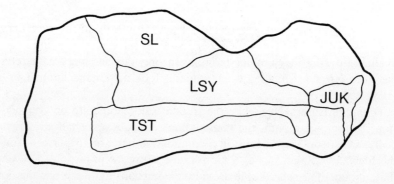

account is not overdue before placing an ad for the customer. Salespeople can not give any discount beyond the volume discount shown in the rate schedule. The rate schedule for *The Battalion* and the Bryan *Eagle* are shown in Exhibit 4.

The commission plan and the sales territory layout have brought complaints from the new salesperson, Sam Lisam. Lisam was hired just before the change in commission schedules. He was anxious to go into sales then and was given an area on the outskirts of Bryan that is beginning to boom.

Two years ago, a Dairy Queen and a local high school were the only major points in the area. Since then, the area has boomed with major commercial development. In the past two months, two new shopping centers have opened and more expansion is expected.

When he started, Lisam impressed Dinarella with his eagerness. However, since the commission change, Lisam has complained about the new setup. Lisam says the commission plan favors large volume and his area presently does not offer much volume. He believes this makes it more difficult for him to do as well financially as the other salespeople. He also points out that some of his customers are reluctant to advertise in *The Battalion* because his area is relatively far from the university. Dinarella is concerned that, if he continues to be dissatisfied, Lisam may not last long.

Dinarella and Jackson must also deal with a heavy demand for advertising space. Advertisers complain to the salespeople they would buy more space if it were available. The salespeople have complained to Dinarella that they could make more sales and more commissions if there were more ad space to sell.

The third department in *The Battalion* is production. *The Battalion* does not own its production facilities, but buys production and press-

Exhibit 4
Ad Rates Per Column Inch

Inches	The Battalion	Eagle
less than 50 inches	2.60	4.04
50 to 100 inches	2.50	4.04
100 to 250 inches	2.40	4.04
250 to 500 Inches	2.30	4.04
500 to 1,000 inches	2.20	4.04
1,000 to 1,500 inches	2.10	4.04
1,500 to 2,500 inches	2.00	4.04
2,500 to 3,500 inches	1.90	4.04
more than 3,500 inches	1.80	4.04

room skills and time from the TAMU Printing Center, a university-owned publications plant. *The Battalion* also pays for supplies used by the printing center to produce the paper.

The leased facilities include a complete composing room where the individual pages are assembled in type, a pressroom where the paper is printed, and loading dock and mailroom facilities from which the paper is distributed.

The Battalion situation in October 1979   *The Battalion* operates on a $480,000-a-year budget. Most of this is generated from advertising revenues, but about $70,000 comes from student subscriptions and $30,000 comes from revenues generated by other student publications. Jackson and his superiors feel the latter $100,000 represents a deficit they would like to see eliminated as soon as possible.

A possible answer to *The Battalion*'s deficit problem would be to increase advertising revenues. As previously mentioned, the rapid growth of the Bryan-College Station area has generated an overwhelming demand for ad space and the advertising department has told Jackson that they could easily fill any additional space given. Where the space would come from is a problem.

Approximately 65 per cent of the space in *The Battalion* is advertising, which is about average for daily newspapers. Jackson's superiors feel it is imperative not to increase the advertising ratio in order to maintain a quality product and continued demand for the newspaper. Postal regulations prevent a newspaper averaging more than 75 per cent advertising from using cheaper bulk rates, and mailed copies account for about 5 per cent of the paper's circulation.

If revenues are increased by maintaining the advertising ratio, but increasing the number of pages, other problems would be involved.

Physical requirements in the pressroom limit the paper to a maximum of sixteen pages per press run. If an issue is over this length, the press has to make two runs, producing two separate sections that then have to be combined in a separate mechanical operation. This double run and insert operation adds about 50 per cent to the pressroom costs for that day's newspaper.

The paper is running at full, 20 sixteen-page capacity, three days a week. Tuesdays and Fridays, the paper is typically twelve pages, with a full press run of sixteen pages on Monday, Wednesday and Thursday. Advertisers favor the mid-week when they get greater coverage because many students leave early for the weekend and Tuesdays have never been good advertising days.

Jackson has discussed with the TAMU printing center the possibility of acquiring a larger press with greater capacity to alleviate the problem. However the cost of a newer, larger press is prohibitive, and there are no capital investment funds available for at least two years because of prior commitments.

Questions

1. What are the problems faced by *The Battalion*, if any?
2. What should be done?

Case 2

Diagraph Bradley Industries, Inc.

"Identifying a package might not seem like an important thing," said Jim Brigham, president of Diagraph Bradley Industries Incorporated, "but when you realize that everything that moves as freight or is identified in cartons on production lines and in storage has to have some kind of mark put on it, then the size and potential of marking tools and supplies takes on an increased importance." The importance of package addressing was first thought about seriously in 1893 by A. J. Bradley, a young St. Louis inventor who had recently patented a paper cutter. Walking to work through part of the wholesale district, Bradley frequently had to make his way around shipping cartons stored on the sidewalk. He found out that the cartons could not be marked fast enough and so overflowed normal storage space.

Soon Bradley had developed and patented a machine he called "the typewriter of the shipping room." It moved a stencil made of thin metal on a carriage that speeded up the cutting of stencils. Nine machines were sold the first year, and the business, incorporated as the Bradley Stencil Machine Company, continued to improve. Stephen Hartog was one of Bradley's first employees. After four years of continuing sales increases, Hartog presented Bradley with an idea for improving the

This case was prepared by Professors Kendall A. Adams and Adam K. Gehr of Southern Illinois University, Carbondale as a basis for class discussion rather than to illustrate either effective or ineffective handling of an administrative situation.

Copyright © 1975 by K. A. Adams and A. K. Gehr.

machine that incorporated interchangeable punches and dies. The cost of making such a machine was considerably lower than that of the present machine and the ease of use could be improved. Bradley rejected the idea and fired Hartog, saying that if he had been doing his work he would not have had time to develop such a thing. Hartog decided to go it alone and manufacture his own stencil-cutting machine which was circular and more compact than Bradley's long carriage machine. In 1898 he went to a well-known St. Louis metal pattern maker, Theodore Remmers, to begin building the required parts. Shortly thereafter Hartog was overtaken by bad times and declared bankruptcy. Remmers satisfied his outstanding claim by taking over the patent rights to the machine. Remmers interested several investors in the possibilities of Hartog's machine and, with the capital raised, formed the Diagraph Company.

The Diagraph Company and American Bakers Machine Company, another firm operated by Remmers, were moved together into a new building in 1900. Production continued satisfactorily for both firms under Remmer's guidance until 1915 when Remmers decided it was time for him to assume fewer responsibilities.

James W. Brigham went to work in the Remmers business in 1913 and assumed full responsibility for Diagraph Company sales in 1915. Soon afterward Brigham began manufacturing ink to be used with the stencils in a basement corner of the plant. Remmers was not encouraging about the ink enterprise, but it was tolerated. Soon after getting underway with ink, Brigham formed the American Oil Board Company which could manufacture a stencil board made of special paper stock impregnated with linseed oil. The stencil board and ink were necessary items for anyone using the Diagraph machine.

Sales progressed steadily and in 1928 Brigham bought the Diagraph Company from Remmers and the other owners. One of the first things he did after the purchase was to add the Brigham Oil Burner to the product line. Within two years the oil burner was declared a failure with $20,000 in losses recognized. Business continued for the stencil machine, ink, and oil board but in an unspectacular way. In 1936 Brigham saw the opportunity to expand sales by buying out the old Bradley Stencil Machine Company, which had more plant capacity and established customers. During World War II demand for stencil cutters and stencil materials increased dramatically. Stencil machine shipments went from 75 per month to 500 per month with almost all sales made to the government.

The war years were good for business, but Brigham began to assess the future of the stencil machine. The first year after the war, sales did decline without much improvement in the second year. The outlook for stencil machines appeared bleak, and Brigham decided to diversify into other products. In 1948 a plant was established in an old ammunitions manufacturing building in Southern Illinois available as surplus through the Federal Government. It was decided to begin by manufacturing a somewhat diversified line of recreation equipment at the new plant and later, as success was identified with certain items, begin to specialize in those items. Brigham enjoyed outdoor sports and imagined that there was an opportunity for improvements in fishing, boating, skiing, baseball, and hunting equipment, and that the future demand in the recreation equipment industry should expand.

The stencil machine, ink, and stencil board facilities remained in St. Louis while Brigham devoted most of his time to the new operation in Southern Illinois. In 1950 a visit by a loan officer from the firm's principal banking source made it quite clear that the bank was going to foreclose on the business unless significant changes in sales and profitability were forthcoming. The new venture in Southern Illinois had failed. Resources accumulated through the war years had been spent. The stencil machine, board, and ink business in St. Louis remained the only bright spot with sales of about $500,000 for 1950. The decision was made to consolidate the business, concentrating on the stencil line, and move the entire operation to Southern Illinois. A new credit line was established with a different bank and the machinery was moved from St. Louis.

Up until the time of the bank representative's visit, James R. Brigham, J. W. Brigham's son, had been working as a salesperson for IBM equipment in the St. Louis area. A series of meetings were called by the president, J. W. Brigham, and his conclusion was to phase out his active participation in company operations. James R. Brigham agreed to begin taking over his father's position.

"The company I took over twenty-five years ago was broke," Jim Brigham said as he looked for a moment at some object on the far wall of his office. "I will never forget that meeting with the loan officer. Dad knew it was coming but it's one of those things that comes as a surprise regardless of how long you expect it. The loan officer said his bank was finished with us, and it was pay up or they would take over the plant. With that Dad took his keys from his pocket and, before anyone could react, he tossed them into the banker's lap saying, 'There it is, if you can run it any better, go to it.' That ended the meeting. The banker put the keys back on Dad's desk and walked out. The Manchester bank took over our account and kept the doors open. Without that bank, we would have closed the doors in a month's time."

"What really saved us," Jim Brigham continued, "was the Korean War. By 1951 our sales for the stencil line were up almost to World War II levels. It seemed that history truly was repeating itself. If so, I knew that a severe slump could be expected at the war's end. I began to appreciate my Dad's position and realized that his venture into the sporting goods line, which at the time seemed pretty ill conceived to me, was his response to the sales slump he knew was inevitable. Stencil system sales simply could not maintain their wartime levels. Something had to take the place of wartime stencil sales."

Product Development "New-product policy was very much on my mind. I knew it was the key to independence from the kinds of war-related cycles we had seen. At the same time I knew the stencil line had been a steady item that had saved us more than once. Since the Korean War demand kept the plant busy and running fairly smoothly, I decided to take advantage of the situation by traveling and visiting our dealer organization. At that time it seemed that we had pretty thin representation in many areas and I wanted to improve that situation. It was during a visit to our sales agent in Portland, Oregon that I noticed something interesting. Someone in their organization had experimented with a roller ink applicator. It was a rubber cylinder that was rolled on an ink pad and then run over a stencil. The inked roller took the place of the ink brush generally used in applying the ink to the stencil. It was a good idea because the ink brush had always been a problem in the system. The roller was neater, faster, and would probably be more durable. The only problem with the roller was that it was not completely satisfactory. The ink disintegrated the latex roller and, because of its watery consistency, smeared the stencil. Anyway, the idea stayed with me and I talked about it with my engineer and others. As the idea progressed, we called in an ink chemist as a consultant and he helped us produce the present alcohol-based ink which was compatible with the latex roller and had the proper consistency. It seems strange that such a simple thing as this roller ink applicator should take so long to develop, but by early 1954 we had the item, called Rol-Flo, ready for sale. It was instantly successful and helped a lot as the Korean War sales dropped."

The applicator had a latex roller fitting a frame that screwed into a plastic bottle holding the ink supply. The alcohol-based ink was not the same as the regular brush-applied ink so that all applicator sales automatically produced extra ink sales at about four times the price of brush ink. None of the applicator features was patentable but even so it was over four years before competition began to copy the latex roller applicator. According to Jim Brigham, the competition just could not believe anyone would pay the higher price for special ink and applicator when the same job could be done with a brush and regular ink.

Soon after the acceptance of the roller applicator was ensured, a salesperson from New Jersey mentioned in a report a fountain pen about the size of a cigar with a felt-tipped point that was being used to apply marking ink. This applicator was used to write on or mark the item free-hand, without a stencil. Samples were purchased and it was quickly seen that this refillable pen was a potentially useful item, but it had a major problem not unlike that found with the roller applicator. When the consistency of the ink was suitable for marking, it was too thin to keep in the pen. As a result, the pen leaked, making it very difficult and disagreeable to handle, carry, and store. The problem was solved by Diagraph's engineer, who developed a metal valve that controlled ink flow and the position of the felt tip. This item was introduced in early 1958 and achieved excellent market acceptance immediately.

Again, as with the roller applicator, the felt pen was not patented, but competition was not quick to respond with a competing item. The Mark-X, as the new pen was called, sold for about eleven dollars per dozen, while ink bought for seven dollars a gallon would supply enough to fill about four dozen felt-tipped pens. The Mark-X was disposable, so refilling was not possible. According to Brigham, the competition was again betting that the trade would not pay such a high price for ink, which is really what they were buying in the Mark-X, but Brigham explained that convenience had been overlooked for years by the marking industry. The customer who bought the Mark-X was actually buying speed, convenience, labor saving, and legibility in his package marking.

While the Mark-X was being developed, there had been talk about the new paper stencils being manufactured by one of Diagraph's principal competitors and another manufacturer of stencils. These stencils were about three by four inches and came with the original and a carbon attached. Their margin was punched to fit the cogs on card-fed electronic print machines used to print invoices. By attaching the paper stencils to the paper invoice stock and feeding both into the printer, one could print the address stencil at the same time the address on the invoice was being printed. The precut stencil would be attached to the shipping room invoice thus eliminating some stencil cutting in the shipping room. Larger stencils would have to be cut by the traditional method.

It began to appear that another industry, the manufacturers of paper forms, had come up with a potentially dangerous competitor to the traditional stencil. However, further investigation turned up some familiar problems. The paper stencil was small, thin, and fragile. Ordinary applicators could not be used to apply ink to the stencil. What had been developed by Diagraph's competitors was a convex pad containing ink. The paper stencil was clipped to the pad and held against the item to be marked. A rocking or rolling motion would force ink through the paper stencil, but the ink did not always behave as desired. Too much pressure or too wet a pad would cause smudging or ruin the stencil entirely. It was clear that the application part of the system had not been worked out satisfactorily by the paper form manufacturers and this is where Diagraph saw an opportunity. The result was the introduction in 1964 of the Duplicator line which consisted of the tissue stencil form, the applicator, called Siphon-Flo, the ink used in the applicator, and a metal-backed inking pad. The stencils came in four forms with five types of inking pad. The Siphon-Flo acted as a handle when attached to an inking pad, making an ink applicator designed specifically for the use of machine cut (either electronic or typewriter) paper stencils. The latex inking pad used a lot of the technology already developed for Rol-Flo. The Siphon-Flo consisted of a non-refillable plastic squeeze bottle with a sealed valve to control ink flow much as in the Mark-X. Faster methods of clipping the stencil to the pad were developed by Diagraph along with storage hangers that kept the ink pad clean and easy to re-use. The Duplicator line was considered successful although somewhat less so than the Rol-Flo and Mark-X because competition had come into the market early in the development of the system. However, the Diagraph entry was technically superior to the competition.

While typical order size for the Rol-Flo, Mark-X, and Duplicator line products was between $25 to $55, there was a built-in repeat sales factor. Each of the items either became used up or required supply items for their use, so that the relatively small orders would often add up to $1,000 annually.

Between 1954 and 1964 the financial success of these three items permitted the acquisition and financing of several distributorships. Two distributorships were acquired outright as subsidiaries, while others were set up by providing financial assistance to former Diagraph salespeople who wanted to go into business for themselves in a territory not presently covered. In this manner Jim Brigham developed what he refers to as controlled distribution, and the maintenance and continuance of this distribution system represents for him, as president of Diagraph, one of his foremost objectives. Controlled distribution was his way of ensuring that customers could depend on Diagraph as a source of supply and maintenance service. While product quality was important, and Diagraph had done a good job in this area, he felt that Diagraph's success during the past ten years was due primarily to the controlled distribution plan. This plan provided customers with a supply-service combination that his competitors had been noticeably unable to match.

At almost the same time that Diagraph became aware of the market entry of paper stencils, they also learned of another new development having potential competitive overtones. Instead of printing stencils that could be used to print address or other labels on boxes or containers, this new machine printed the label on a piece of paper that could be glued and stuck to the container or, if the paper stock was already glued, the label could be moistened with water and applied. It was actually a mini printing press, weighing about thirty-five pounds, that could print two by four to about four by four inch labels rapidly. Each label would have exactly the same information on it and be precut to the same dimension. Normally about one hundred labels could be printed per minute using this machine. The type on the print cylinder could be changed quite easily when label information had to be changed.

One of the machines was purchased and examined for possible design improvements. The machine was found to be well designed and attractively encased in a blue-gray steel housing resembling the new electric typewriters that had gained so much acceptance. After some study the Diagraph engineer and his staff came up with two principal recommendations that they thought would increase the usefulness of the machine. The inking system on the competitive machine could be improved and an adjustment could be built into the machine that would make it possible to adjust the length of the label. Of the two, the adjustment of label length was thought to be the more important improvement.

With the possibilities of these improvements in mind, Jim Brigham decided, after consultation with various people whose judgment he respected, to go ahead with development of a label-printing machine. Diagraph's machine, called the DiPrinter, was available for sale in 1968.

The DiPrinter featured a choice of two printing methods. One method incorporated a rubber mat in which pressure sensitive type could be inserted to quickly make up whatever message was desired. The rubber mat locked to a brass cylinder that rotated against a visible inking fountain and then against the paper stock on which the message was printed. Besides being clearly visible, the inking fountain could be detached easily for refilling and its very precise metal metering devices could be adjusted easily without tools to ensure an even flow of the correct amount of ink.

The DiPrinter's other printing method used a stencil that was attached to a rotating brass cylinder similar to the one used with the rubber mat. However, the ink supply for the stencil was contained in an ink-impregnated, disposable latex mat that is slipped over the drum before the stencil is attached. The latex mat is similar to the one used for Rol-Flo.

While the DiPrinter was considered market ready and shown in the catalog in 1968, sales results were disappointing. Prior to listing, a few machines had been field tested, with some minor mechanical modifications resulting. The machine was considered by users, Diagraph's engineering staff, and salespeople to be sound mechanically. The only remark made by users was a request for more accessory equipment and a greater variety of stencils and inks. Diagraph management anticipated expanding accessories and supplies as the DiPrinter became established, so this request was not a surprise. However, the negligible sales were not anticipated, and Brigham knew he had to find out why they were low.

Very soon after introduction Brigham became aware that this machine did not fit the selling methods used for the other products. If he hired salespeople to specialize in selling the DiPrinter, he ran the danger of antagonizing his present sales force. On the other hand, the sales force was not selling the item. Brigham thought that if he knew more about customer purchasing behavior for an item such as this, he could devise better policies for sales management and salesperson training. Two consultants did field interviews for him on this topic, but the results were inconclusive. By inquiring around, it was found that the sales manager of the competing label-printer manufacturer, Art Wagner, might be interested in a move. Shortly thereafter, Wagner was hired and given a vice-presidential position with full sales authority for the Diagraph DiPrinter. Sales began to improve almost immediately.

Shortly after the DiPrinter was introduced, information was received in a salesperson's report about a friction-operated marking machine to be attached to roller or power conveyors. This machine utilized a printing plate, moveable type faces, and a cylindrical ink-impregnated plastic inking pad similar to the one used on the DiPrinter. Diagraph contracted with the present manufacturer to make some machines under Diagraph's DiCoder brand. A purchase agreement was reached quickly with the manufacturer, Gottscho, so that the DiCoder was available for marketing in 1968. The only limiting stipulation in the agreement was that the DiCoder was not to be sold in foreign countries.

A complete and installed DiCoder would cost the purchaser about $350. While noticeably less than that of the DiPrinter, this purchase price was still considerably higher than the price of the older Diagraph products. Furthermore, the DiCoder was an equipment item, not a supply item, and the purchase decision was frequently complex. It was more suited to manufacturing applications, while the traditional Diagraph line was used in the shipping room. Brigham asked for a review of the Gottscho agreement during a conversation with the company lawyer, and was subsequently told that the agreement was not binding because it contained expired patents. Thus, by 1972 Diagraph was in a position to manufacture and market its own DiCoder.

The New Sales Manager   George Buys was moved to the home office to take over as DiCoder sales manager after eight years of exceptional selling performance for a Diagraph distributor. George traveled extensively demonstrating the DiCoder to salespeople and assisting in

DiCoder sales to prospects when his assistance was requested. Sales increased slightly but soon leveled off even though Buy's efforts in introducing and demonstrating the machine were really quite remarkable. In 1974 George decided to go into business for himself, buying out the wholesale distributor in Minneapolis who handled the Diagraph line along with other non-competing products.

Brigham realized that this opening was one of more than usual importance. Of course he wanted to fill the position with a good person and preferably one who had previous experience with the product line and selling philosophy of Diagraph. However, he also realized that the DiCoder, like the DiPrinter, presented unusual marketing problems. He was not satisfied with the acceptance of the DiCoder by the sales force. As had been true with the DiPrinter, experienced salespeople seemed to be reluctant to prospect for businesses that could use the DiCoder. They preferred to establish a set customer group and concentrate on repeat selling to this group. Also, Diagraph had specialized in products used by shipping room personnel. It was an important part of the Diagraph selling strategy for salespeople to build friendships with shipping room personnel. Purchase approval would be obtained from the shipping room foreman rather than the purchasing agent. The DiCoder, like the DiPrinter, was not a shipping room item, but was more of an item for office or production use. Some sales personnel seemed to be able to cross over and sell in other parts of a customer's plant, but others were not doing it satisfactorily. This uneven acceptance of the DiCoder by the sales force had been a problem from the first, and it had not been resolved. However, a solution was more critical now because of the necessity to fill George's position and to increase sales to take advantage of having acquired all rights to the machine.

Organizational Realignment   Brigham's response was a fairly complex organizational realignment in which Art Wagner took over managership of the Los Angeles sales subsidiary, one of the company's largest and most profitable; John McKevitt became sales vice-president with responsibility for all product lines; and Don Harris was given the title of product manager, with his principal assignment being field sales training and assisting McKevitt in other tasks as assigned. Both McKevitt and Harris came to these headquarters' posts directly from field selling jobs. McKevitt had managed a Diagraph sales branch and Harris had been a salesperson for a Diagraph sales subsidiary.

While the DiCoder did face competition from other similar conveyor driven marking machines, it is important to point out that the competitors (Kiwi, Gottscho, Control Print, Belmark) were all aiming for a different portion of the market. Belmark specialized in marking consumer film-wrapped packages, while the other three firms specialized in large systems application in which the conveyor driven marking machine was only a small part of the system. For the time being, Diagraph was reaping somewhat of a bonus from the sales of the large systems sellers. Evidently so much concentration was going into the systems that, once a system was put in operation, little follow-up selling of needed supplies for the system was occurring. Diagraph salespeople had spotted this opportunity and were selling ink, rollers, and other supply items for use with conveyor driven marking machines sold by competitors.

As Jim Brigham talked about the DiCoder, it was easy to see that he had a lot of satisfaction in the knowledge that Diagraph supplies were being sold to users of competitors' machines. "The way I view the company and its success is not that so much is due to our products as to our sales organization. Fortunately for us, the success of the Mark-X and roller stenciling products provided sufficient revenue to build up our sales force. For example, we just landed an agreement to supply all of Pabst Brewing inking cartridge requirements for the friction driven coders (like the DiCoder) sold to them by one of our competitors. Generally, our competitors just have not solved the problem of sales organization sufficiently to pick up the supply business as well as the machine business. We are the only suppliers of a friction driven coder that can also supply sales and service through a national sales organization." Diagraph management foresaw a potential for expansion into what they perceived to be a vast area of coding specialization while their competitors seemed to be going in the direction of marking systems specialization. Specializing in systems seemed to result in competitors being more interested in selling a series of interrelated coding machines and equipment rather than a single machine, such as the DiCoder, and the supplies for a single machine.

Production All machines produced at the Herrin plant are bench assembled. Addition of a new product to the line calls for pushing together four tables into a square, adding such tools as may be needed to assemble and test the machines, training a man and, perhaps, an assistant to assemble and test the machines. Demand for the DiCoder is low enough that one man can produce enough to fill all orders. The man doing the assembly is given the orders to fill from the warehouse and can schedule himself to produce the needed mix of types of DiCoders. Almost all parts for all machines are made in the machine shop of the plant. There is a complete set of machinery, some automated and semi-automated, to produce any sort of machine part, leaving only the casting and forging to be contracted out. Tools and dies for the machine shop are produced by tool and die makers in an area off the machine shop. The tool and die makers have sufficient slack time that little additional labor cost is incurred in adding new parts to the production line. (The shop workers, indeed, accuse the tool and die makers of taking a perpetual vacation.)

Thus, the addition of a new machine to the line involves the design and manufacture of the necessary tools, calculating EOQ's for the various parts, and putting them into the production schedules for the various machines.

The machines currently used are sufficiently under-utilized so that additional runs may be scheduled without scheduling an extra shift. Diagraph has not had trouble locating machinists as needed. Few skilled production jobs are available in the Southern Illinois area, and natives who have gone to Chicago or elsewhere and taken skilled jobs are generally anxious to leave the city if they can obtain skilled jobs that allow them to enjoy the less pressured life style of Southern Illinois.

The plant is currently not unionized and employee relations and employee morale are good. Although the physical facilities of the plant are old, the care taken about employee safety in the past has enabled Diagraph Bradley to meet current OSHA requirements with a minimum of expense. No further trouble is anticipated with OSHA authorities.

The remainder of the plant is used for warehousing of parts, warehousing of finished goods and shipping materials, housing a shipping department, and manufacturing paper products.

Paper is bought in bulk. That used for stencil board is passed through an oil bath, cut, and dried on special drying racks. Paper for the DiPrinter has to be cut to proper size and spooled.

Finance Exhibits 1 and 2 present the 1974 and 1975 income statements and balance sheets for Diagraph Bradley.

The long-term debt is scheduled to be retired at a rate of $25,000 a year through 1979 and $17,000 a year thereafter. Although the debentures are convertible, it is assumed that the debt will be retired rather than converted. The preferred stock was issued to purchase two wholly-owned subsidiaries: Shippers Supply Company, and Diagraph Bradley of New England. The preferred stock is voting and pays a 7 per cent cumulative dividend. In addition to the liabilities shown on the balance sheet, Diagraph Bradley also has non-cancelable lease commitment that cost $185,283 in 1971 and $160,251 in 1973. The long-term notes payable consist of a revolving credit agreement at ¾ per cent over prime of $343,750 and two 8 per cent loans totaling $211,000 with repayments of $23,000 per year required, along with a few other minor notes and contracts.

Exhibit 3 provides the sources and uses of funds for Diagraph Bradley.

Exhibit 1
Diagraph Bradley Industries, Inc. and
Subsidiaries Consolidated Statement
of Income and Expense 1974 and 1973
Year Ended May 31

	Year Ended May 31		Increase or [Decrease]
	1974	**1973**	
Net Sales	$9,990,461	$8,898,809	$1,091,652
Less cost of goods sold based on direct costs	5,039,508	4,431,043	608,465
Gross profit based on direct costs	4,950,953	4,467,766	483,187
Less direct selling costs	1,250,438	1,096,421	154,017
Profit after direct selling costs	3,700,515	3,371,345	329,170
Less operating expenses:			
Herrin (home office)	1,710,612	1,525,636	184,976
New Jersey	213,488	199,064	14,424
Philadelphia	179,582	158,461	21,121
Metairie	69,432	56,532	12,900
Detroit	69,043	64,009	5,034
Houston	71,176	71,399	[223]
Rochester	52,054	47,338	4,716
St. Louis	53,711	43,338	9,777
Chicago	350,637	318,650	31,987
Ft. Wayne	78,328	76,663	1,665
Los Angeles	98,548	92,494	6,054
Herrin (Midwest branch)	68,410	65,267	3,143
Boston	155,763	144,449	11,314
Total departmental expenses	3,170,784	2,863,896	306,888
Net operating profit	529,731	507,449	22,282
Less net other expenses	108,491	99,946	8,545
Net income before federal income tax	421,240	407,503	13,737
Less provision for federal income tax	190,140	188,415	1,725
Net income for the year	$ 231,100	$ 219,088	$ 12,012
Earnings per share:			
Assuming no dilution	$ 2.31	$ 2.19	$ .12
Assuming full dilution	2.01	1.90	.11

Exhibit 2
Diagraph Bradley Industries, Inc. and
Subsidiaries Condensed Consolidated
Balance Sheets 1974 and 1973
Year Ended May 31

	Year Ended May 31		Increase or [Decrease]
	1974	1973	
Assets			
Current Assets:			
Cash on hand and in bank	$ 379,958	$ 373,507	$ 6,451
Notes and accounts receivable:			
customers (net)	1,159,630	1,067,652	91,978
Other notes and accounts receivable	9,366	17,802	[8,436]
Inventories	1,814,366	1,530,363	284,003
Other current assets	81,194	58,176	23,018
Total current assets	$3,444,514	$3,047,500	$397,014
Investments	160,430	143,369	17,061
Fixed Assets:			
Cost	1,122,429	1,058,495	63,934
Less accumulated depreciation	773,820	719,059	54,761
	348,609	339,436	9,173
Other Assets	117,238	123,875	[6,637]
Total assets	$4,070,791	$3,654,180	$416,611
Liabilities and Net Worth			
Current Liabilities:			
Notes and contracts payable	$ 327,114	$ 114,358	$182,756
Accounts payable: trade	603,498	553,036	50,462
Accrued expenses	285,681	335,661	[49,980]
Other current liabilities	50,432	33,514	16,918
Total current liabilities	$1,266,725	$1,066,569	$200,156
Other liabilities	13,563	11,858	1,705
Long-term debt	796,617	765,986	30,631
Net Worth:			
Capital stock	727,028	727,028	—0—
Paid-in surplus	48,710	48,710	—0—
Retained earnings	1,218,148	1,034,029	184,119
Total net worth	$1,993,886	$1,809,767	$184,119
Total liabilities and net worth	$4,070,791	$3,654,180	$416,611

Exhibit 3
Diagraph Bradley Industries, Inc. and
Subsidiaries Consolidated Statement
of Changes in Financial Position
1974 and 1973 Year Ended May 31

	Year Ended May 31	
	1974	**1973**
Source of Funds:		
Operations:		
Net income from Exhibit 1	$231,100	$219,088
Add [or deduct] items not involving the flow of funds during the year:		
Depreciation and amortization	66,510	61,433
Increase in deferred investment tax credit	1,705	[966]
Unrecovered cost of equipment sold	844	933
Provision for bad debts applicable to non-current notes	[497]	[756]
Funds derived from operations	299,662	279,732
Increase in long-term debt	30,631	—0—
Refund of prior year federal income tax	2,852	—0—
Decrease in non-current notes receivable	995	1,513
Total funds provided	$334,140	$281,245
Application of funds:		
Purchase and construction of fixed assets	69,479	40,183
Dividends paid	43,580	23,580
Increase in sinking fund for debentures	10,000	10,000
Increase in cash value of life insurance	7,560	7,753
Payment of prior year's state taxes	6,253	—0—
Increase in long-term deposits	275	—0—
Patent and trademark costs	135	722
Decrease in long-term debt	—0—	7,277
Total funds applied	$137,282	$191,730
Net increase in working capital	$196,858	$191,730

Analysis of Changes in Working Capital

Increase in current assets:		
Cash	$ 6,451	$149,472
Notes and accounts receivable (net)	83,542	137,772
Inventories	284,003	230,142
Other current assets	23,018	[5,572]
	$397,014	$511,814
Less increase in current liabilities:		
Notes payable	$182,756	[43,269]
Accounts payable	50,462	200,632
Accrued expenses	[49,980]	155,509
Other current liabilities	16,918	7,212
	$200,156	$320,084
Net increase In working capital	$196,858	$191,730

Sales   Sales have expanded from $5 million in 1970–71 to $8 million in 1974–75. Dollar sales by product line is given in Exhibit 4. It should be noted that the sales figures represent both sales to subsidiaries at wholesale and sales by branches at retail. Thus, proportions are slightly distorted if the distribution of sales between these two channels changes. Exhibit 4 also gives gross profit as a percentage of sales for each product line.

Product line definitions in Exhibit 4 include both machines and supplies. Thus, for example, the stencil machine category includes both the machines themselves and the stencil board which is sold for use in the machines.

Building the Sales Force   The introduction of the Mark-X and the roller stencil gave Jim Brigham the funds he needed to begin building a sales force that could be more closely controlled. Up until then, all sales had been through distributors who could handle other products along with Diagraph Bradley. Now Brigham bought out, over a period of three years, two of his largest distributors by exchanging preferred stock for their outstanding common. He also began setting up branches across the country through which Diagraph Bradley sold directly, using its own sales personnel. Finally, Brigham began the practice, which is still continued, of helping long-time employees set up their own distributorships. This has had two beneficial effects. First, it has enabled the corporation to give opportunities for advancement to a number of employees. This is difficult in a closely held small firm. Secondly, it has given Diagraph Bradley a set of highly loyal distributors. Today over one-half of all distributorships are run by former employees. Brigham refers to this distribution system as a "controlled sales force," and strongly believes that it is in a large part responsible for the present strong competitive position of Diagraph Bradley.

Diagraph Bradley sells through three wholly-owned subsidiaries: Diagraph Bradley of New England, Diagraph Bradley of California, and Shipper Supply Company; and through networks of distributors and branches. Distributors are independent businesses with exclusive selling rights in certain areas. Sales to distributors are, of course, at wholesale.

Distributors also may handle lines of closely related, but, of course, not competing products. The distributors' salespeople receive training at Diagraph Bradley. Sales to subsidiaries are recorded at wholesale and profits are paid to the parent corporation as a dividend. The corporation records sales of branches at retail and profits are recorded by Diagraph Bradley.

Exhibit 5 shows the distribution network of Diagraph Bradley.

Questions

1. How is Diagraph management identifying its product development needs and goals?
2. How does Diagraph's product policy relate to sales management?
3. What market and production differences and similarities exist between the traditional Diagraph products and the DiPrinter and DiCoder? How were these differences reconciled? What should management's response be to future product differences and similarities?
4. Evaluate Brigham's feeling that sales expertise is the company's strong point.

Exhibit 4
Percentage of Sales by Product Line

	70–71	71–72	72–73	73–74	74–75	% margin 74–75
Stencil Mach.	12.4	11.5	12.4	11.3	11.8	27.9
Stickfast	1.8	1.8	1.6	1.5	1.4	30.8
Outside Contracts	1.2	.7	.6	.5	.5	– 9.6
Rol it on	7.1	6.5	6.0	5.8	5.1	50.2
Rol-Flo	2.7	2.1	2.1	2.0	2.0	42.6
RIO ink	10.3	9.6	9.4	9.4	8.6	35.
Stencil Bd.	8.1	7.7	6.9	7.3	8.0	27.
Ink Glue	7.4	6.9	7.0	5.1	4.8	33.
Brushes Markers	11.0	10.0	9.8	9.5	8.1	49.2
DiPrinter	1.2	1.6	1.7	2.1	2.5	30.5
Printers	.7	.5	.4	.5	.3	26.9
Label Moisteners	.2	.1	.1	.1	.1	33.3
Aerosols	—	—	—	2.8	3.3	38.4
Duplication	3.2	3.0	3.1	3.1	3.1.	37.3
DiCoder	3.3	4.8	5.9	6.5	6.5	42.2
Duplicating line	12.2	13.3	12.7	12.3	12.3	43.3
Label paper	2.4	3.1	3.8	4.7	5.7	11.6
Jobbing	9.6	12.5	13.7	12.4	12.3	15.9
Staple line	3.7	2.9	1.7	2.6	2.8	—
Duplicating, other	.2	.1	.1	*	*	
Mylar line	1.0	1.1	.8	.5	.6	48.5
Tape mach-el	.1	*	*			
Stitcher		*	*			

Exhibit 5
Diagraph Bradley Distribution Network

	Distributors	Branches	Subsidiaries
AL	Birmingham		
AR	Little Rock		
CA	San Leandro		Commerce (DBC[a])
CO	Denver		
CT		New Haven	
FL	Hialeah		
GA	Lithonia		
IL			Worth (SS[b])
			Pekin (SS)
			Rock Island (SS)
IN	Indianapolis		Fort Wayne (SS)
IA			Davenport (SS)
			Des Moines (SS)
KY	Marcraft		
LA		Metairie	
ME			Portland (DBNE)[c]
MD	Baltimore		
MA			Canton (DBNE)[c]
MI	Grand Rapids	Madison Heights	
MN	St. Paul		
MO	North Kansas City	St. Louis	
NE	Papillion		
NH			Manchester (DBNE)[c]
NJ		Union	
NY		Buffalo	
		Rochester	
		Syracuse	
NC	Fayetteville		
OH	Cincinnati		
	Dayton		
	Cleveland		
	Columbus		
OK	Oklahoma City		
	Tulsa		
OR	Canby		
PA	Pittsburgh	Philadelphia	
RI			Providence (DBNE)[c]
SC	Mauldin		
TN	Nashville		
TX	Dallas	Houston	
	Fort Worth		
	San Antonio		
UT	Ogden		
VA		Richmond	
		Roanoke	
WA	Seattle		
WI	New Berlin		

[a]Diagraph Bradley of California.
[b]Shippers Supply Company.
[c]Diagraph Bradley of New England.

Case 3

Shulton Industries

Shulton Industries is composed of a group of subsidiaries serving the world-wide energy industry through the marketing of top quality products and services. The two major subsidiaries are Oilteck, located in Houston, Texas, and the Forney Corporation, located in Richmond, Virginia. In 1972, a division of Forney was formed to complement their present line of products. This division, Elcon, was located in Houston.

Oilteck was acquired in December 1975 and was Shulton's first operating subsidiary. Its products included pipeline measurement systems, meter testers, custom-engineered rubber products, and replacement components for compressors used in the petroleum, petrochemical, industrial gas, and mining industries.

In November 1977 Shulton acquired the Forney Corporation. Forney's product lines included armored electromechanical cable used primarily in oil and gas well logging and perforating. Forney also manufactures wire rope, to be used by construction, mining, fishing, and oil and gas drilling companies. Elcon markets a broad range of electromechanical cable terminations and connectors to complement Forney's electromechanical cable lines.

Company and personnel names have been changed.

Marketing Plan and Forecasts

Oilteck's projected sales for fiscal 1979 were $22.6 million. Rubber products sales increased from $5.4 million in 1977 to $7.6 million in 1978. The 1979 profit plan projects rubber product sales of $9.9 million. Rubber products will enter fiscal 1979 with a backlog of $3.8 million. Two of Oilteck's largest customers have announced major expansion programs for 1979. During 1978 these two customers accounted for 23 per cent of total rubber products volume.

Oilteck's sales of pipeline/compressor products increased to $11.7 million in 1978. This was a 46 per cent increase over the $8 million in 1977. The majority of this increase could be credited to pipeline measurement systems which accounted for 47 per cent of total pipeline sales. The company entered fiscal 1979 with a backlog of $1.6 million and a sales forecast of only $4.9 million in pipeline systems. This meant that a significant amount of business had to be booked during the first six months of 1979 to reach the desired company-wide sales of $22.6 million.

Finally, sales for compressor parts were projected to be $1.9 million in 1979, up from $1.6 million in 1978.

The Forney Corporation found itself in a position to exploit the unusual opportunities created by the decision of U.S. Steel and ITT to terminate production of electromechanical cable. The total domestic market for this product in 1977 was $48 million. Approximately $20 million of this was in the oil fields, with Forney having 70 per cent of the available market. This represented 86 per cent of the production of electromechanical cable, with the remainder being sold to oceanographic companies. The electromechanical market was expected to grow to $105 million by 1985.

The Forney Corporation considered lack of technical research, limited manufacturing capacity and versatility, and lack of product diversification to be major weaknesses. The division's primary strengths were the excellent quality of the products, and excellent service reputation. Electromechanical sales were projected to reach $2.04 million in 1979. The electromechanical division expected to obtain 90 per cent of the $4 million market left by U.S. Steel, therefore sales percentages would be extremely high in 1979 and 1980 with a leveling off in subsequent years.

The total sales for the industry for wire rope in 1977 was $418 million. Forney's sales were $9.2 million or 2.2 per cent of the market. Seventy-four per cent ($309 million) of the industry total was produced by the eleven major manufacturers of wire rope in the United States with the balance coming from imports. Forney ranked ninth out of eleven with 3 per cent of total domestic sales. The 1979 projection showed $1.7 million in drilling rope sales. Management considers its small percentage of the market to be the major weakness. The five-year forecast for wire rope was based on growth of existing product lines and penetrations into energy-related markets in which the company has had only minimal sales. Mining, quarrying, and construction represented 75 per cent of wire rope sales.

Corporate Goals Dick Vaughan, Chairman of the Board, stated to stockholders, in their 1978 meeting, that Shulton was a profitable, growing manufacturer that found itself in a position to double the size of operations and sales in three or four years.

> Development and implementation of a sound, orderly, and comprehensive growth program is essential to supply the market represented by the former U. S. Steel and ITT customers. Through expanded facilities our customers will be made aware that Shulton can meet their needs, competition will be discouraged, and a broader base of new and diverse product lines will be introduced.

He went on to say, "We are presently considering the following actions:

- capacity expansion.
- penetration of the markets left by the withdrawal of ITT and U. S. Steel from the electromechanical cable area.
- increasing market share in weak areas such as oceanographics and marine support for the electromechanical cable market. Increasing the amount of market share we hold in the wire rope market.
- expansion and diversification of product lines in all areas. This should include creation of a formal Research and Development Department.
- redefining the company from serving only the energy-related markets to serving many diverse markets.
- the development of distribution channels to complement the expansion into new markets, the development of new product lines, and the increase in the amount of products that will be flowing through these channels.
- additions to both the work force and management to provide the proper supervision for these new areas.
- reorganization to expand our present sales personnel or use the services of an industrial middleman."

Shulton's Sales Organization

Shulton had grown so rapidly due to the U.S. energy crisis that little thought had been given to the formal development of a sales organization. Jimmy Brewer had been with Shulton since it began in the early 1960s, and has served as a sales coordinator. His job has been to hire, train, and coordinate the activities of Shulton's eight salespeople: five for Oilteck, two for Forney, and one for Elcon. Several of the management personnel in each of these companies, along with Brewer, are also responsible for selling. The role of the sales personnel has mainly been that of service to customers, giving technical advice on the installation, usage, and repair of the products. Customers come to Shulton without Shulton having to seek them out.

Shortly after Vaughan's talk to the stockholders, Brewer was asked to review the possibility of using a middleman to sell Shulton products. After a careful review of the advantages and disadvantages of using a middleman, Brewer explained his findings and made a recommendation to Dick Vaughan, as shown below.

To: Dick Vaughan
From: Jimmy Brewer
Subject: Hiring a manufacturer's agent to sell Shulton Products

You have asked me to look into the use of middlemen (manufacturer's agents) to sell our products. The following report contains my findings and recommendations. I would welcome the opportunity to further discuss my recommendations with you.

The five agents I contacted each have a sales force of adequate size to sell our products. They solicit orders, charging commission rates ranging from 8 to 12 per cent. The rate depends on the product's selling price, sales volume, and services they perform, and is based on the price paid by the customer. Three of the agents prefer a drop shipment arrangement with the agent making the sale and sending the order to us. Two of the agents will buy from us and provide warehousing; however, their commission rates are higher than those of the others.

The following are what I consider the advantages and disadvantages of using an agent. In essence it depends upon cost, the need for fast market coverage, and the amount of control needed to aggressively sell the product.

Advantages to Using a Manufacturer's Agent   The major advantages to using agents are as follows:

1. Requires fewer resources to enter a market. Less personnel and money would be needed. This is important to new companies, and to companies with little knowledge of how to operate and manage a sales force.
2. Agents already have a sales force, which may be calling on customers that compose our target market. This becomes an easy chan-

nel to quickly obtain geographical sales coverage of target accounts.

3. Sales of a product or product line may be too low to generate enough profits to operate a sales force.
4. An agent may be presently handling "companion" products that would aid in selling our line.
5. We may receive better market information, e.g., on competition, customer needs, potential for new products.

Disadvantages of Using a Manufacturer's Agent   After considering the advantages, we should also consider the following disadvantages of using an agent.

1. The agent, not us, has direct control, i.e., over hiring, firing, and paying the salespeople.
2. It is the agent's salespeople who build the good will and personal relationship with customers, not us.
3. The agents may call on only the easiest to sell, large customers, not the small and medium-sized customers that may make up the bulk of the target market.
4. Because agents sell many product lines, they may be reluctant to aggressively train, promote, and sell our products unless they are high profit, and/or high volume, and/or easy to sell.
5. Agents may be costly to us if their employment results in such things as low selling effort, poor market coverage, little market information feedback, or misrepresenting the product to customers.

How can Shulton get its money's worth? We must carefully select the agent. The agent's present customers should be contacted, along with their clients to see whether an effective selling job is being done. Credit checks, future growth potential, and management resources of the agent should be researched. A specific, formalized business agreement between principal and agent should be developed. All functions to be performed by the agent (e.g., exclusive distribution with agent, training, promotional support, commission rates) must be determined. A fair and equitable commission rate should be paid. If needed, bonuses and contests could be offered. Selling material should be provided to the agents, e.g., catalogs, order forms, suggested sales presentations.

Conclusion   After careful review I do not feel we should use an agent. For us, the disadvantages outweigh their advantages. We could lose our excellent reputation if we chose the wrong agent, and they are expensive. We could go a long way towards developing a quality sales force using the money spent on agents' commissions. We do not need market coverage immediately because our plants are presently producing near capacity. I would like to have the opportunity to discuss with you several ideas I have on developing a quality sales force consistent with your goals for Shulton Industries.

Brewer's Presentation

Two weeks later Vaughan called Brewer and asked him to begin developing a sales program for the corporation. Brewer asked whether it would be possible to first present his general philosophy and ideas to see whether there was agreement. If he was on the right track then he would like to have an opportunity to develop a more detailed sales program. Vaughan agreed and asked that Brewer be present at the board of directors meeting two weeks from Tuesday. He would be allowed one hour on their agenda, of which fifteen minutes would be allocated to his presentation and the remainder of the time spent discussing his ideas.

After careful consideration Brewer decided on six areas for discussion.

Exhibit 1
Shulton's Sales Program

1. Hire one salesperson for every $500,000 in sales.
2. Hire the most qualified people in the job market.
3. Compensate salespeople on a straight commission basis.
4. Develop a market information system.
5. Establish a quality training program.
6. Create one or more sales organizations.

---

1. *Hire one salesperson for every $500,000 in sales.* Brewer reviewed the past sales of Shulton's divisions, examined the role of salespeople, looked at future expected sales, analyzed the size of the competition's sales forces, and came to the conclusion that this "sales to personnel" ratio would be most appropriate.
2. *Hire the most qualified people in the job market.* At a minimum, he wanted an individual with a college degree in engineering who had a reasonable grade point average and a good school record. He was unsure about hiring women, but believed that qualified women should be considered. He was willing to consider applicants with other majors, such as business, but he felt that such individuals should possess high mechanical and selling aptitudes. Over the past four years Brewer had developed friendly relationships with the department heads of several universities who could help supply quality people. He was certain that, with their help and his excellent

judgment of applicants, he would have no difficulty in choosing people who would be successful.

3. *The best compensation for salespeople was a straight commission.* A commission plan has a maximum motivating effect on salespeople according to Brewer. Selling costs were basically in proportion to sales, allowing for the development of an average sales-cost ratio. By using straight commission, the initial expansion of the sales force would be less expensive than it would be with a straight salary plan. If Shulton had limited capital for the development of the sales force, a commission program would require little or no cash outlay until sales were generated. However, trainees could be started on a salary until their earned commission surpassed their salary. If the salesperson could not quickly develop to that level, then increased training and supervision would be required. Salespeople would be expected to work long and hard hours. If performance continued to be low, then Brewer felt it would be best for that person and the firm to part company.

4. *Shulton Industries should develop a marketing information system to support its salespeople.* Brewer felt that a marketing information system would help the company to better analyze its markets, forecast sales, keep track of competition, and inform sales personnel of geographical areas and specific customers with high sales potential. In this manner salespeople would not be on their own in identifying their potential customers. This suggestion would necessitate hiring someone experienced in sales analysis.

5. *Salespeople should be extensively trained on Shulton and competitive products, in addition to selling techniques.* In the past very little emphasis had been placed on training. Brewer felt that, to attain high performance, the sales force must be well informed. This would require an initial training program and ongoing training for experienced salespeople. He also wanted to set up a "Selling Newsletter" as a continuing source of information to salespeople. Brewer also wished to establish a yearly national sales meeting, and either bimonthly or quarterly regional or divisional sales meetings.

6. *One or more sales organizations should be created within the Shulton corporation.* A single organization would mean that all salespeople would sell all products. A sales organization for each division would allow more specialization. However, its resulting duplication of efforts would be costly. For example, decisions would have to be made as to whether each division would have its own functional groups, such as training and sales analysis. Elcon's sales did not appear to be adequate to support those costs. Brewer felt he needed direction from Vaughan on this matter.

In making his proposal Brewer wanted to go with the best, or "ideal" sales program and then adjust downward if necessary. His goal was to develop a sales force of reasonable size that was highly trained and motivated by competent managers. To finance his proposal, Brewer felt that 9 to 12 per cent of total sales would be a reasonable budget figure for marketing. Due to the importance of personal selling, he was quick to propose that 80 to 90 per cent of the marketing budget be allocated to the sales force.

Questions

1. What are the business philosophy and goals of Shulton Industries? Is the corporation production or market oriented? Would you consider this good or bad?
2. Jimmy Brewer has made a good case for the development of the company's own sales force. Do you agree with each of the six parts of his sales program plan? Why?
3. Assuming Dick Vaughan approved Brewer's plan, develop a more detailed sales program for Shulton Industries.

Case 4

Reid Scientific

In the fall of 1977, sales for Reid Scientific, a division of the Reid Hospital Supply Corporation, were declining and market share was reduced. The industry was growing at a rate of 15 per cent while Reid managed only a 9 per cent growth, barely above the inflation rate. Tom Brooks, a vice-president of the division and the Southwest Area manager, wondered whether the present organizational structure of Reid Scientific was best meeting the needs of customers and supplying the company with the new products and the personnel needed to grow.

Reid Hospital Supply Corporation   The Reid Hospital Supply Corporation is one of the largest distributors and manufacturers of health care products in the world. The health care market represents around 10 per cent of GNP, or approximately $150 billion, and includes such markets as hospitals, clinical laboratories, universities, and industry. Sales last year were $1 billion. The financial community considers Reid a growth company, meaning sales and earnings grow at a rate above 15 per cent per year. Reid is divided into three major operating groups: medical products, hospital, and science/business. The Medical Products Group consists of subsidiary manufacturing companies that produce highly technical products, including artificial limbs and organs, and heart valves. The Hospital Group has two primary manufacturers that supply the distribution arm, Reid Hospital Supply Division, with all products needed to support a hospital from bed pans to intravenous solutions. The Science/Business Group has one primary manufacturer that produces the biologicals and reagents used in scientific laboratories and other common laboratory products such as glassware. Science/business products are distributed through the Reid Scientific Division. Each of these three groups operates as an independent division with warehouses and office facilities throughout the world. Reid Hospital Supply Corporation handles more than 120,000 different items and operates in all fifty states and twenty-six foreign countries.

Reid Scientific Division   The Reid Scientific Division is the largest division of the Reid Hospital Supply Corporation, representing approximately 25 per cent of corporate sales or $500 million in 1977. Reid Scientific has twenty-six regional sales and distribution centers in strategic locations throughout the country. The complete product line consists of 55,000 different items for the three major markets: clinical, industrial, and educational.

Their Markets   The clinical market consists of laboratories located in hospitals and diagnostic centers, where specialized medical tests are performed for physicians; blood tests and urine analysis are common examples. These tests help the doctor with diagnosis, and the cost is usually 50 per cent or more of the health care bill. In the last few years there has been increasing public pressure on clinical lab technicians for more accurate testing, with malpractice suits beginning to affect the clinical labs. Equipment to ensure the quality of tests can cost from two cents for a test tube to $112,000 for a blood analyzer that performs eighteen blood tests at one time. Approximately 80 per cent of Reid Scientific's sales are generated in this market segment.

Industrial market laboratories are specialized labs that perform the research and development needed by businesses for new product growth. Companies like Texas Instruments use laboratory equipment that is specially adapted for their purposes to run tests in the area of electronics. For example, the clinical labs use tissue and bone slicing machines to aid in making microscopic observation. Texas Instruments needs a similar apparatus that will slice silica, a quartz-like mineral that is used in the manufacturing of electronic parts. Through the '70s, the energy problem has sparked massive research and development efforts by companies such as Exxon, Shell, and Dow Chemical to develop substitutes for oil products. Their labs need equipment and supplies for these research efforts.

The last market center is educational institutions, i.e., universities and high schools. Most schools, especially at the college level, offer chemistry and biology courses for students. In the course work, laboratory equipment, consisting mostly of glassware and chemicals, is used for various experiments. Medical schools also represent a sales opportunity because students need sophisticated and specialized equipment for proper training.

The Sales Force   The sales force represents Reid Scientific's major marketing strength. There are over 500 sales representatives nationwide, each receiving special training from Reid and from the manufacturers whose products he or she sells. The training is continually supplemented with seminars, workshops, and sales meetings. These keep the sales personnel aware of new developments in instrumentation and laboratory techniques which enable the sales representatives to better serve the customers' needs. Reid Scientific sales representatives are among the best compensated sales people in the industry. The pay method is straight commission based upon contribution to gross profit, which is sales less the cost of products sold. After five years' experience, the average salesperson can earn $30,000 each year.

Reid Scientific is organized geographically into five areas throughout the United States. A vice-president is placed in charge of each area with region managers located at the regional offices to control the sales force. Funding, direction, and sales quotas come from the division headquarters. Each regional office assigns quotas to sales representatives based upon the previous year's performance and corporate quota expectations.

The sales representatives' territories are also based on geographic boundaries. Each representative is assigned a particular territory and is responsible for all potential accounts in that territory. The territories contain, usually, a mixture of clinical, educational, and industrial customers that the sales representative must serve. Few territories are so large that the sales rep cannot return home every night, and most sales territories offer the potential for new sales. The sales representatives call upon their customers regularly, and the accounts receive the knowledgeable, personalized service upon which Reid Scientific's reputation is built.

The Situation in the Fall, 1977   Several things had occurred that prompted Tom Brooks to review the organizational structure. Many industrial companies were trying to "catch the tide" and move into new, expanding areas, e.g., oil and chemical product research. Big sales could potentially be generated in this industrial market, but it was difficult to get the sales representatives to go out of their way and make calls, knowing that the sales dollars were two and three months down the road. The sales representatives were making their commissions on existing clinical accounts, where sales were steady and assured. Brooks and other members of Reid management recognized the potential growth in this type of industrial account and acknowledged the fact that Reid needed to place some sales emphasis there.

Brooks talked about the attitude that permeated the entire marketing organization, which was that "all labs were the same," but this simply was no longer true. Out of necessity, laboratory technicians were becoming very specialized in their respective fields. These technicians in clinical and industrial labs had vastly different requirements and needed different sales representatives who knew how to solve their technical problems. Brooks commented that "a local blood bank, Texas Instruments, Mobil Oil, and Parkland Hospital, a large medical teaching hospital in Dallas, all have basic lab equipment like a microscope, pH meter, and spectrophotometer; but each of them represented different disciplines. The ancillary items they used were different, and so were the reagents they required. One was dealing with blood, one was dealing with silica, one was dealing with urine, and one was dealing with oil. The customer who was trained as a laboratory technician suddenly was getting very sophisticated. This was because technology was moving so swiftly that, to stay knowledgeable in a field, the technician had to become a specialist. When some of our salespeople talked to technicians in siliconology, they did not know what it was or why it was."

The management of Reid Scientific realized that the members of the sales force must become dedicated to specific markets or customers. The sales reps had to become specialists just to call on any particular customer. Because new technology was advancing so fast, to remain well positioned with the customer, Reid Scientific must enter many new fields with new products to satisfy customers. Brooks made the statement that to "continue a high growth rate, if you are as well positioned as we are, and if the customer was growing into new technologies, if you did not have items to feed these needs, you would gradually get less and less of his business and not grow as fast as he was growing."

New Products Committee   Reid Scientific had a ten-member new products committee at the divisional level consisting of: product managers from all three market areas; staff people, e.g., warehouse managers to determine whether the product could be physically handled; and line personnel, e.g., area vice-presidents to determine whether the product is profitable enough for the sales representatives to carry. There was such a diversity of interests on the committee that companies might be hesitant to come to Reid with a new product. For the product to be accepted, all members must approve it, which seemed impossible. "Who needs the trouble of going to Reid with a new product and trying to convince them," was a remark Tom Brooks heard a few times from companies with new products. Even established manufacturers had trouble because the committee was trying to direct funds into coming areas like oil research. On the other hand, when the blood bank industry came up with a new plastic tube that would automatically sell if the sales representatives just "had it in inventory," they could not get the attention of the committee and a competitor picked up the product.

A meeting was scheduled for all vice-presidents and the divisional staff to further assess the problems and come up with some viable solutions. In Tom Brooks' mind, there were three available alternatives: 1) to divide Reid Scientific into two separate companies, industrial and clinical; 2) to reorganize Reid Scientific by major market centers, educational, clinical, and industrial, and remain one company; 3) undergo no changes at this time and assume a "wait and see" policy. Brooks was to present his views on a working solution to increase sales and growth rates at the meeting.

Question

1. What would be your solution if you were Brooks? Why?

Part 2
Sales Planning

Case 5

Colorange, Ltd.

Colorange Ltd. is one of Australia's leading manufacturers of surface coatings. The firm has grown steadily since its founding in 1912. By 1978, Colorange had factories in seven states and employed nearly 3,000 people.

Although the company has been introducing new products and developing its own chain of outlets, it is regarded as a conservative company. Public and trade surveys show that its products are considered high quality, but the firm is not perceived as progressive compared with its major competitors. The company offers a complete range of interior and exterior paints for domestic and commercial use. In addition, it has a wide range of stains and varnishes. Colorange Ltd. also markets specialty lines for industrial, automotive, and marine purposes.

The company's products are sold principally through hardware and department stores. In recent years, the firm has reluctantly let its products be sold by selected discount and chain stores. Colorange also has made large investments in a network of company owned and operated "Colorange–the Beautifier" stores that serve as both retail and trade

This case was prepared by M. J. S. Collins, Senior Lecturer in Marketing at the Caulfield Institute of Technology (Australia); David L. Kurtz, the Thomas F. Gleed Chair in Business and Finance, Seattle University; and Louis E. Boone, Professor of Marketing, University of Central Florida, as a basis for classroom discussion and not to illustrate either effective or ineffective handling of an administrative situation. This case was revised for this text, with permission of the authors, by Professor Darrell R. Hankins, University of Alabama in Birmingham.

outlets. Colorange has a special sales force to run these outlets and to sell to professional painters. Other specialist sales personnel handle the industrial, automotive, and marine markets. The independent outlets are the responsibility of the retail or decorative sales force in each state.

The Setting Michael Allen, the sales manager for decorative products in Victoria, was distressed as he examined the latest sales figures. For the third consecutive month, his brand had not made the sales quota, and he knew the head office would be expecting explanations and a plan for corrective action. Certainly the economic climate explained the poor growth in demand. Minor companies, particularly the price cutters, were showing marked gains; but other major competitors were not being hurt as badly as Colorange. Allen began to analyze the data he had available.

The Market—Retail Over the past two years the market in Victoria had barely grown; but the smaller paint companies, largely through aggressive discounting practices, have shown considerable expansion.

Retail Paint Sales—Victoria			Million Liters[a]
	1977	1978	Year-to-Date: April 1979
Colorange	3.78	3.57	1.18
Competitor A	2.67	2.76	0.93
Competitor B	2.70	2.72	0.90
Competitor C	1.33	1.38	0.53
Others	3.27	3.50	1.22
	13.75	13.93	4.76

[a]A liter equals 1.057 quarts.

Colorange's sales by main product groupings are shown in thousands of liters below:

	1977		1978	
Product	Colorange	Industry	Colorange	Industry
Interior Full Gloss	624	2,385	652	2,508
Exterior Full Gloss	914	2,786	819	2,647
Interior Semi-Gloss	585	2,842	563	2,697
Undercoats	418	1,170	384	1,226
Flat Plastics	835	2,647	666	2,758
Stains/Varnishes	(168)		(203)	
Other	(234)	1,922	(279)	2,090
	3,778	13,752	3,566	13,926

Although demand varies somewhat with economic and weather conditions and certain sales peaks exist, such as during the Easter season, overall sales tend to be spread evenly over quarters.

The retail market, identified as the reseller market, represents all sales made though retail outlets. Currently it is estimated that industry retail sales are divided as follows and account for approximately 40 per cent of paint volume. The remainder is sold direct to painters:

Independent hardware outlets }	
Hardware groups }	45
Discount specialist paint stores	10
Mass merchandisers & department stores	20
Specialist company outlets	15
Other	10

Generally, the share held by the hardware segment is decreasing while the mass merchandisers and specialist outlets are gaining market share. To halt this trend away from hardware stores, many outlets have banded together to form major buying groups, and these groups are increasing in importance.

Management of the Colorange Sales Force   The total budget set according to the marketing plan for 1979 was designed to hold market share and assumed an industry growth rate of approximately 4.9 per cent. The first four months' results for Victoria were:

	January	February	March	April	Year-to-Date
Sales Forecast	$395	$395	$440	$620	$1,850
Units (000s liters)	270	270	300	420	1,260
Actual sales	423	369	418	558	1,768
Units (000s liters)	276	245	282	377	1,180

Units refer to total weighted sales volume of all lines of paint. Colorange's retail sales of paint over the past several years have been as follows:

1972	1973	1974	1975	1976	1977	1978	1979	(Year-to-date April)
				(000s liters)				
2,905	3,077	3,272	3,455	3,590	3,780	3,570	1,180	

Monthly sales over the past two years have been:

	Jan.	Feb.	Mar.	Apr.	May	June	Jul.	Aug.	Sept.	Oct.	Nov.	Dec.
	(000s liters)											
1977	284 ↓	260 ↑	309 ↑	420 ↓	325 ↓	279 ↓	261 ↑	320 ↓	275 ↑	355 ↓	352 ↓	340
1978	285 ↓	250 ↑	287 ↓	370 ↓	298 ↓	265 ↓	245 ↑	312 ↓	282 ↑	340 ↓	334 ↓	302
1979	276 ↓	245 ↑	282 ↑	377								

While the industry sales were projected to be the following:

1972	1973	1974	1975	1976
		(000s liters)		
10,962	11,354	11,963	12,665	13,050

The Sales Job   Sales representatives are paid a straight salary. Newly appointed sales personnel are paid $A9,000 per year and after approximately three years are given a "mature" grading with a range from $A10–12,000. A few representatives are given senior sales status with a higher salary, based on service and performance. In 1977, an Australian dollar was worth approximately $U.S. 1.10.

The representatives have cars, but must pay for all private mileage at 2¢ per mile. They also are given an advance of $115 for expenses and report actual expense on a monthly basis. Expenses in metropolitan areas are not expected to exceed approximately $6 per week.

From time to time, sales representatives are given the opportunity to earn additional rewards through contests. These are used to push a particular product or range and generally take the form of cash based on sales over a given quota. Occasionally merchandise is given instead.

Apart from sales and budget figures, sales representatives are evaluated against objectives they set in conjunction with their sales manager. The objectives are normally of a qualitative or descriptive nature to reflect the way each representative intends to develop a territory. The company philosophy is to make representatives act as managers of their territories and so establish their own plans and strategies. The structure and function of the reseller field sales force is indicated in the following job description:

Job Description
Colorange Reseller Sales Representative
(Ballarat Territory, Victoria)

Accountability Objective: Promotes and sells the Colorange decorative market range to users and resellers to achieve sales forecast within expense budget.

Dimensions: Responsible for a territory comprising the following:

Sales volume	$133,000 annually
Customers	Units 90,000 annually
Distributor/retailers)	
Painters)	177
Architects	5
Government departments & local authorities	8

Nature and Scope of Position: The reseller sales force concentrates its activities on all decorative sales not made through the "Colorange–the Beautifier" organization. Direct sales of decorative products usually involve selling to the end user through the local reseller, and selling to the resellers for stock purposes.

The incumbent is one of seventeen reporting to the sales manager, decorative products. Eleven are metropolitan representatives who service the greater Melbourne area. Five are country representatives, of which the incumbent is one, servicing other areas of Southern and Central Victoria in a similar capacity to the metropolitan representatives except that the country representatives usually have a broader function and responsibility. The seventeenth position reporting to the sales manager is the market officer, decorative products who provides clerical and office support for the field staff.

The incumbent reports weekly to the sales manager on such items as calls made, mileage, cost/mile, entertainment, competition and the like. The incumbent handles all customer complaints and problems of a minor nature in the territory. For problems involving technical factors beyond the representative's knowledge, the sales manager requests technical assistance from the laboratories.

The incumbent is required to provide support for general company promotions including point-of-sale materials, merchandising and the like. Should he or she require special assistance for a promotion, he or she must approach the sales manager. The representative can initiate special promotions for a territory and implement these once approval has been obtained. Again, additional support must be requisitioned through the sales manager.

The incumbent is relatively free in terms of how to sell the product, providing such methods are not detrimental to company image or policies. Pricing of the product is done according to a chart supplied by the firm. Prices vary according to customer classifications. The representative is not involved with setting prices.

An overall sales budget is set for the decorative market by the sales manager. Sales representatives set their own budgets in accordance with this overall budget. Before it comes into force, it must be approved by the sales manager who may make alterations in consultation with the field salesperson. Once the budget is set it remains current for twelve months. The representative can not alter the budget.

A company vehicle is supplied to the incumbent. This is replaced after four years or 50,000 business miles.

The incumbent is required to help resellers with store and layout problems, merchandising stock levels, and the like. He or she is also expected (where requested) to provide color schemes and/or product specifications for householders and others. The representative keeps customer record sheets and sales statistics as well as making note of competitors' activities in the territory.

Summary of Principal Tasks:

1. Promote company image to ensure ready acceptance of products;
2. Maintain customer files to provide a reliable history of customers for himself and others;
3. Initiate and implement territorial promotions to maintain sales performance;
4. Handle any problems arising in the territory, referring only the larger, more difficult problems to the sales manager.

Questions

1. The forecast for 1979 is 3,700,000 liters. On the basis of the data in the case you are required to:
   a. Review the forecast for 1979 and give an "expected actual."
   b. Provide a forecast for 1980.
   Your forecasts should show the approach taken and method(s) used. You should then critically evaluate these and indicate what other methods, information, and procedures you would use, if available, to make a more accurate forecast.

2. Examine Allen's situation and make recommendations on how he can improve performance.

Case 6

S B & H
Microcomputers, Inc.

Henry Burke, S B & H national sales manager, has just been given the
job of restructuring his four sales regions with the aim of providing
better customer service and reducing selling costs. A major goal is to
improve the efficiency of the sales force by allocating salespeople based
on sales potential, in order to increase sales and profits.

The Company Last year S B & H sales reached $30,128,000 with the
design, production, and sale of a microcomputer for homes and businesses. Previous sales over the past five years have increased an average
of 15 per cent each year. As shown by *last quarter's* financial statement
in Exhibit 1 management has three major marketing costs: advertising,
sales promotion, and the sales force. Typically, 10 per cent of sales are
allocated to these marketing expenses. Of this, advertising receives 10
per cent, sales promotion 20 per cent, and the sales force 70 per cent.
However, these percentages often change from quarter to quarter in
response to competition based upon management's judgment.

 The S B & H microcomputer is used in the home and in small businesses. S B & H's list selling price to its customers is $6,000. Costs of

This case is designed to be used in two parts. Marketing research information can
be purchased or furnished by the instructor. It was developed by Professors
Charles M. Futrell and Richard T. Hise of Texas A&M University, and William M.
Smith, consultant. The first author can be contacted, if a computer assisted
solution will be used. Copyright 1980.

Exhibit 1
Company Sales and Marketing Expenses

Total Quarter Sales			$7,782,000
(Unit Sales = 1,297)			
Marketing Expenses		$778,200	
Advertising	$ 77,820		
Sales Promotion	$155,640		
Sales Force	$544,740		
Sales Manager's Salary			
Base Salary	$ 35,000.00		
Commission	$ 38,910.00		
Salespeople's Salary			
Base Salary	$287,500.00		
Commission	$116,730.00		
Recruiting and Training	0		
Severance	0		
Sales Support	66,600.00		

goods sold (total manufacturing costs and changes in inventory values) have been approximately 66⅔ of the list selling price. Salespeople can lower or increase the price based on the competitive situation. They are not allowed to sell the product for under $4,000.

The Microcomputer Market　The market for microcomputers is extremely competitive. Most customers perceive them as basically the same. Thus, marketing is important to stay competitive. There are two markets for S B & H. The industrial market is composed of small and medium-sized businesses. The consumer market is the household.

Businesses can use the S B & H for such things as payrolls, inventory control, general accounting, word processing, and mailing lists. Consumers can use it in their homes for financial and educational purposes, as well as for games.

There are nearly 3 million small businesses in the U.S. having annual sales under $500,000 so the sales potential for microcomputers is large. Also, the price is such that most businesses can afford it. Between $5,000 and $10,000 will buy a complete business system including low-cost application packages containing the software and user's manuals necessary to implement accounting and payroll processes, as well as various data base management systems. One important feature involves on-line access to outside resource material and data bases. For example, the user can arrange to tie into large computer faculties, such as those found at universities, with a telephone. The computers may also be programmed to monitor and manage the heating, cooling, and electrical systems in small businesses and homes.

The home market is predicted to be slow in developing because prices are still relatively high; there are few accessories; user skills are low; and the mystique and actual fear people have about the computer being too complex to ever be able to use it properly. Hopefully this will change as industry invests in product development and provides easy to follow product instructions.

The Sales Force   Burke's sales force consists of forty-six men and women located in the four sales regions, shown in Exhibit 2. The Central, South, and Northeast regions each contain one manager and eleven salespeople; the West region has thirteen salespeople. Basically one salesperson has been hired for every $600,000 increase in sales.

Compensation   All sales personnel are on a base salary plus incentive program. Each sales manager is paid a base salary of $2,916.67 a month plus one-half of one percent (.005) of the region's sales. Salespeople receive a base salary of $2,083.33 each quarter plus a 1.5 commission on the region's sales. For the last quarter, monthly salaries for salespeople averaged $2,929.20 and for managers averaged $6,159.67.

Exhibit 2
Four SB&H Sales Regions

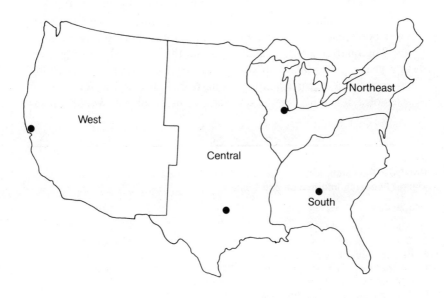

• Regional Offices located in San Francisco, Dallas, Atlanta, and Chicago.

Sales Support In addition to salary, salespeople receive a monthly allowance for automobile expenses, plus selling aids such as product brochures. Every four months sales personnel attend a sales meeting in their regional sales office. Here they learn of product improvements, new marketing plans, and work on improving their selling skills. Management has assigned approximately 12 per cent of the total sales force budget for sales support expense. Last quarter this averaged approximately $1,448 per salesperson or 12.2 per cent of the sales force's budget. Management would like to increase the sales support budget; however, they are not sure if they can afford it.

Market Research In order to help in restructuring sales territories, Burke contacted six national marketing research firms to receive competitive bids on information he felt would help him make his decision. This was such an important decision that he felt he could afford all information necessary. However, due to the high cost of marketing research Burke only wanted to purchase information that he actually needed to make his decisions. The lowest bid was from Goodyear Research. The market information and their relative costs are shown in Exhibit 3. Exhibit 4 presents examples of the actual research reports that can be purchased from Goodyear. The following is an explanation of each report.

1. An industry sales forecast for the following year for microcomputers.
2. A quarterly industry sales index for microcomputers. This indicates what percentage of yearly industry sales are forecast for each quarter. The quarterly index equals 100 and the sum of the four quarters in a year equals 400. With yearly industry forecasted sales of 10,000 microcomputers, for example, a quarterly index of 100 forecasts sales of 2,500 units for the quarter. An index of 150 would forecast

---

Exhibit 3
Goodyear Research, Inc.
Market Research Information and Costs

Information	Cost
1. Industry sales forecast	$10,000
2. Quarterly sales index	$ 5,000
3. Regional quarterly sales potential	$10,000
4. Competitive prices last quarter	$12,500
5. Competitive advertising expenditures last quarter	$12,500
6. Regional size of competitor's sales force last quarter	$12,500
7. Competitor's compensation methods last quarter	$12,500
8. Competitor's sales support last quarter	$10,000

Exhibit 4
Examples of Research Reports

Report 1: Industry Sales Forecast in Units (Next Year)

Report 2: Quarterly Sales Index for Each Quarter of the Year

Quarters			
1	2	3	4

Report 3: Regional Quarterly Sales Potential for Each Quarter of the Year

West				Central				South				Northeast			
1	2	3	4	1	2	3	4	1	2	3	4	1	2	3	4

Report 4: Competitive Price for Last Quarter

Company	Microcomputer Prices
A	$
B	
C	
D	

Report 5: Competitive Advertising Expenditures for Last Quarter

Company	Advertising Expenditures
A	
B	
C	
D	

Report 6: Size of Competitor's Force by Region for Last Quarter

Number of Salespeople

By Company	West	Central	South	Northeast
A				
B				
C				
D				

Report 7: Competitor's Compensation Methods as of Last Quarter

Company	Salary Only	Salary Plus Commission	Salary Plus Commission and Contests
A			
B			
C			
D			

1 = salary only
2 = salary plus commission
3 = salary plus commission and contests

Report 8: Competitor's Sales Support Last Quarter

Company	Dollar Amount
A	$
B	
C	
D	

quarterly sales of 3,750 microcomputers. This segments the yearly sales forecast to aid in being more precise.

3. A quarterly sales potential for microcomputers in each region. This helps answer the question, "Which sales region has greater potential for sales?" For example, if the quarterly sales index for microcomputers was 100 there are potentially 2,500 units that may be sold. Regional indexes of 25, 20, 25, and 30 for the West, Central, South, and Northeast regions respectively show that the Northeast region has the greatest sales potential followed by the West and South with the Central region having the lowest industry sales potential.

4. Actual average quarterly prices being charged by your four major competitors.

5. The level of competitive quarterly advertising expenditures by your four major competitors.

6. The size of the sales force the four major competitors have in each region.

7. Salespeople's compensation methods of the four major competitors.

8. The dollar estimate of sales support competition spends on the sales force.

Burke felt all of the information would be useful. He had never worked with sales forecasts and always relied on his own estimate. However, studies 1, 2, 3 would help in numerous activities, as shown in Exhibit 5. Goodyear also furnished him with their guidelines for effective sales forecasting, shown in Exhibit 6.

The other five studies would show exactly what his major competitors were actually doing. Although some of this information could be collected through the sales force, Burke felt that that method would take too much time for him to make his decisions.

Questions

1. Which information would be the most cost effective and should be purchased from the marketing research consultant? (Not all research need be purchased every quarter). What would be the total marketing research expenditures for one fiscal year? Give reasons for all decisions.

2. Are there any other types of marketing research that could be purchased that would help S B & H to make their sales force more productive?

3. What alternatives might Henry Burke suggest, other than purchasing the research?

Exhibit 5
Importance of the Sales Forecast

1. Foundation of all planning and budgeting activities in the marketing area and firm.
2. Purchases
3. Inventory levels.
4. Manpower needs.
5. Cash budgets.
7. Product-line expansion.
8. Product elimination.
9. Company objectives.
10. Acquisitions.
11. Research and development effort.
12. Sales quotas.

Exhibit 6
Guidelines for Effective Sales Forecasting

1. Constantly check for accuracy.
2. Consider alternative independent variables.
3. Consider the marketing mix, the market, competition, and the economy for independent variables.
4. Computer usage is a must.
5. Use breakdown and build-up approaches as check on sales forecast.
6. Trend analysis and correlation analysis are probably more appropriate for consumer goods; user's expectations, executive opinion, and sales force composite approaches are probably more appropriate for industrial products.
7. Weigh cost of forecasting approach against benefit obtained.
8. Choose independent variables that logically should predict sales.
9. Consider correlation forecasting options in the following order: simple-linear, simple-curvilinear, multiple-linear and multiple-curvilinear.
10. Greater deviation of actual from predicted sales is likely to occur as the forecast time period increases.
11. Standard error of the estimate should be used to predict a range of sales volume.
12. Assumptions underlying the forecast should be explicitly stated.
13. As a general rule, one should only forecast a period equal to one-half of the number of years of sales history available.
14. Various forecasting approaches should be tried to see whether a consensus can be reached.
15. Quantitative forecasts need to be balanced with one or more of the judgmental approaches.

4. Assuming Burke purchased the information you suggest, how should he allocate his limited dollars and personnel resources in order to improve the efficiency of S B & H's sales force? Develop a financial statement showing your projected total and unit sales for each region and the various costs involved in implementing your decision.

Part 3
Time and Territory Management

Case 7

ChemGrow, Inc.

By September 18, 1979, John Kee, vice-president of Agricultural Sales, will be presenting his newly conceived Dealer Marketing Plan and Evaluation Program to the president of ChemGrow, Inc., William Joseph.

Company History

Production   ChemGrow is one of the largest fertilizer manufacturers in the world. It is basic in phosphate rock, and manufactures phosphoric acid, anhydrous ammonia, and other mixed fertilizer products. In the past ten years, the company's production characteristics have shifted dramatically from a manufacturer of specialized NPK (nitrogen, phosphate, and potash) materials in over forty plants to the production of high analysis fertilizers in a few, very large capacity installatons.

Manufacturing Plants   ChemGrow's major production facilities are in Florida, Louisiana, and Arkansas. They are located on or close to river or ocean transportation, and can therefore take advantage of low-cost barge transportation to supply large terminal points and thus supply the market at the lowest possible cost (Exhibit 1).

Expansion   During late 1976 and 1977, ChemGrow evaluated future fertilizer demand and found the need to develop a large scale expansion program. The $250 million project included a new 425,000 tons a year anhydrous ammonia plant at Verdigris, Oklahoma (cost: $35 million); expansion of the phosphate rock mining facilities that it bought from Southern Gas at South Pierce, Florida; and construction of a 400,000-ton phosphoric acid plant near Donaldsonville, Louisiana, as well as a sulfuric acid, nitric acid, and urea granulation facility, and several formulating facilities.

Much of the ammonia made at Verdigris will start flowing early next year through ChemGrow's own 4,900-mile pipeline that runs from Oklahoma up through the fertilizer hungry Midwest farm states and into North Dakota, Minnesota, and Ohio. ChemGrow's present expansion activities alone should boost its fertilizer output 50 per cent over the 3.7 million tons of products it made in 1977.

The key to capacity growth for ChemGrow has been its control of its raw materials. ChemGrow has enough phosphate rock reserves to maintain its present phosphate production levels for seventy years. For the nitrogen side of its business, early last year ChemGrow signed a seventeen-year natural gas contract with Oklahoma Natural Gas Company. ChemGrow's expansion program also includes exploration for natural gas in seven off-shore Texas and Louisiana tracts.

ChemGrow has been very optimistic about fertilizer growth; but on the other hand, there have been critics of the company—mostly competitors—who believe that ChemGrow's fertilizer expansion is atrociously ill timed. They feel that after last year's boom, when buyers feared shortages and seized all the fertilizer they could find, the industry may now be on the verge of a world-wide glut, perhaps comparable to the agonizing oversupply of 1972–1974.

Management Team   At the headquarters of ChemGrow, Inc. in Tulsa, Oklahoma, William Joseph has built a winning managerial combination for an industrial empire. Joseph believes that when it comes to executives, the best are the cheapest for a company in the long-run and that you do not make money by being a scrooge.

In selecting top people, he has looked for such qualities as initiative and drive; then he provides them with the tools with which to work and with an incentive. Money is an incentive, but Joseph also believes they must have pride in the company. The job of a chief executive includes creating the atmosphere in which these people can operate successfully. Joseph has built on the managerial philosophy that in order to

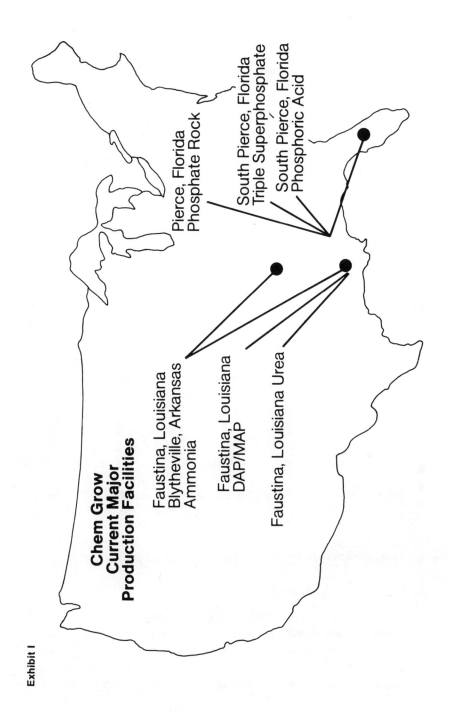

Pierce, Florida
Phosphate Rock

South Pierce, Florida
Triple Superphosphate

South Pierce, Florida
Phosphoric Acid

Chem Grow
Current Major
Production Facilities

Faustina, Louisiana
Blytheville, Arkansas
Ammonia

Faustina, Louisiana
DAP/MAP

Faustina, Louisiana Urea

Exhibit I

succeed in any venture, you do not need a team of people, you need the right man to head up the effort and then he will develop his own team.

Agricultural Sales   John Kee is one of Joseph's leaders who is now in the process of reevaluating and developing his own marketing team. His first step was to define a basic outline for the Dealer Marketing Plan and Evaluation Program. Some of the major aspects of the plan are outlined below.

Marketing Plan Outline

1. ChemGrow's Marketing Philosophy, including various statements on channel trade goals, major emphasis products, customer classification and qualifications, and price strategy.
2. Analyze Present Position, using historical sales data, customer/product/territory profiles, defining major and minor competition's supply network, and describing ChemGrow's strengths and weaknesses compared to each competitor.
3. Project Future Environment, by product tons consumed per acreage, industry projections for product mix, favorable and unfavorable trends, and future competitive programs.
4. Marketing Regions Goals, account manager develops goals for product tonnage for the long and short term; plans strategies to attain these goals by increasing customer growth, increasing the market share in the region by obtaining new customers, and identifying new areas for expansion.
5. Support Required to Obtain Goals, including manpower requirements, supply and distribution requirements, marketing programs, training programs, and extra services needed.

Kee felt that the overall basic plan for marketing was specific in terms of the company's primary interests in growth, but too general for the region managers to put into action, so another outline was developed for the sales manager.

Mechanics: Account Manager Marketing Plan

1. Prior to Customer Call: outline your territory, locate and identify present customers and their trading area, locate yours and competitor's supply points, and identify prospective areas of concentration for new customers.
2. Steps to be Completed with Customers: complete sales forecast,

update sales history for each customer, and complete customer profile with prospective customers.

3. Steps to Summarize Territory Marketing Plans: prepare product profile for present customers, prepare marketing plan work sheet, and prepare sales volume forecast for the territory.

4. Your Territory Plans: make up six months time allocation schedule, make up a monthly calendar, prepare first call action plan for prospective customers, and get regional approval and support for plans and needed help.

Current Issues

Kee is pleased with the marketing plans he has outlined, but he knows that getting the appropriate information to complete and implement the plans may be a problem. In the past, efforts at sales analysis have always been done on a "crisis" basis; whenever he absolutely needed a certain form of information, an analyst was assigned to the problem and the answers were developed on a one-time basis. There was little *systematic* evaluation of the sales data that was available in the company. Kee knows that this void needs to be filled if adequate information is to be available for decisions concerning sales effort planning and control.

Kee's general concern about the present quantitative evaluation program has recently been highlighted by an upcoming deadline. He knows that at the end of the month decisions need to be made involving: (1) a special bonus plan for the most productive region, (2) a ten-day vacation to Mexico for the most outstanding salesperson in each region, and (3) a list of "most valuable" customers who will be invited to participate in a luxury dealer council meeting. At the beginning of 1977, when Kee set up the program that included these sales promotion incentives, he was intentionally vague about how the customers, salespeople, and regions would be evaluated in arriving at the award decisions. He knows that time is running short and that these evaluations must be made soon. Yet, he is also sensitive to the fact that the salespeople and customers alike will be irritated if the award decisions do not appear to be fair. He wants whatever decisions are made to be objective and consistent.

Kee has expressed his frustration to several of his aides; he is in need of sales analysis information and once again it must be assembled on a crisis basis. He said in his last staff meeting that he is placing high priority on developing a usable, accessible computerized information system so that problems of this sort do not arise in the future, and so that in the future ongoing sales analysis reports can provide systematic inputs for sales force decision making.

In recent years, all quantitative sales analysis has been done manually under the direction of Kee's assistant, Richard Evans. Evans has never enjoyed these jobs in the past. It always seemed that he was spending his time on what appeared to be work that was clerical in nature, or worse yet that could have been done more rapidly, accurately, and completely by computer. This time, however, Evans feels a new sense of intellectual challenge in the job. While he knows that he faces the immediate task of identifying the best performing territory overall, the best salesperson in each territory, and the list of key customers, he also sees that he can contribute to the design of an integrated sales analysis system. He knows that he can work himself out of this recurring drudgery if he does a good job of figuring out what information is needed, and in communicating that need to the computer personnel in the firm. In fact, Kee has told him that he wants a memorandum from Evans outlining his thoughts on what sales analysis reports they can request starting in the immediate future.

The Available Information   In preparing for his assignment, Evans has talked with several others on the sales management staff and he has been sensitized to the fact that his problem is not a simple one. For example, he has been reminded that each salesperson sells three different products and that each product has a different gross margin associated with it. Moreover, the sales department is concerned with its sales (and margin) growth over time, so Evans wants to be certain that he does not take a static view in evaluating performance.

Unfortunately, not all of the information that he would like is currently assembled in one place. From the accounting department he is able to get good estimates of the gross margin per ton of sales for each of the three major products (ammonia, phosphate, and potash) sold in this division. These gross margin figures are summarized in Exhibit 2.

Exhibit 2
Dollar Gross Margin Contribution
for Each Product

Product	Gross Margin 1975	1976	1977
Ammonia	$ 8	$14	$20
Phosphate	12	12	12
Potash	16	9	5

Evans knows that different salespeople tend to sell these products in different proportions, however. In fact, several months ago this was raised as a concern. Kee felt that some of the salespeople were selling primarily the products that were easy to sell, rather than a complete product line in general and a profitable mix of products in particular. At that time, Evans had done an analysis on that issue, and it occurred to him that it might be useful to check his files for the report he prepared then. With the report in hand, Evans is reminded of what he had done. First, he tabulated for each different salesperson what proportion of total ton sales were in each of the product lines. The summary table from his report is reproduced here as Exhibit 3. He also remembers that he had found that for each salesperson these proportions tended to be relatively stable, even across different customers and during different time periods. Evans puts that report to the side, but makes a mental note that this information can be helpful to him in his current assignment.

Finally, Evans goes to the accounting department to get sales information on different customers. They are helpful, and tell Evans that they will be pleased to get whatever information that they can for him, but that right now they are in the middle of an audit and that they will not be able to respond to his requests until after his immediate deadline. However, G.N. Ieshades, the head of the accounting department, suggests that the distribution center may have some of the information he needs.

Exhibit 3
Average Percentage of Total Sales for
Each Product by Each Salesperson

Region	Salesperson	Ammonia (%)	Phosphates (%)	Potash (%)
Eastern	McFee	60	35	5
	Collam	5	20	75
	Parks	80	10	10
	Dow	100	0	0
Central	Thums	80	20	0
	Cook	25	50	25
	Block	20	30	50
	Fowler	75	20	5
Northwest	Vans	70	20	10
	Sciffman	65	20	15
	Lukbore	80	10	10
	Wilkie	20	10	70
Southwest	Goodie	5	5	90
	Stubber	5	15	80
	Holden	0	0	100
	Macke	10	20	70

At the distribution department, Evans does in fact find some helpful information. They are able to give Evans an alphabetical computer printout summarizing the total tons of products shipped to each customer in 1975, 1976, and each quarter of 1977.

Back at his office, Evans' secretary volunteers to reorganize the information on the computer printout, and to group the different customers according to the salesperson that sells to them and the region in which they are located. The secretary prepares a different summary table for each region, and gives them to Evans. These are shown here as Exhibits 4 through 7.

Evans knows that more information would be better, but realizes that for now he has to work with what he has. At this point, it is not clear whether he would be able to get more complete information, even if he had the time to wait. As he sits down to work on his analysis, he focuses on the immediate evaluations that he needs to have completed by the end of the month; but he also writes down his more general thoughts about what computer generated reports the sales department will want in the future. In fact, he finds that in organizing some of his current analysis he is developing good formats and specifications for the reports that he will suggest in his memorandum to Kee.

Exhibit 4
Sales Analysis at the ChemGrow Company
Sales to Each Customer Over Time

					Eastern Region			
Obs	Sales-person	Cus-tomer	Sales 75	Sales 76	1st Qtr. 1977	2nd Qtr. 1977	3rd Qtr. 1977	4th Qtr. 1977
1	Collam	EPF	6,523	4,800	2,800	3,000	2,635	2,635
2	Collam	FEV	3,010	4,550	4,740	10,000	0	0
3	Collam	FSC	1,505	4,100	3,685	5,000	3,025	3,030
4	Collam	HFC	3,261	4,350	3,000	3,000	633	0
5	Collam	M	8,028	13,000	5,000	15,000	3,000	584
6	Collam	PI	2,760	4,650	0	2,948	0	0
7	Dow	CSS	517	2,165	1,000	2,000	500	0
8	Dow	FSC	3,430	5,065	1,500	1,500	0	0
9	Dow	FSI	10,756	8,400	1,050	1,000	1,000	1,000
10	Dow	OSS	7,097	5,470	800	1,200	950	900
11	McFee	CFS	1,395	2,490	950	1,000	723	0
12	McFee	EGS	4,161	6,410	500	4,500	1,500	925
13	McFee	FCS	2,963	3,360	1,485	1,485	1,485	1,485
14	McFee	LAS	15,694	9,030	2,500	2,500	1,500	34
15	McFee	OI	10,076	7,500	1,705	1,783	1,780	1,780
16	Parks	JCS	427	2,800	500	500	500	35
17	Parks	LBC	1,373	7,120	1,605	2,000	500	500
18	Parks	MFS	5,628	4,395	900	1,200	800	170
19	Parks	PFF	12,409	0	3,000	10,000	415	400
20	Parks	SFM	193	3,350	0	1,535	0	0
21	Parks	VT	2,878	5,700	1,640	1,500	1,500	1,500
22	Parks	WT	3,663	6,600	0	0	0	0

Exhibit 5
Sales Analysis at the ChemGrow Company
Sales to Each Customer Over Time

				Central Region				
Obs	Sales-person	Cus-tomer	Sales 75	Sales 76	1st Qtr. 1977	2nd Qtr. 1977	3rd Qtr. 1977	4th Qtr. 1977
23	Block	CR	8,650	2,940	600	700	700	0
24	Block	LFS	17,350	7,549	200	1,400	1,050	350
25	Block	LSF	8,750	2,526	1,920	400	100	80
26	Block	TCF	5,100	1,623	0	0	0	0
27	Block	WDB	11,400	9,167	3,500	3,000	1,500	1,500
28	Cook	BFH	2,711	3,110	1,000	1,500	1,070	1,000
29	Cook	FFA	2,575	3,730	200	4,000	1,000	284
30	Cook	HD	3,170	3,465	1,500	2,700	2,070	1,500
31	Cook	JC	2,145	6,450	5,000	5,280	0	8,000
32	Cook	PF	1,980	1,190	0	456	0	0
33	Cook	RBR	2,880	1,275	600	675	510	500
34	Cook	TLA	3,375	2,935	3,000	3,855	0	0
35	Fowler	FGC	8,429	7,493	1,020	1,020	0	0
36	Fowler	GFS	9,164	5,994	450	4,245	1,005	800
37	Fowler	MSF	11,284	6,368	1,535	2,470	1,085	960
38	Fowler	RAP	3,843	12,175	0	1,610	0	0
39	Thums	FWM	1,084	2,700	1,260	2,120	1,000	300
40	Thums	WW	3,458	3,100	300	4,000	0	1,004
41	Thums	WWN	3,709	3,400	1,500	1,500	1,420	1,408
42	Thums	YF	15,315	8,660	4,500	9,000	1,200	588

Exhibit 6
Sales Analysis at the ChemGrow Company
Sales to Each Customer Over Time

					Northwest Region			
Obs	Sales-person	Cus-tomer	Sales 75	Sales 76	1st Qtr. 1977	2nd Qtr. 1977	3rd Qtr. 1977	4th Qtr. 1977
43	Lukbore	BAS	6,200	7,444	2,875	3,596	2,485	74
44	Lukbore	MVF	4,800	7,603	1,650	1,550	1,500	1,710
45	Lukbore	SCF	9,300	5,648	2,500	2,500	1,360	0
46	Lukbore	WFL	5,500	3,555	0	6,050	1,460	0
47	Sciffman	HF	11,300	6,764	3,595	3,740	2,460	605
48	Sciffman	JN	2,100	4,194	0	5,000	0	380
49	Sciffman	LS	4,200	1,044	800	820	840	820
50	Sciffman	RM	4,300	3,890	2,160	564	2,010	66
51	Sciffman	VF	5,500	4,747	345	568	327	300
52	Vans	AGC	4,600	2,200	1,550	1,550	0	0
53	Vans	CF	5,900	5,400	1,875	1,875	1,875	1,875
54	Vans	DBI	2,200	2,100	1,265	864	871	0
55	Vans	ECG	8,500	4,620	2,467	3,495	2,140	898
56	Vans	OFC	2,800	6,080	6,591	3,140	719	100
57	Wilkie	ASI	4,800	5,230	2,100	1,565	346	1,889
58	Wilkie	BG	11,150	11,160	3,800	3,800	4,000	3,600
59	Wilkie	CF	4,100	3,700	0	2,600	0	0
60	Wilkie	CI	4,350	15,720	4,860	10,400	5,140	0
61	Wilkie	F&R	13,000	5,720	0	2,250	0	0
62	Wilkie	IO	8,750	2,690	1,200	1,240	1,200	1,200
63	Wilkie	LF	5,100	3,100	1,125	1,695	2,433	2,147

Exhibit 7
Sales Analysis at the ChemGrow Company
Sales to Each Customer Over Time

				Southwest Region				
Obs	Sales-person	Cus-tomer	Sales 75	Sales 76	1st Qtr. 1977	2nd Qtr. 1977	3rd Qtr. 1977	4th Qtr. 1977
64	Goodie	BSF	6,350	4,500	900	700	400	362
65	Goodie	GFF	6,540	8,350	2,465	1,245	1,240	2,500
66	Goodie	KMA	0	0	0	904	0	0
67	Goodie	LCS	3,650	3,840	1,105	1,365	750	981
68	Goodie	PGC	8,510	9,125	2,500	3,262	2,500	2,500
69	Goodie	RGC	19,280	7,240	4,750	20,000	300	671
70	Holden	AGS	2,324	2,505	1,125	3,685	1,038	662
71	Holden	FCS	3,150	5,370	0	5,500	0	0
72	Holden	GF	4,195	5,190	2,531	2,530	2,400	2,664
73	Holden	IFS	5,800	3,340	4,659	3,178	993	0
74	Holden	OFS	2,811	5,935	3,418	8,650	67	0
75	Macke	CE	4,600	2,505	621	652	262	0
76	Macke	CF	3,400	8,670	12,512	3,150	1,013	200
77	Macke	DG	5,900	2,765	850	855	850	855
78	Macke	FER	2,200	2,495	650	650	610	600
79	Macke	SCG	8,500	4,620	2,350	1,240	1,175	1,180
80	Macke	TMN	2,800	3,279	0	5,525	0	0
81	Stubber	BAC	4,505	4,820	1,000	1,000	1,080	1,080
82	Stubber	DPC	2,810	2,600	1,975	1,975	0	0
83	Stubber	GCC	8,125	8,150	5,000	5,000	775	0
84	Stubber	GSS	4,015	3,050	575	685	834	181
85	Stubber	HDS	6,050	5,530	2,475	3,156	1,004	240
86	Stubber	TPS	8,933	6,286	365	2,010	0	83

Case 8

Allen Shoe Company

The Allen Shoe Company is a moderate-sized, midwestern-based manufacturer of children's shoes. The company originally produced only orthopedic shoes, but has subsequently expanded its line to include all kinds of footwear for children up to age fifteen.

Allen's brands include Allen Shoes for infants and small children, Hopscotch shoes for growing girls, and Playtime shoes for growing boys. Allen's shoes are manufactured with orthopedic features such as straight and reverse lasts, supinator, arch supports, Thomas heels, and long counters. The company also imports a line of sneakers and sandals.

The Allen shoes are positioned as medium priced, medium quality shoes within the better grade (non-discount store-marketed) footwear industry. Allen competes almost directly in price and quality with its major competitors, while the very high quality, high priced market segments are dominated by smaller firms.

The company markets its product lines directly to its approximately 1,500 retail distributors, most of which are family and children's shoe stores. As a matter of marketing policy, Allen prefers shoe specialists as retail dealers; thus department and clothing outlets are avoided when

This case was prepared by Professors Conway Rucks and John E. Mertes of the University of Arkansas at Little Rock. This case is designed to be used as a basis for class discussion rather than to illustrate either effective or ineffective handling of an administrative situation.

possible. With sales of about $20 million in 1975, Allen is the second largest domestic manufacturer of children's shoes.

Allen's marketing department consists of a vice-president of marketing, who supervises a director of marketing communications and a sales manager. The director of marketing communications is primarily responsible for the company's extensive promotional programs directed toward its dealers. The sales manager supervises the company's twenty field salespeople.

Marketing management recognizes field salespeople as the core of their marketing effort; consequently they have developed sophisticated plans for motivating and supporting salespeople and analyzing their performances. Allen's sales force is compensated by a salary and bonus plan. With this plan, salespeople receive a lump sum bonus if they attain biannual quotas placed on both manufactured and purchased shoes. They receive an additional bonus for every 500 pairs sold over their quotas. Finally, salespeople receive a 5 per cent commission on all merchandising materials. These include shoe polish, promotional toys and displays, and store supplies.

All salespeople are evaluated according to the following sales criteria: (1) quota attainment; (2) merchandising material sales as a percentage of total pairs sold; (3) product mix evaluation, a salesperson's total sales of a randomly selected line as compared to last year's sales of the same line; (4) account penetration, the number of pairs per dealer a salesperson sold as compared to last year; (5) time spent detailing doctors; (6) the number of new accounts opened; and (7) the ratio of expenses to sales. The salesperson rated best across all these criteria is designated "salesperson of the season," and is given an additional $1,500 bonus.

By Spring, 1980, Tom Elder, the vice-president for marketing, became concerned over the firm's sales systems, particularly sales territory allocation which affects all other dimensions of sales performance. He expressed this concern in the following memo to the rest of the marketing management staff and to the company president.

To   Marketing Staff
From Tom Elder
Subject Territory Analysis

INTRA-COMPANY CORRESPONDENCE Date

Over the past few weeks, we have talked off and on about territory analysis and the various steps to be taken. As we discussed, it was about ten years ago that we set up our present system and during that period of time sufficient changes have taken place to warrant an evaluation of our total system. I consider this to be the most important project that we have. In order to accomplish it on time and in an orderly manner, it will be necessary to develop an outline and time table.

I have expressed ideas about our objectives and various elements that should be included. In this memo, I am setting forth a rough outline as a suggestion, which you can use to build from.

OBJECTIVES:

It is my personal feeling that our present system has evolved to the point that we have certain built-in inequities. In principle we state that all territories offer about the same opportunity for growth and salesperson earnings when in fact we know this is not the case.
I see our major objectives as being two-fold.

1. To provide the company with the most economical and comprehensive sales coverage possible. We need to ask how many salespeople we should have and how their territories should be arranged for maximum efficiency in coverage.
2. To provide our sales force with a reasonably equal opportunity for above industry average earnings. As inflation soars, all incomes suffer and perhaps the salesperson is more aware of this than most. I know that if we do not provide above average opportunity we will suffer greatly in turnover and this is costly in many ways.

SECONDARY GOALS:

In order to accomplish our primary objectives, we must obtain a great deal of information that will be used to evolve secondary goals. Each of these should be given special consideration as they, in total, make up our objectives. I am not presenting these in any order of importance but rather as they come to mind.

1. Territory Alignments: There are several major questions that we need to ask about the general philosophy of our territories. Unless we learn how to move mountains, it is impossible to have twenty territories exactly equal. On the other hand, we are able to achieve some better balance than we now have. How many territories should we have? At $20 million, we have twenty territories, do we need twenty-four or should it be twenty-seven? At $24 million, what would be a reasonable alignment? Which is the more important criterion, number of dealers, size of dealers, total volume, or all three? When we have one salesperson who ships $1.5 million and another who ships less than $500 thousand there must be something

wrong. Can a salesperson with fewer than fifty accounts be considered to have the same work load as the salesperson with one hundred accounts? All of these factors and more must be considered in a new territory alignment.

2. Sales Potential: Naturally this is closely related, and certainly affects territory adjustment. However, I think we should deal with it as a separate goal because it is so important and complex. In essence, we are asking what our potential is within each account or each territory. We have accounts in all stages of development. There are some in which we are getting the majority of the business and we have little opportunity for growth. In others, we have just gotten a good start and can look forward to many years of increased volume, while others will never use Allen as their major resource. We need to evaluate every one of our accounts in this light and see just what potential is there. Another area of sales potential would be those dealers we do not sell to. Just how many accounts are there in a territory that we can sell? Certainly company stores such as Brand A Booteries and others must bear heavy consideration. We have to look hard at our franchise practice which limits the sales in certain cities. From this study, I would hope to develop some sort of a penetration index and a competitive index.

3. Quotas, Compensation, New Salesperson Measurements: From all of these studies, we know that changes will be made, and these changes will affect quotas, which affect compensation, etc.

Our present system is highly growth oriented. Not that growth should not play a big role; but we know that there is limited growth, and we should recognize it in our quotas and bonuses.

With more reliable and detailed information, I am sure we can establish more realistic sales quotas. It is true that our present method of assessing five-year performance does cover many variables, but it can be improved upon. The heart of our system is the quota; therefore it should receive a great deal of consideration. Another area that needs careful examination is our compensation/bonus system. We expect a salesperson to earn at least 20 to 25 per cent of his or her income via bonuses. Therefore, this naturally plays a big role in a salesperson's earnings. Perhaps we need more than one type of compensation. Perhaps we have some territories that simply involve a "maintenance" job as opposed to others that still have great growth potential.

One of the keys to the management of any sales force is motivation, how to cause a person to reach the ultimate of his or her sales ability. The greatest tool we have developed is our Salesperson Measurement

Program or Salesperson of the Season award. We know that in our present system there are many inequities. With greater balance, and more accurate information, I am sure we can make this an even greater tool for motivation.

As you can see from this outline, and I'm sure it is not complete, this is a very serious and involved project. This is why I consider it so important to establish a project plan and time table.

To meet these objectives, I suggest the following plan of action.

Phase 1. Develop Model.

Before we put in a tremendous amount of time and effort, I think we should develop a complete test model to see whether our approach is valid and gives the needed information. In order to accomplish this, I suggest that we use the state of Ohio (the home base of the company). I suggest several areas be considered.

1. All cities of over 10,000.
2. All cities with a trading area over 25,000.
3. Buying Power Index[1] for each city.
4. Footwear Buying Index for each city.
5. Retail sales for each city.
6. Better grade juvenile footwear for each city.

From the above we should be able to develop a projection of potential sales by city and state.

Phase 2.

After we have gathered all data, I suggest that we consider each item and its relevance to the final decision. Finally we apply Allen sales figures to determine what our penetration is of the market and how that corresponds with the accumulated information.

Phase 3.

Of course, the development of phase three would largely depend on the results and development of phase two. From this we would develop our total plan and time table.

---

[1]The Buying Power Index, published by *Sales and Marketing Management*, is a weighted index of effective buying power, population, and retail sales data broken out by state, county, and metropolitan areas of over 40,000 persons.

I'm sure there is some question as to the reliability of this plan. In order to prevent a lot of errors and unwarranted effort I have asked Dr. Rucks to meet with us to discuss the methods we intend to use.

This meeting is scheduled for 9 A.M., Thursday, May 27.

The overall objective of sales territory reallocation was to insure maximum volume and growth potential for the company. A subordinate objective was to provide salespeople with "equal" territories: territories that would give all salespeople equal opportunities for earnings.

It was decided that, before territories were restructured, a comprehensive analysis would be made of the present and potential volume in each trading area (SMSA) in the United States. The executives of the company developed the following documents to be used in that analysis.

To   Marketing Staff
From   Tom Elder
Subject   Market Analysis

INTRA-COMPANY CORRESPONDENCE   Date
ALLEN MARKET ANALYSIS INSTRUCTIONS

Form 1.
Fill in questions 1 through 10 and 12 from available secondary information.

Question 11 is arrived at by multiplying #10 (number of children) by 2.25 pairs consumed.

Question 13 is arrived at by multiplying #12 (family per cent) by #10 (number of children).

Question 14 is arrived at by multiplying #13 (number of children in quality market) by 2.25 number of pairs sold of quality shoes.

Forms 2 & 3.
Both forms 2 and 3 concern information about the stores.

There are no computations to be made.

Form 4.
Fill in information on 1 and 2.

Question 3 is a total of all competitive pairs from forms #2 and #3.

Question 4 will be the same except for instances in which some of the stores are owned by a manufacturer and we are prohibited from selling to the store. In these instances, you will subtract this pairage from the total of #3 to arrive at a lower figure for #4.

Question 5 is the total of all Allen sales from form #3.

Question 6a. Add all competitors' pairs (item 3) plus Allen's (item 5).
      6b. Add independent competitors' pairs (item 4) plus Allen's (item 5).

Question 7 is the per cent of Allen's (item 5) to total pairs (item 6a). Take item 5 and divide by 6a.

Question 8 is the per cent of Allen's (item 5) to independent pairs (item 6b) take item 5 divide by item 6b.

Question 9, from form 3, the per cent of Allen (item 29) to the total (item 31).

Allen Market Analysis Instructions

FORM 1. Now we return to the lower half of form 1.

Question 15. Take from form 4 item 6.

Question 16a. Total pairs into market (item 15) as a percentage of quality shoe potential (item 1).

Question 16b. Total shoes into market (item 15) as a percentage of total children's shoes (item 11).

Question 17, from form 4, item 4.

Question 18, from form 4, item 5.

Question 19, from form 4, item 8.

Question 20, from form 4, item 9.

Question 21, from form 3, item 20 + 22 + 24.

Question 22, from form 3, item 26 + 28.

Question 23. Growth potential (line 21 + 22) as a percentage of Allen pairs (line 29).

    The first pages explain how the document is used. A "dealer" form (form 3) was to be completed for each Allen dealer in each trading area and a "competition" form (form 2) was to be completed for each dealer in competitive brands in each trading area.
    Form 2 was completed from company sales records for the Allen information and by the salesperson in the trading area's territory for the information about competitive brands. The salesperson was completely

responsible for the completion of form 2. Form 1 was completed from available secondary data. The company's executives decided to restrict the total consumer market to children in families with an annual income of $17,500 or more. The number 2.25 represents the average number of "better grade" shoes consumed per child, according to the executives' best estimates. The marketing executives all believed that the salespeople were qualified to estimate the pairage of competitive shoes in each store. They were to make these estimates based on the square feet of space in the stores, the number of chairs in the shoe department, the displays of shoes, etc.

After the potential in each trading area has been determined, the total potential in various combinations of proximate cities will be analyzed to determine trading areas. One tentative territory, for example, is an area that includes most of the states of Arkansas, Alabama, and Mississippi and portions of Louisiana and Florida. Another tentative territory included only metropolitan New York, Newark, and a small portion of Connecticut.

Questions

1. Explain the effect of an Allen salesperson's territory on how he or she will be evaluated and how much he or she will be paid. Include all evaluation criteria used by the company in your answer.

2. (a) Is it possible to construct sales territories that are equal in all the criteria Allen uses to evaluate salespeople? Why or why not?
   (b) If it is not possible, which criteria should be most important?

3. Evaluate the territory reallocation technique used by Allen. What are its strengths and weaknesses?

4. What are the advantages and disadvantages of having salespeople collect the required in-store data?

5. Outline the procedure that should be used to determine sales territories once the market analyses are completed for all trading areas. Assume that equal sales potential in the territories is the only objective.

City (1)_____   State (2)_____

     Population (3)_____

County (4)_____

SMSA (6)_____

Buying Power Index (7)_____

Footwear Buying Index (8)_____

Better-Grade Junior Footwear (9)_____

Number of children 0–15 in market (10)_____

Total children's shoes consumed (11) _____

Percentage of families with income over $17,500 (12)_____

(10) × (12) equals number of children eligible (13)_____

(13) × 2.25 equals quality shoes sold in market (14)_____

Total pairs going into market (15)_____

Percentage of market in Better Grade Junior Footwear (16)_____

Competitor pairs in market (17)_____

Allen pairs in market (18)_____

Allen percentage of market (19)_____

Allen in-store penetration (20)_____

Growth potential in store in Allen pairs (21)_____

     in Hopscotch & Playtime pairs (22)_____

Growth potential (per cent) (23)_____

Form 2
Allen Market Analysis
— Competition —

City (1)_____   State (2)_____

Store Name (3)_____

Street Address (4)_____

Family (5)_____   Independent (8)_____

Juvenile (6)_____   Part of Independent chain (9)_____

Brace Shop (7)_____   Controlled by Manufacturer (10)_____

Volume (11)_____   Owned by Manufacturer (12)_____

                                                      Department Store_____

Brands Carried   **Approximate Pairage**

Brand A (13)_____   _____

Brand B (14)_____   _____

Brand C (15)_____   _____

Brand D (16)_____   _____

Brand E (17)_____   _____

Brand F (18)_____   _____

Other (19)_____   _____

Total (20)_____   _____

Is there an opportunity for Allen in this store?

                    (21) ☐ Yes   (22) ☐ No

If so, how many pairs? (23)_____

Form 3
Allen Market Analysis
— Allen Dealers —

City (1)_____   State (2)_____

Store Name (3)_____

Street Name (4)_____

Family (5)_____   Juvenile (6)_____   Brace shop (7)_____

Volume (8)_____   Volume (9)_____   Volume (10)_____

Other Brands Carried	Approx. Volume Pairage	Growth Potential
Brand A (11)_____	_____	_____
Brand B (12)_____	_____	_____
Brand C (13)_____	_____	_____
Brand D (14)_____	_____	_____
Brand E (15)_____	_____	_____
Brand F (16)_____	_____	_____
Other (17)_____	_____	_____

Total all Pairage (18)_____

Allen Product Lines Carried	Pairage for 1979	Growth in Pairs
Regular _____	(19) _____	(20) _____
Arch Feature _____	(21) _____	(22) _____
Specialty _____	(23) _____	(24) _____
Hopscotch _____	(25) _____	(26) _____
Playtimes _____	(27) _____	(28) _____
Allen _____	(29) _____	(30) _____

Total other brands plus Allen (31)_____

Growth potential Allen (32)_____

Form 4
Allen Market Analysis
— Recap —

City (1)_____   State (2)_____

  I. Market being served by our type of dealers.

     All competitors' estimated pairs (3)_____

     Independent competitors' estimated pairs (4)_____

     Allen's pairs (5)_____

     TOTAL PAIRAGE (6) _____

  II. Better Grade Juvenile Footwear Index: What percentage is Allen getting of the total better grade juvenile market?

                     (7)_____

  III. Competitive Index: What percentage is Allen getting of the better grade juvenile market that is being served by independents?

                     (8)_____

  IV. Penetration Index: What percentage of the better grade juvenile market is Allen getting of the stores that carry Allen shoes?

                     (9)_____

Case 9

Allis Machinery Corporation

Allis Machinery Corporation expects to sell $7.6 million of capital goods this year, which represents a slight decline in sales. Sales management was asked whether the present seven sales territories shown in Exhibit 1 adequately cover AMC's accounts. The reply was yes. "We feel we know who are our potential customers and where they are located. Furthermore, our salespeople call on each customer an average of three times a year," replied the national sales manager, Mike Day. Because their customers are often quite separated geographically, each person averages two sales calls a day. Luckily most of the larger accounts are in metropolitan areas. Salespeople work an average of 48 weeks each year, so they make approximately 480 sales calls yearly, which is about right for this industry. The company's president, Jay Stanton, asked Day why sales were declining. "Is it the quality of your sales force? Industry sales are increasing! Our sales need to increase next year."

A Study of the Market

Stanton formed a group to study the market. The group was composed of Stanton's administrative assistant and representatives of marketing, planning, and operations research.

It quickly became apparent that salespeople were selling according to their own leads. There was no coverage of the Southeastern region of

Exhibit 1
Allis Machinery Corporation's
Sales Territories

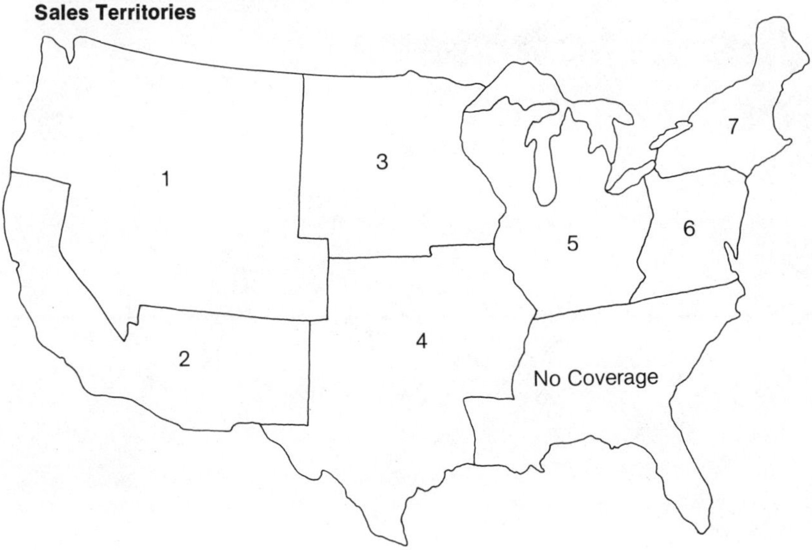

the United States because sales management considered it an area with low market potential.

An outside consultant provided information based on government surveys, census information, trade publications, customer feedback, and limited sampling. This information resulted in examining SIC codes 10 through 39 involving firms with twenty or more employees by: (1) SIC code; (2) plant name; (3) address; (4) phone number; (5) estimated sales; (6) number of people employed; and (7) name of the parent company. Also, consumption estimates per employee for specific products were provided. This was done by:

1. Establishing a relative order of magnitude of a product's consumption by SIC code based on consumption tables published by the census bureau;
2. Applying an adjustment factor based on a comprehensive study of the product;
3. Revising the consumption estimates based on inputs from customers.

This resulted in a yearly estimated sales potential per employee for plants based on their SIC code. Next, the study group and salespeople developed target industries based on the codes. Taking the consumption estimate per employee and multiplying it by the number of employees for a plant resulted in the sales potential estimate for each plant by SIC codes.

Development of Customer List

The information was analyzed by computer and a report was developed showing the estimated product sales potential by state, county, and individual industrial plant. The report was reviewed by three key experienced salespeople who thought that it accurately reflected business potentials in their territories.

Analysis of Current Territories

The next step was to relate the information to current sales territories to determine whether potential customers were being adequately contacted by salespeople. If needed, better sales territories could be developed in terms of territory potential and salespeople having equivalent sales potential. Finally, the revised territory structure would be refined through study group discussions and inputs from sales. Once agreement is reached, sales force decisions can be finalized and plans implemented. Constraints to be considered were budget, feelings of current salespeople, and operations sales management requirements. Mike Day wanted his two best senior salespeople to have larger territories based on sales potential. One of these would be Al Crawford, whom he wanted to stay based in Chicago.

Summary of Findings

It was found that contacting customers in states having a potential less than 0.8 was unprofitable due to the high costs involved in the sale. In fact, these states contained a total of only 225 small accounts. Exhibit 3 is a summary of present customer's sales. It was found that actual sales were highly correlated with sales potential. Accounts, other than the small customers, were experiencing a slight increase in sales.
It was determined that the small accounts need to be located close to the larger customers to make sales calls profitable. As shown in Exhibit 2, the southeastern states were found to have substantial sales potential. Day felt that one, maybe two, salespeople should be hired. One for the Southeast and perhaps one for territory 3. Territory 3 had two people quit in the last three years. When Day visited the salesperson in Minneapolis, Greg Scott, Greg said he was considering an offer from the Massey Corporation because his salary expectations had not been

Exhibit 2
Summary of Sales Potential By State

State	Sales Potential[a]	State	Sales Potential[a]
Alabama	3.0	Nebraska	1.0
Arizona	0.5	Nevada	0.05
Arkansas	1.0	New Hampshire	1.0
California	6.0	New Jersey	5.0
Colorado	0.05	New Mexico	0.5
Connecticut	1.5	New York	5.78
Delaware	1.0	North Carolina	2.0
Florida	4.0	North Dakota	0.001
Georgia	3.0	Ohio	4.0
Idaho	0.05	Oklahoma	1.5
Illinois	6.0	Oregon	1.0
Indiana	3.0	Pennsylvania	5.0
Iowa	1.0	Rhode Island	1.5
Kansas	1.5	South Carolina	2.0
Kentucky	1.0	South Dakota	0.009
Louisiana	2.0	Tennessee	1.0
Maine	1.0	Texas	7.0
Maryland	1.0	Utah	0.05
Massachusetts	1.0	Vermont	1.0
Michigan	5.0	Virginia	2.0
Minnesota	2.0	Washington	2.0
Mississippi	2.0	West Virginia	1.0
Missouri	1.0	Wisconsin	3.0
Montana	0.005	Wyoming	0.005

[a]Weighted percentage of total estimated U.S. market potential.

Exhibit 3
Summary of Customer Sales

Account Size	Number of Accounts	Total Sales Volume	Relative Sales Trend
Extra Large	28	$3,800,000	increasing
Large	63	$2,680,000	increasing
Medium	308	$1,064,000	increasing
Small	70	$ 56,000	decreasing

met. Even though AMC's commission rate of 12 per cent was 2 per cent higher than Massey's, Scott was not earning the income he expected. When Day returned to the office and reviewed his records, he found Scott's salary to be around $38,400. This was less than half the $84,000 average salary AMC paid their other salespeople.

Mike's salespeople.

Day had to meet with Stanton in one week to suggest ways his sales personnel can help the company increase sales.

Questions

1. How would you evaluate AMC's present manpower planning program for its sales personnel?
2. Assuming you were the sales manager, Mike Day, what would you suggest to improve AMC's personal selling efforts?

Case 10

Western Sports Incorporated

In the summer of 1971, Mr. Harold Johnson, recently appointed vice-president in charge of Sales of Western Sports Incorporated (WSI), was concerned about the company's sales trend in its fifth district. The fifth district is comprised of Michigan, Indiana, Pennsylvania, Ohio, and Wisconsin. The company's other four districts were generating an increasing total sales figure on a continuous basis. Although, as a whole, WSI was showing an annual sales increase, Mr. Johnson felt that the fifth district could equal or match any of the other four districts in total sales. He decided to review the fifth district and its success in meeting the competition of other sporting goods manufacturers selling within this five-state area. He also considered whether a change in distribution and/or pricing policies would be beneficial in increasing total sales volume in district five. Mr. Johnson wondered whether the trend in district five could affect the sales in other districts. (See Exhibit 1.)

The Firm In 1930, WSI established its sporting goods manufacturing firm in Sacramento, California. By the beginning of 1940, the firm had a total of five different manufacturing sites. They are Sacramento, California; Phoenix, Arizona; Minneapolis, Minnesota; Grand Rapids, Michigan; and St. Louis, Missouri. Each of the additional four plants

Exhibit 1
States Comprising the Five Districts

District I
  California
  Oregon
  Washington
  Idaho
  Montana

District II
  Wyoming
  Colorado
  Arizona
  New Mexico
  Utah

District III
  North Dakota
  South Dakota
  Nebraska
  Minnesota
  Iowa

District IV
  Oklahoma
  Kansas
  Missouri
  Illinois
  Texas

District V
  Michigan
  Indiana
  Ohio
  Pennsylvania
  Wisconsin

Submitted by James F. Van Dam, Law Student, Cooley Law School.

had been a former competitor of Western. WSI purchased each business to facilitate growth in these new areas and reduce the transportation costs of finished goods distribution. (Previously WSI had been producing sporting goods manufactured in the Sacramento plant and distributing them to retailers throughout the five districts.) Currently, each district is operated as a separate entity with each manufacturing plant being the central headquarters for its own district. The home office remains in Sacramento, and it is here that district performance is analyzed and evaluated in terms of (1) past history and (2) comparison to other districts.

Sporting Goods   WSI manufactures eight different lines of sporting goods. These range from baseballs to bowling balls. Because WSI's policy has always been to sell sporting goods that far surpass the official sporting rulebook's specifications on quality, their products have been widely used by many professional and semiprofessional sports organizations (such as the National and American Baseball, Football, and Basketball Leagues). With professionals using Western's products, Western has been able to build an image of quality in the market for their products. Many promotional campaigns have been organized around a popular professional athlete's endorsement of a particular WSI product. This has aided the firm's market standing among amateur users, who make up approximately 85 per cent of WSI's total end sales (approximately 15 per cent of sales are to professional and semiprofessional sports organizations).

The Research and Development Department of WSI has been recently attempting to expand the product line offered. Top management has also suggested developing two separate quality products to gain a larger share of the market. These projects are now in the innovative stages of development.

Distribution and Pricing   Distribution at WSI is directly from the manufacturing plant to the retail outlet or sports organization. Each district has one district manager with one senior salesperson and junior salesperson per state. The sales force calls on prospective buyers who are order takers from established accounts within their state. Most sales people have their own office staff within their state that can take telephone orders from customers or can help with customer problems. This sales office staff also facilitates the product flow from manufacturer to consumer. The follow-up procedure is to give prompt and efficient delivery and to insure customer satisfaction. The function of the typical sales office staff as a distributive link is shown more clearly in Exhibit 3. Once the orders have been made through the salesperson to the manufacturing plant, the goods are delivered by a truck-transport network that operates from the central office in each district. Delivery time is usually ten days or less from the date the order is placed.

The pricing policy is determined by the district's central office. The markup normally fluctuates from 10 to 20 per cent for the products sold. Prices are occasionally adjusted to meet the prices of competitive sporting goods of similar quality.

As mentioned earlier, WSI sold goods to retail outlets at a 10 to 20 per cent markup on gross cost of goods with a 5 to 15 per cent net profit on sales. The retailers in turn have a markup on the items that they sold. The athletic association usually paid 3 to 5 per cent more for goods than the retailers. The credit terms offered by the manufacturer are 1/10/n30. There is no shipping charge; this cost was absorbed by WSI.

The Fifth District   The fifth district's sales manager is Mr. Peter Kroeshell. Mr. Kroeshell has been with the firm since 1948, when he began as a junior salesperson. His responsibility as sales manager is to insure good selling practices (according to company policy) and to see that his sales force is adequately covering the market. The district's research and development projects on a monthly basis a sales forecast for each person's territory. This forecast is accomplished with the assistance of the salesperson involved. Through this person's feedback on

Exhibit 2
Sales per District of Eight WSI Products, 1970–75

Year	Baseballs	Footballs	Basketballs	Soccer Balls	Tennis Balls	Bowling Balls	Golf Balls	Hand Balls	
1970	60,000	54,800	31,300	2,800	31,000	14,000	29,000	4,200	*District I*
1971	76,400	59,500	39,600	4,700	39,600	18,600	31,200	6,500	
1972	69,600	68,300	39,900	10,900	47,200	21,400	39,600	11,400	
1973	78,300	74,700	45,800	12,700	48,100	31,100	47,400	14,800	
1974	84,200	79,000	51,200	13,800	55,300	31,600	49,300	18,600	
1975	91,000	31,600	59,700	15,000	69,000	31,800	57,600	19,400	
1970	54,000	39,400	31,700	3,900	35,000	19,500	27,300	4,900	*District II*
1971	63,000	47,300	35,200	4,600	39,600	21,300	28,200	4,700	
1972	71,400	49,900	39,600	9,100	41,700	30,100	41,000	10,600	
1973	79,600	56,700	43,400	14,600	49,600	32,000	47,400	11,400	
1974	81,200	61,300	49,900	19,300	60,700	34,700	51,300	15,300	
1975	86,000	68,000	58,400	26,900	71,000	35,300	59,400	20,100	
1970	67,000	41,600	33,000	4,100	39,000	19,300	21,300	4,100	*District III*
1971	69,700	50,600	35,000	4,600	39,000	20,300	22,400	4,900	
1972	80,100	51,900	39,700	9,100	47,300	29,600	41,700	5,700	
1973	84,000	63,200	46,300	10,900	59,400	31,300	49,600	7,300	
1974	91,300	69,100	49,100	12,400	71,200	33,300	51,900	9,100	
1975	98,300	71,300	59,600	17,000	84,000	39,000	60,400	16,000	
1970	57,000	61,000	31,000	3,700	27,300	14,400	22,600	3,900	*District IV*
1971	69,400	63,300	39,300	4,700	29,200	15,400	29,600	4,600	
1972	71,300	65,000	41,700	9,100	47,000	19,200	41,200	4,700	
1973	76,000	71,000	43,200	10,600	49,400	31,400	47,600	9,600	

Exhibit 2—*continued*

Year	Baseballs	Footballs	Basketballs	Soccer Balls	Tennis Balls	Bowling Balls	Golf Balls	Hand Balls	
1974	79,000	72,400	47,600	14,300	51,200	39,700	49,000	14,300	*District V*
1975	89,000	74,000	48,000	15,900	59,600	46,000	59,600	19,700	
1970	59,400	47,000	39,000	3,300	29,700	15,800	25,400	4,200	
1971	47,100	39,600	29,900	2,700	21,000	14,300	19,600	3,600	
1972	46,400	38,400	19,600	1,900	19,600	12,200	15,200	2,500	
1973	39,300	35,000	14,400	2,100	19,300	11,700	14,900	1,900	
1974	37,900	34,300	14,600	2,000	17,900	10,400	13,800	1,800	
1975	35,900	49,900	13,400	1,900	16,800	9,600	12,700	1,800	

Exhibit 3
Function and Organization Chart

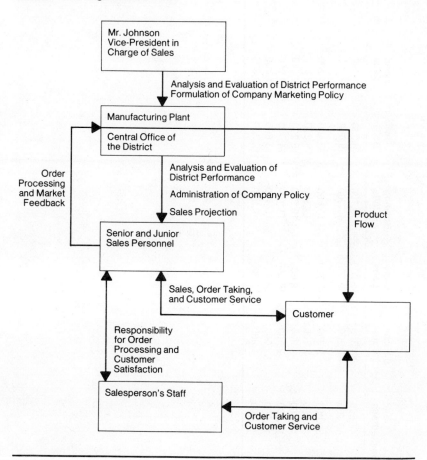

market changes, top management attempts to gain a more precise insight into shifts in demand.

In this district, the average senior salesperson's salary is $15,000 per year and the average junior salesperson's salary is $9,500 per year. They each receive one-half of 1 per cent on their total dollar sales, plus a liberal expense account. The senior sales force is made up of people whose years of service with WSI range from fifteen to thirty years. The greatest percentage of their accounts have been developed by their hard work and have been standing accounts for many years. The five junior salespeople in the fifth district have been with the firm for an average of four years. Many of their accounts have been taken over from the senior salesperson (the result of the territory becoming too large for one person to cover). Because of the high-caliber sales personnel recruited by WSI, the attrition rate is extremely low. Due to a record of top-quality products and excellent service, WSI salespeople have an outstanding working relationship with many of their customers. Each customer is called on at least once a month, with large accounts called on as often as once a week.

The retail outlets vary from small hardware stores to some of the largest chain stores in the United States. The chain department stores are some of the largest accounts that WSI has on the books. Four of the largest buyers are Sears, Roebuck and Company, Montgomery Ward and Company, W. T. Grant Company, and J. C. Penney Company. For a breakdown of customer types and major accounts, see Exhibit 4. Two of these accounts (Sears and Ward) were WSI's largest customers in 1970. Late in that year, however, they began producing their own sporting goods that were competitive with WSI's products. Both of these firms have decided to produce sporting goods for their department stores on a limited basis. They have sold their own manufactured sport products east of Chicago from 1970 through 1975. According to informed sources, they planned in 1970 to expand their production to cover the entire United States market, if the first five years were successful.

Competition and the Future   Mr. Johnson was concerned over the tremendous drop in sales due to Sears' and Ward's sporting goods production. He also anticipated the possibility of a reduction in sales in the other districts due to the expected expansion. This fear was based on the high level of purchases made by these and other chain department stores in the other four districts. Because the general distribution of customer types was similar throughout WSI's districts, the new sporting goods producers could do great harm to WSI's total sales volume.

Some Alternatives Considered

1. Wholesale trade as middleman. For the last two years, both Rogers Wholesalers, Inc., and B. P. Distributors have been attempting to take on the WSI line of sporting goods. [Both] of these firms are national chain wholesalers and insist they could increase market coverage and total sales of the Western line. The plans offered by Rogers and B. P. were very similar. They would purchase WSI's sporting goods at 5 to 7 per cent below the prices retail outlets were now paying. They offered the following advantages:
   a. Transport to retailers (This would reduce WSI's delivery costs which now totaled 5 per cent of total sales.)

Exhibit 4
**Customer Types and Per cent of Sales
in WSI's Fifth District**

Customer Categories	Per cent of Total Sales					
	1970	1971	1972	1973	1974	1975
Hardware stores	8%	8%	7%	4%	4%	4%
Discount stores	2%	3%	3%	4%	4%	3%
Athletic organizations	14%	16%	12%	15%	14%	15%
Sports shops	6%	12%	12%	13%	14%	14%
Chain department stores	65%	55%	50%	49%	49%	48%
Independent department stores	5%	6%	16%	15%	15%	16%
Total	100%	100%	100%	100%	100%	100%

**Sales (in dollars) of Chain Department Store Accounts in District 5
(1970–75)**

Customer Accounts	Sales in Dollars					
	1970	1971	1972	1973	1974	1975
Sears, Roebuck and Company	4,700,000	3,900,000	3,000,000	2,200,000	1,900,000	1,600,000
Montgomery Ward and Company	3,200,000	2,700,000	2,200,000	1,800,000	1,500,000	1,300,000
W. T. Grant Company	1,000,000	1,100,000	1,100,000	1,300,000	1,400,000	1,400,000
J. C. Penney Company	800,000	850,000	850,000	875,000	900,000	900,000
All others	900,000	900,000	950,000	100,000	150,000	1,100,000

Exhibit 5
Sales Mix

Customer Categories	Sales to Customer Categories (in Number of Items Sold)					
	1970	1971	1972	1973	1974	1975
District I						
Hardware stores	41,000	46,000	49,000	42,000	46,000	41,000
Discount stores	11,000	12,000	15,000	17,000	19,000	26,000
Athletic organizations	50,000	56,000	47,000	49,000	49,000	56,000
Sports shops	30,000	40,000	47,000	51,000	54,000	57,000
Chain department stores	87,000	90,000	91,000	94,000	96,000	111,000
Independent department stores	32,000	47,000	49,000	61,000	67,000	69,000
District II						
Hardware stores	36,000	37,000	37,000	45,000	48,000	46,000
Discount stores	14,000	15,000	16,000	19,000	26,000	29,000
Athletic organizations	52,000	53,000	54,000	58,000	59,000	65,000
Sports shops	37,000	41,000	56,000	59,000	94,000	73,000
Chain department stores	69,000	71,000	78,000	91,000	98,000	102,000
Independent department stores	31,000	30,000	37,000	39,000	35,000	42,000
District III						
Hardware stores	31,000	36,000	36,000	39,000	47,000	47,000
Discount stores	19,000	21,000	29,000	34,000	36,000	39,000
Athletic organizations	51,000	50,000	54,000	55,000	59,000	61,000
Sport shops	30,000	34,000	39,000	47,000	50,000	51,000
Chain department stores	78,000	84,000	89,000	94,000	97,000	103,000
Independent department stores	31,000	34,000	37,000	34,000	41,000	42,000

Exhibit 5—*continued*

Customer Categories	Sales to Customer Categories (in Number of Items Sold)					
	1970	1971	1972	1973	1974	1975
District IV						
Hardware stores	27,000	29,000	41,000	46,000	46,000	46,000
Discount stores	16,000	21,000	23,000	29,000	29,000	32,000
Athletic organizations	59,000	60,000	61,000	47,000	42,000	47,000
Sport shops	31,000	34,000	41,000	41,000	43,000	47,000
Chain department stores	79,000	81,000	88,000	89,000	95,000	99,000
Independent department stores	27,000	28,000	29,000	34,000	39,000	39,000

Exhibit 6
Firms of Similar Sales Volume and
Similar Size to WSI, 1970–75

Firm Name	Dollar Sales					
	1970	1971	1972	1973	1974	1975
McKinsy, Inc.	62,400,000	62,900,000	67,000,000	69,300,000	67,000,000	69,900,000
LaVern and Son, Inc.	75,800,000	75,900,000	76,100,000	77,200,000	77,200,000	78,400,000
W. A. Nielson Co.	86,400,000	86,900,000	87,400,000	89,100,000	89,900,000	91,200,000
W. H. Rochester, Inc.[a]	67,900,000	65,700,000	63,200,000	69,900,000	76,000,000	76,800,000
Montery Sports, Co.	63,000,000	63,800,000	64,100,000	65,200,000	65,800,000	65,900,000
Western Sports, Inc.	75,000,000	77,200,000	78,100,000	79,900,000	79,800,000	79,800,000

[a]Since 1973 this firm has sold sporting goods through its own exclusive sports shops.

b. Some degree of advertising and sales promotion of the WSI product (At this point, only the large retail chains offered any amount of advertising and promotion.)
2. Reduce prices and offer product at a lower price than competition.
3. Increase the sales force so as to increase the coverage of the market area. This alternative would break down the area of responsibility for each salesperson. This would increase the amount of time each salesperson could spend with a customer. Although this might produce some increase in total sales, it is questionable whether the increased profit could exceed the increased expense. There is also the problem of reducing the accounts and the income of the established area sales personnel.
4. Expand the firm's markets to include areas of the eastern United States.
5. Establish WSI sporting goods shops that are exclusive merchants of the WSI products. (W. H. Rochester, Inc., a competing sporting goods manufacturing firm of similar size to WSI, developed an exclusive chain of dealers in 1973. Their degree of success has been quite substantial, according to some of WSI's retail customers and available statistical data.)

Questions

1. To what is the decline in the fifth district due: sales force, department chain store's changes in operating policy, the economy, etc.? Justify your answer.
2. Establish a sales force evaluation system for Western. What are the most important factors?
3. If competition is the cause of the decline, which one of the alternatives suggested (or other possibilities) would be the best strategy to increase sales? Justify your answer.

Case 11

Hi-Po Drugs

David Lucke was a little worried. He had recently discussed the performance of his sales district with his immediate supervisor, Mike Summer, the manager of Hi-Po Drugs' Southern region. During their conversation, Mike had remarked that he felt David's district had room for some improvement. He based this belief on his personal knowledge of the area. Mike had been the district manager of David's territory for ten years before being promoted to regional manager; thus, he knew the area well. David defended his district's performance by pointing out that sales had been increasing by 5 to 10 per cent per year over the last five or six years. Mike acknowledged that sales had increased but argued that the district still had a way to go before achieving its full potential. Mike ended the conversation on this note:

> Look, I worked that area for years as both a salesperson and district manager. I think I know what the area is capable of producing. I know that demand has increased for all our product lines and I believe you could be doing better.
> I'm not trying to be overly critical. Actually, I'm trying to be helpful. So, why don't you take a close look at your operations and let's talk about it then. OK?

This case was developed by Professor James L. Taylor, Department of Management and Marketing, University of Alabama. Copyright © 1980.

David Lucke was the district sales manager of a four-state area making up the East South Central United States. The four states composing the territory included Alabama, Kentucky, Mississippi, and Tennessee. Four sales representatives covered the marketing area, with each representative having one of the states assigned as a territory. These sales representatives were paid an annual salary plus a 5 per cent commission on all sales above an assigned quota. The average salary among the sales reps was $18,500 a year.

Hi-Po Drugs was a national company that specialized in a wide range of nonprescription drugs. The company's offering was organized around four product lines. One line included a variety of vitamins, minerals, and tonics; another line was made up of various cold remedies and cough syrups; a third line included antacids and laxatives. Several types of pain relievers comprised the fourth line.

The vitamin-mineral line of products was targeted toward the price-conscious consumer. Generally, the products included in this line were sold below the average retail price of similar competitive products. The other three product lines were competitively priced but not oriented specifically toward the economy-minded buyer. However, the products in these lines were moderately priced and targeted at the value-oriented consumer.

Sales representatives of Hi-Po sold to several types of customers. These customer types included drug wholesalers, drug stores, discount stores, and supermarkets and other food stores. Some chain stores were also called on, but Hi-Po had achieved only limited success with this type account.

David Lucke's conversation with Mike Summer prompted him to conduct a sales analysis of his district. He wanted to determine just how well or poorly his area was faring. First, he compiled from company records Hi-Po sales for his district and for the company as a whole. Next, he turned to published industry data on sales of nonprescription drugs throughout the United States. These data are presented in Exhibits 1 and 2.

Finally, David temporarily hired a marketing analyst to test various general indexes to determine which best described past potential in his area. The market analyst examined sales over a thirty-year period and found that a coefficient correlation of .93 existed between total sales in the states and *Sales and Market Management* magazine's Buying Power Index (BPI). High correlations also were found between the sales of individual product lines and the BPI. For the vitamin-mineral line, a better statistical fit was obtained between sales and the BPI when the measure for economy-priced products was used. The best fit was obtained with the BPI for moderate-priced products in the case of the other three lines. These indexes are reflected in Exhibit 3.

David Lucke felt that he now had the information needed to conduct his sales analysis. He decided to do the work himself as opposed to paying the analyst additional money. He reasoned that the sales analysis would be conducted on a periodic basis, and he did not want to hire an analyst every time it was to be done.

Questions

1. Conduct the sales analysis for David Lucke with the information provided.
2. Discuss your interpretation of the results and their implications for managerial attention.
3. What are the shortcomings of the analysis?

Exhibit 1
District and U.S. Sales &
Nonprescription Drugs

	District[a]		U.S.[a]	
Year	Hi-Po	Industry	Hi-Po	Industry
1971	$3.8	$15.0	$70.0	$250
1972	4.0	15.1	73.1	252
1973	4.2	15.6	78.0	260
1974	4.3	16.5	79.8	275
1975	4.8	18.4	89.9	310
1976	5.3	19.8	100.0	330

[a]All figures are in millions.

Exhibit 2
District Sales for 1976 by
Territory and Product Line[a]

Territory	Vitamins	Cold Remedies	Antacids	Pain Relievers	Total
Alabama	$517	$557	$246	$290	$1,610
Kentucky	513	513	234	250	1,510
Mississippi	370	355	45	160	930
Tennessee	225	400	275	350	1,250
District	$1,625	$1,825	$800	$1,050	$5,300

[a]Sales are in thousands.

Exhibit 3
Sales & Marketing Management
"Buying Power Indexes" by
State and Region, 1976

	Graduated Buying Power Indexes		
Territory	Economy-Priced Products (EPP)	Moderate-Priced Products (MPP)	Premium-Priced Products (PPP)
Alabama	1.9479	1.6570	1.3763
Kentucky	1.8356	1.4916	1.2143
Mississippi	1.3500	.9588	.7886
Tennessee	2.2818	2.0345	1.6583
Region	7.4153	6.1419	5.0375

Source: "Survey of Buying Power" *Sales & Marketing Management* (annual issue), 1977, page 2–1. Reprinted with permission.

Case 12

Representative Rubber Company

Learning Objectives

1. To gain experience in time management.
2. To learn how to plan a route which meets the requirements of servicing current accounts, developing prospective accounts, and minimizing travel time.

Advance Preparation   Read the Overview, the Representative Rubber Company case, and the Procedure.

Overview   An important ability of successful sales representatives is to know how to efficiently use their time, plan their routes, service accounts, and develop prospective accounts. Conflict often arises between the sales representative and the sales manager in developing time schedules and route plans. This exercise demonstrates how such plans should be developed, and why it is necessary to coordinate such efforts between the sales manager and the sales representative.

The Representative Rubber Case

Company Background   Representative Rubber Company is one of several rubber producing firms in the United States. It produces a full line of tires and tubes along with other rubber products such as hot water bottles, tennis sneakers, industrial rubber products, etc. The firm is divisionalized, and the Tire Division sells tires and tubes to several thousand independent franchised dealers, as well as through company-owned retail tire stores. The Tire Division has sales of approximately $300,000,000 in tires, tubes, and repair materials.

Approximately 300 sales representatives are employed to cover the forty-eight continental states. Hawaii, Alaska, Canada, and Mexico are handled by the firm's International Division. Several years before, the firm divided the sales territories of its 300 sales representatives according to the sales volume then coming from each area. That is, sales representatives were assigned to enough counties to give each of them about $1,000,000 in sales.

The Rubber Manufacturer's Association, a trade association to which nearly all tire manufacturers belong, annually collects the tire sales data of each of its members for each county in the United States. These county data are needed for each contributor and distributed to each member. Each member, then, knows his or her sales and the total industry sales in each county.

Sales Representative's Effective Working Time   Sales representatives are expected to work five days a week. Any sales meetings are held on Saturday mornings and *need not* be worked into the travel schedule.

Approximately forty-five hours, including travel time, are available to a sales representative each week. Occasionally, a sales representative is expected to work more than the average nine hours a day, but is not expected to work more than forty-five hours in a week.

All sales representatives live within the confines of their territorial assignment, and are allowed to return home each night.

Prospecting Time   The company has decided that to ensure future business, a minimum of a sales representative's time must be spent on prospecting for new dealers. This involves making calls on competitive accounts, bankers, and others who might either be prospective representative dealers or who would know of such prospects.

Dealer Calls   Current dealers must be called upon at the rate of *two hours per month per $50,000 of annual current business*. This time is spent counting inventory, taking orders, training retail salespeople, helping prepare advertisements, inspecting returned tires, etc.

Data about your territory are given in Exhibits 1–4. In Exhibit 1, you will find broad county data on auto registrations, total tire sales in dollars last year, and our firm's sales in each county. Exhibit 2 breaks the county sales down into major city and township components, and shows the total number of tire dealers in each city. Exhibit 3 is a roster of our active accounts and their sales for last year. Finally, Exhibit 4 is a map of the territory and a mileage chart for the towns.

Procedure

Step 1. Before class, read the Representative Rubber Company case and answer the questions on the page titled "Criteria for Time and Route Management for Sales Representatives."

Step 2. Also before class, complete the "Routing Form (prepared by Sales Representative)." Be sure to comply with the rules prescribed by the company, and develop the routing schedule over a four-week period. An example of how to fill in the form is shown below the routing schedule.

Step 3. In class, the administrator will divide the class into groups of three students per group by asking class members to count off by three. Each number one is the territorial sales manager, each number two is the sales analyst, and each number three is the sales representative in the territory. (5 minutes)

Step 4. Each group (comprised of a sales manager, a sales analyst, and a sales representative) will meet to develop a routing schedule that meets the rules prescribed by the firm for the sales representative over four weeks. (20–40 minutes)

Step 5. Fill in the "Routing Form (prepared by Sales Manager)." All three participants will help in developing the routing schedule; however, the sales manager is in charge and will have final authority in filling out the routing form. (5 minutes)

Step 6. Complete the form "The Objectives and Criteria, Model, or Framework Used in Sales Representative Routing Procedure."

Step 7. General class discussion and instructor comments:
a) What differences exist among groups in the decisions they reached? Why? b) Were differences between sales representatives' goals and company goals resolved? If so, how? c) From the company's point of view, what is an optimum routing solution for sales representatives? Why?

**Criteria for Time and Route Management
for Sales Representatives**

1. Assume you are a sales representative for Representative Rubber Company. Choose a home town for yourself on the basis of where you would like to live and which would be centrally located insofar as covering the territory. Why did you select the town you did? (Note: you should plan to stay overnight at some time during most weeks, but certainly not every night.)

   I would choose to live in _____.

   The reason(s) for my choice is(are): _____

   _____

   _____

2. What *criteria* would you use in devising a scheme for dividing your prospecting time among the counties in your territory?
   Criteria:

   1. _____

   2. _____

   3. _____

   4. _____

   5. _____

   6. _____

   7. _____

   8. _____

   Which, in your opinion, are the *three most important criteria*? Why these?

   1. _____ 2. _____ 3. _____

   These criteria are the most important because: _____

   _____

   _____

   _____

Routing Form
(prepared by Sales Representative)

Week	Monday			Tuesday			Wednesday			Thursday			Friday		
	Start		Hours	Start		Hours	Start		Hours	Start		Hours	Start		Hours
1	End		—	End		—	End		—	End		—	End		—
	Start		Hours	Start		Hours	Start		Hours	Start		Hours	Start		Hours
2	End		—	End		—	End		—	End		—	End		—
	Start		Hours	Start		Hours	Start		Hours	Start		Hours	Start		Hours
3	End		—	End		—	End		—	End		—	End		—
	Start		Hours	Start		Hours	Start		Hours	Start		Hours	Start		Hours
4	End		—	End		—	End		—	End		—	End		—

Example: **Monday**

	Hours
Start—Jefferson City	
Jefferson City Tire	4
Prospecting	4
Travel	0
End—Jefferson City	8

Routing Form
(prepared by Sales Manager)

Week	Monday		Tuesday		Wednesday		Thursday		Friday	
	Start	Hours	Start	Hours	Start	Hours	Start	Hours	Start	Hours
1	End	___	End	___	End	___	End	___	End	___
	Start	Hours	Start	Hours	Start	Hours	Start	Hours	Start	Hours
2	End	___	End	___	End	___	End	___	End	___
	Start	Hours	Start	Hours	Start	Hours	Start	Hours	Start	Hours
3	End	___	End	___	End	___	End	___	End	___
	Start	Hours	Start	Hours	Start	Hours	Start	Hours	Start	Hours
4	End	___	End	___	End	___	End	___	End	___

Example: **Monday**

	Hours
Start—Jefferson City	
Jefferson City Tire	4
Prospecting	4
Travel	0
End—Jefferson City	8

Exhibit 1
Selected Territory Data for
Representative Rubber Company

County Name	County Auto Registrations	Representative's Current Sales	Total County Tire Sales Last Year
Washington	12,000	$100,000	$ 900,000
Jefferson	11,000	450,000	750,000
Fillmore	10,000	250,000	1,200,000
Arthur	4,000	200,000	260,000

Exhibit 2
Estimated Sales by City Last
Year, and Dealer Census

County and City	Estimated City Sales	Estimated Number of Dealers	Our Dealers
Washington			
Adamsville	450,000	5	0
Krepston	450,000	4	1
Jefferson			
Jefferson City	450,000	6	4
Wilson	150,000	3	1
Newton	75,000	2	
Ayerville	38,000	3	1
Eaton	37,000	2	1
Fillmore			
Athens	960,000	18	4
Sparta	130,000	4	2
Rhodes	110,000	2	1
Arthur			
Lincoln	260,000	2	1

Exhibit 3
Record of Dealer Sales for
Last Year in this Territory

Dealer Roster	Estimated Sales
Adamsville	
Krepston	
Pioneer Tire Sales	100,000
Jefferson City	
Jefferson City Tire	150,000
Main Street Tire & Appliance	100,000
Acme Supply	50,000
Jones and Laughter, Inc.	50,000
Wilson	
American Automotive	60,000
Ayerville	
Ace Recap Company	20,000
Eaton	
Little Accessory Corporation	20,000
Athens	
Athens Supply	50,000
Holsten and Holsten	40,000
Dearborn Tire Company	25,000
North American Auto Supply	15,000
Sparta	
Greek Gifts & Automotive	60,000
Goodbody Tires	15,000
Rhodes	
Rhodes Tire & Appliance	40,000
Lincoln	
J. W. Booth & Sons	200,000

Exhibit 4
Map and Mileage Chart for this Territory

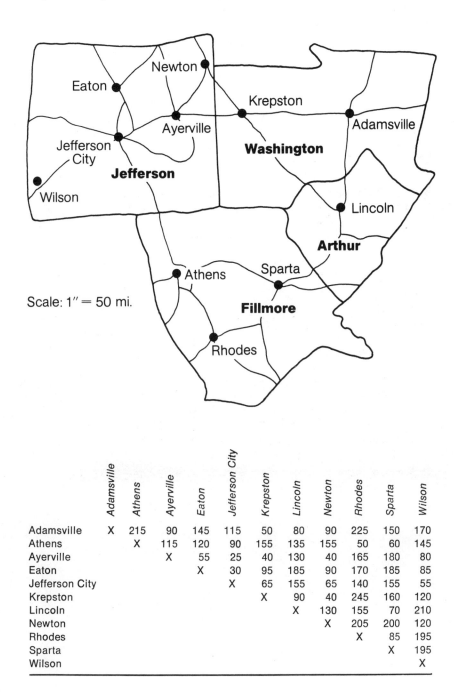

Scale: 1″ = 50 mi.

	Adamsville	Athens	Ayerville	Eaton	Jefferson City	Krepston	Lincoln	Newton	Rhodes	Sparta	Wilson
Adamsville	X	215	90	145	115	50	80	90	225	150	170
Athens		X	115	120	90	155	135	155	50	60	145
Ayerville			X	55	25	40	130	40	165	180	80
Eaton				X	30	95	185	90	170	185	85
Jefferson City					X	65	155	65	140	155	55
Krepston						X	90	40	245	160	120
Lincoln							X	130	155	70	210
Newton								X	205	200	120
Rhodes									X	85	195
Sparta										X	195
Wilson											X

**The Objectives and Criteria, Model, or
Framework Used in Sales Representative
Routing Procedure**

1. The objectives we are trying to achieve for our sales representative routing schedules are:

   (1) _____

   (2) _____

   (3) _____

   (4) _____

2. The criteria, model, framework, and/or approach we are using for achieving these objectives are:

   _____

   _____

   _____

   _____

   _____

3. a. The sales representative is: (circle one)
   (1) very satisfied with the scheduling
   (2) somewhat satisfied with the scheduling
   (3) somewhat dissatisfied with the scheduling
   (4) very dissatisfied with the scheduling

   b. The reason for his or her satisfaction (or dissatisfaction) is:

   _____

   _____

   _____

4. Describe the interaction that took place in your group in developing your routing schedule.

   _____

   _____

   _____

   _____

Part 4
Staffing and Training

Case 13

Automotive Supply Products, Inc.

Two people from the Equal Employment Opportunity Commission (EEOC) have recently completed an audit of Automotive Supply Product's (ASP) sales force personnel files. Of the firm's 550 salespeople, none are female or members of minority groups. This week the company received a recommendation from EEOC that their hiring practices be changed. The report stated that minorities must be hired immediately and moved into management within two years. In six months EEOC will visit ASP to follow-up on their recommendations.

Changes in Recruiting Practices

Top management had seen this coming for a long time. Each district manager has always been allowed to recruit and hire his own people. However, it was felt this had to change.

In order to better comply with governmental regulations, and in an effort to centralize employment activities, each region's assistant regional sales manager was given the responsibility of college recruiting. This would allow district managers more time with their salespeople.

This case was developed by Teresa Scoggins as a requirement for her MBA at Texas A&M University under the supervision of Professor Charles M. Futrell. The company name and individual names have been changed.

The Atlanta Sales Region   Dave Appleby had been with ASP for nine years, and has been the assistant regional sales manager for the last two years. Appleby met with each district manager in the Atlanta region to assure them that he would do his best to screen and select the very best applicants for them to choose from. The district manager would still make the final hiring decision. Appleby also asked each manager how many people he would need and for characteristic preferences for salespeople.

Approximately 80 per cent of ASP's sales candidates are recruited from colleges. Each December personnel forecasts are made for the coming year. This includes estimates of both new positions and turnover. On-campus interviewing takes place in March, July, and October resulting in over two hundred students being interviewed each year. Typically four students are usually selected for each opening and undergo an in-depth interview at the local district office. After taking tests and interviewing with office personnel, the four are ranked, with the top candidate asked to work for a day with a local salesperson. That person usually receives the first job offer.

Candidates for the Miami District   Archie Burkett is the sales manager for the Miami district. Burkett is fifty-five years old and has worked for ASP for twenty-five years. During his fifteen years in management, Burkett has gained a reputation for doing a good recruiting job. Several of the people he has hired have been promoted into the New York office. At times Burkett would confess that he had trouble making up his mind on whom to hire. However, he looked for people with ego drive, empathy, and a need to achieve success. It seemed to work for him so he used those three characteristics as a guide. Burkett's own yearly performance appraisal always included his hiring success and costs. In addition, hiring successful people meant better sales for his district which resulted in a higher yearly bonus for Burkett and his salespeople.

When the new personnel selection system was announced, Burkett could see advantages and disadvantages. However, he realized that the move would bring minorities into ASP's sales force. Given twenty-seven years of sales experience, Burkett knew men could do a good job. He was unsure of women. He felt he might find it difficult to train and work with a woman. What would happen if he had to criticize her? He could see her begin crying. Also, what about his yearly bonus? If her sales drop, so does his salary. Burkett remembered the comments of several members of his sales force when two women were hired by a competitor. They said women could not stand the pressure; would not stay out overnight; were not dependable; and would only work for a short time, quitting in order to raise a family. Furthermore one salesperson felt that customers would not like a woman trying to sell them ASP's products. Burkett himself had always felt a woman's place was in the home.

In December Burkett asked for and received approval to hire two new salespeople. His sales had increased so that two new territories could be created. In March, Appleby called Burkett to ask when would be the best time for him to interview three students for the two jobs. Burkett was surprised at having so few to interview. However, Appleby felt these were the best candidates with qualifications well above those of the others. All three applicants were to be interviewed the second week in April. Appleby said he had already mailed all applicants' paper work to Burkett for review.

As Burkett examined the applications he was startled to see that two of the three candidates were women, and he felt very uneasy anticipating his first interview with a female. How should he act? Well, he would worry about that when the time arrived. For now he developed a summary of the three people as shown in Exhibit 1. Archie ranked the people in this order Green, Davis, then Glenn.

The Interviews   One applicant was interviewed a day. The interviews took place on Tuesday, Wednesday, and Thursday. As they arrived in the morning, Burkett's secretary met them and administered several tests which took about three hours to complete. Burkett took them to lunch and from approximately 2:00 to 4:00 people in the office interviewed them. For the first time Archie asked two salespeople John Bryant and Larry Billingsley, to also interview the applicants.

John Bryant had been hired by Burkett eight years ago. He and Burkett had become close friends and each year spent one week of their vacation fishing together. Larry Billingsley had been hired by Burkett one year ago. Burkett felt he was bright, hard working, and an excellent

---

Exhibit 1
Biographical Data on the Candidates

1. Kevin Green. Age 23. Industrial distribution major at the University of Alabama; GPA 2.86; earned 80 per cent of money for school working part-time and summers. Played offensive end on Alabama's national championship team under Coach Bear Bryant.

2. Clara Davis. Age 24. Marketing major with BBA and MBA from the University of Florida; GPA 3.85 undergraduate and 4.0 graduate. No work experience. School activities include president of sorority and vice-president of the student body. Likes sports and reading.

3. Susan Glenn. Age 23. Psychology major with 3.56 GPA from Georgia State University; hometown Miami; worked in retail sales for father's small automotive parts store part-time for eight years. No school activities.

salesperson. In fact, Burkett considered Billingsley as top management material. Both Bryant and Billingsley were excited about the opportunity to help recruit. All three candidates would be interviewed and the three men would meet the next week to review all material.

After interviewing Kevin Green, Burkett was excited about hiring him. They had spent almost an hour talking about what it was like to play football at Alabama. Bear Bryant was always Burkett's image of the ideal coach. Even though Green worked in the summers in his father's grocery store, he had a lot of free time to fish. The only drawback to hiring Green was that he might be in the professional football draft.

Wednesday, Burkett interviewed Clara Davis. When Burkett first saw Clara he could not believe it. She was one of the best-looking girls he had ever seen. She had a good firm handshake, constant eye contact, beautiful smile, and a charming personality. Burkett had trouble carrying on a conversation with her. She should be in the movies, not in sales, he thought to himself. She asked pointed questions on training, compensation, and advancement. Davis had broken off her engagement a year ago and decided that she wanted to be in sales management at the corporate level. Davis was astonished that ASP had no female salespeople. However, she left no question in Burkett's mind that if she were offered a job and if she accepted it, she would work night and day to advance quickly in the corporation and Burkett believed her.

The next day Burkett visited with Susan Glenn. He had his back to the door when his secretary and Glenn entered the room. As his secretary introduced Glenn, Burkett turned to shake hands. He was speechless when he saw that Glenn was an attractive, black female. This possibility had never entered Burkett's mind. The interview was shorter than the others. Like Davis, Glenn was personable and witty. She asked several questions about training, advancement, and opportunities for women at ASP. Burkett discussed their three-week training program, compensation, and mentioned that ASP would hire qualified women who had the potential for management positions.

What Decision to Make   Burkett was glad the interviewing was over. This experience was something he felt he would never forget. The next week he, Bryant, and Billingsley met to discuss the applicants. Appleby was also in town so he was invited.

Exhibit 2 shows the categories of psychological traits that the applicants were graded on, based on tests they had taken. Scores were reported in terms of a standard score scale with a mean of 50 and a standard deviation of 10. The testing company that graded the tests reported the scores and gave a summary for each person. It appeared to Burkett that each of the candidates had scored basically the same. Based

Exhibit 2
California Psychological Inventory

1. Dominance
2. Capacity for status
3. Social presence
4. Self-acceptance
5. Sense of well-being
6. Responsibility
7. Socialization
8. Self-control
9. Tolerance

10. Good impression
11. Communality
12. Achievement via conformance
13. Achievement via independence
14. Intellectual efficiency
15. Psychological mindedness
16. Flexibility
17. Femininity

on the test results, Burkett saw very few differences. He told Bryant, Billingsley, and Appleby that the tests made his job more difficult because they did not screen out anyone. On a blackboard, Burkett developed the preferences for the applicants shown in Exhibit 3. Burkett was openly upset at the differences in preferences. Even though he felt forced to rank the two women second and third, Burkett did not want to hire either of them. When Appleby said let's hire them all, Burkett left the room. Appleby caught him in the hall and calmly reminded him that, if the firm did not hire qualified minority applicants, it would be guilty of government affirmative action violations.

Exhibit 3
Preferences for Applicants

Interviewers' Ranking	Kevin Green	Clara Davis	Susan Glenn
Archie Burkett	1	2	3
John Bryant	2	1	3
Larry Billingsley	3	1	2

Questions

1. What should Burkett do?
2. How would you rank the applicants?
3. Assuming you could only hire two people, whom would you hire?
4. Discuss personnel practices and laws pertaining to this case.
5. What are the problems in the case, if any? If there are problems, what would you recommend?

Case 14

Data Products International

Fred Johnson was turning into a true believer in Gumperson's Law which states that the probability of any given event is inversely proportional to its desirability. Not only are those things you wish to avoid most likely to occur, but the events you anxiously anticipate never seem to materialize. Fred was feeling somewhat depressed because equal opportunity had finally come to roost in his office. He is the manager of the San Francisco sales office of Data Products International. One of his primary responsibilities is recruiting and hiring new sales representatives. Up to now, he had managed to avoid the issue of women.

Data Products International (DPI) is a large firm, although dwarfed by some of the giants in the data processing industry. It is headquartered on the East Coast and has sales offices in almost every major U.S. city. Several of the larger metropolitan markets are serviced by multiple sales offices. DPI was growing rapidly as primary demand for the industry's products expanded. This rapid growth brought about constant pressure to recruit new salespeople.

DPI followed a fairly established recruiting pattern. Almost all of its recruiting activities involved college placement offices, and most candidates were recent college graduates. Although DPI preferred business graduates with some math or science background, a few of the more

This case was prepared by Barbara A. Pletcher, California State University at Sacramento.

recent recruits had degrees in political science and economics. Each September Fred prepared a forecast of his hiring requirements for the next spring. This included both new positions and replacements for people who either left the company or were transferred. On the basis of this forecast, he scheduled visits to area colleges. He had several favorite schools from which he had hired a number of successful sales representatives in the past. He liked to visit the University of the Pacific in Stockton, San Luis Obispo, California State University, Sacramento, Chico State, and the University of Nevada at Reno. On-campus interviewing usually took place between January and March. Until now, he had conducted all the on-campus interviews personally, so he also was responsible for initial screening. After seeing between twenty-five and thirty-five students over the normal campus season, he would invite as many as three students per anticipated position to a follow-up interview in San Francisco. The purpose of the office interview was to get a better look at the person in an actual business setting, complete a few tests, and give the potential employee a better chance to evaluate the company. Fred always gave the student some time alone with one of the newer sales representatives. He hoped that the student would ask some questions which might seem too frivolous or dangerous to ask the sales manager. He often was surprised that these young people asked so few questions when they had such important decisions to make, both about the company and the nature of the selling job. Finally, after conferring with any people who had met the applicants and reviewing the applicant's qualifications, he would rank them and start to make offers. The first offers usually went out during the first week of May.

Although the recruiting process was long and sometimes frustrating, Fred was proud of his record. He could point to a number of young men he had brought into the company who had continued on to management positions. Although making decisions that directly affect the future of others can be a heavy burden, Fred assumed that he must be doing something right. It was not easy to decide who would be successful in sales and who would not. Fred had read lots of books on the subject over the years. Most of the advice boiled down to two simple terms: ego drive and empathy. Ego drive has been described as the need to make the sale, the need to succeed, and the need to win. Empathy is the ability to understand another person's position and feelings. Although Fred never doubted that these were important qualities, he often wished someone would come up with a foolproof way to measure them in people. Not only did he worry that he might damage some other person either by hiring a person who was not qualified and would fail, or by failing to hire someone who would have been successful. He worried about his own future.

Fred's effectiveness in the hiring process affected his future in two very direct ways. First, as manager of the San Francisco office, he was held responsible for productivity. If his people were not good in the field, he would hear about it from headquarters. Secondly, his compensation was directly tied to his sales force. He received a small base salary; however, the majority of his compensation was an override on his salespeople's commissions. If his people didn't sell, he didn't get paid.

This year things were different. A new position had been created that had brought about some significant changes in the recruiting process. All of the DPI sales offices were clustered into regions. San Francisco was part of the Western Region which included eleven western states. In a move to ease some of the sales manager's recruiting burden, a staff person from the regional office had assumed the college interviewing duties. There was some justification for this in that the manager typically saw as many as ten students for each person hired. If the initial screening process could be completed by someone else, the sales manager would have more time to devote to developing new salespeople. Although, like many of the sales managers in the district, Fred could see both advantages and disadvantages to this system, he had not anticipated the difficulty which developed. In effect, he was brought face-to-face with a fact which to this point he had chosen to ignore. He knew that DPI was under pressure to implement affirmative action. All of the advertisements of job openings included the phrase "We are an equal opportunity employer M/F." He had always hoped that managers of the other offices would hire enough minority people so that he would not have to move in that direction. It was not that he had any evidence that women could not do the job as sales representatives, it was just that all his experience proved to him that men could. After all, his livelihood depended on his sales force.

The Staff Recruiter   Jack Cartwright had been with DPI for almost thirty years. He had started out as a salesperson in the Philadelphia office and had managed the Cleveland, Ohio office for twelve years. After a recent heart attack, he had been ordered to cut back on his levels of activity and stress. His needs dovetailed with the DPI plan to introduce a regional staff recruiter. Management decided that it might be a good idea to test this concept using a person with experience in selling and sales management, and years of knowledge about the company and the industry. Jack looked upon his new position as an opportunity to give the careful attention to screening applicants that he had always hoped for but never had time to accomplish while managing the Cleveland office.

Having some organizational sense and recognizing that innovation often collides with vested interest, one of Jack's first activities was to meet with each of the managers of each of the offices in the Western district to assure them that his only purpose was to save them time by screening applicants so that only qualified people would be seen by the individual managers. He emphasized that the final decision, as always, would rest with the individual manager. He stressed the advantages of the new system. He honestly felt that this would save time and result in a more efficient recruiting process. Under the former system, each manager visited a few schools. There were some schools that never were covered and others that were visited by more than one manager. Not only was the company in competition with itself, but it was somewhat confusing for the student, who was never sure whether to schedule interviews with each manager.

Another of Jack's important objectives for the initial meeting with each manager was to determine the manager's needs for people for the coming year and to encourage the manager to discuss preferences and priorities regarding the selection process. He summarized the responses for future reference (see Exhibit 1). Because the managers' opinions seemed consistent with his own, he moved to the next step and scheduled interviews at campus placement centers across the region.

Candidates for the San Francisco Openings Fred Johnson anticipated two openings on his sales staff. Growth in the sales volume in the minicomputer line justified one position, and one of the men in the office products area would be retiring in June justifying the other position. At the end of February, he received a telephone call from Jack Cartwright who asked about the best schedule for follow-up interviews in San Francisco for the five students he had selected as most qualified for the positions. Fred was pleased that the recruiting process was ahead of schedule and that Jack had delivered on his promise to leave the final choice up to the individual manager. Because all five people were from the Northern California area, they decided to schedule the interviews on five consecutive days during the second week in March. Jack promised to send the papers on each candidate immediately so that Fred could be prepared for the interviews. They agreed that Jack might as well schedule the interviews with the candidates since there was no apparent reason to see them in any particular order and they all knew Jack. (See Exhibit 2.)

When Fred received the materials on the candidates, his initial reaction was surprise. For a few moments, he had the urge to call Jack to see if the interviews had been scheduled. If they had not, he intended to suggest that Jack need not bother to schedule one for Joan Channell. It did not take long for him to realize that he could not do that. It is

Exhibit 1
Managers' Responses

1. Appropriate education	Business degree, MBA preferred
	Some science or math courses
	Economics or Political Science is acceptable
2. Work experience	Sales experience preferred
	Work should have involved people contact
3. Drive	Should be involved in extra activities
	Should have earned part of school expenses
	Should show leadership experience
	Sports is a good indication
4. Enthusiasm	Interest in sales
	Confidence in abilities
	Adventuresome spirit
	Should have ventured off the safe paths
5. Self-reliance	Demonstrated ability to take care of oneself
	Independent spirit
6. Interpersonal skills	Some group activities
	Preference for "people jobs"

one thing to avoid women, but it is an altogether different matter to reject them once they have passed the initial screening. When *he* had been doing the interviewing, he had avoided this problem. He decided he would have to go through with the interviews, but he believed that there was little chance that he would offer one of the positions to Ms. Channell.

The issue of Joan Channell stuck with him throughout the day, and he spent some time thinking about the objections he had heard whenever the topic of women in sales had come up in managers' meetings. Absentmindedly, he jotted down a list of comments (see Exhibit 3.) As he looked at his list, he realized that he was in a vulnerable position. If he did not treat this female properly in the interviewing process, he could open up the possibility of action against himself and/or the company. He resolved that he would read some materials on interviewing women and set up some standard questions to avoid problems.

To prepare for the interviews, Fred called in several of his salespeople and told them that since a woman would be coming in for an interview, he felt it was time to standardize the interviewing process. Until now, most interviews had been considered an opportunity to get to know the candidate. In the past, he had encouraged applicants to discuss the job with one of his salespeople but felt that this would no longer be possible. Fred prepared a list of standardized questions, care-

Exhibit 2
Application Materials

DATA PRODUCTS INTERNATIONAL

EMPLOYMENT APPLICATION

Applicant's Name – *Please Type or Print*

Channell	Joan	Linda
Last	First	Middle

POSITION APPLIED FOR	REASON FOR APPLYING
sales representative	my qualifications meet your requirements and I think this position represents an excellent opportunity

an Equal Opportunity Employer who hires without regard to race, religion, sex, color, national origin, or age.

Home Address 22346   Burt Road
Number   Street

Fairfield   California   94533
City   State   ZIP Code

Home Phone 353-4063   Business Phone 362-1986

Referred By ☐ employee ☐ newspaper ☐ agency

☒ other college placement center

Social Security Number 4 0 2 – 2 3 – 1 5 1 2

Do you have the right to work in the United States on a permanent basis? ☒ Yes ☐ No

Do you have relatives employed by DPI?
☐ Yes ☒ No   If yes, who? _____
   where? _____

Have you ever been employed by DPI?
☐ Yes ☒ No   If yes, when? _____
   where? _____

RECORD OF EMPLOYMENT

Employer Business and Address	Dates FROM (Mo.-Yr.)	Dates TO (Mo.-Yr.)	Salaries BASIC MONTHLY SALARY OR DRAW ACCOUNT	OVERTIME BONUS COMMISSION	Position and Basic Duties	Reason for Leaving
MacDonalds 3065 N. Main, Fairfield	6/72	5/73	$2.30/hr		Counter clerk	better job
Stereo Record Center 29375 Elm, Fairfield	6/73	8/74	$2.65/hr		Sales clerk	better job school
Macy's Sacramento,	9/74	6/76	$3.25/hr		Sales clerk	graduate school
California State U. Sacramento	9/76	12/77	$320		graduate assistant	graduation

Have you any income in addition to your salary? ☐ Yes ☒ No   If yes, explain _____

EDUCATION

	Name	Dates Attended From	Dates Attended To	Major	Minor	Degree
HIGH SCHOOL	Howard Taft, Dayton, OH	9/69	6/72	College prep		diploma
COLLEGE	Solano County C.C.	9/72	9/74	communications		A.A.
	Cal. State. U., Sacramento	9/74	12/77	Marketing	Finance	B.A., M.B.A.
OTHER TRAINING						

MISCELLANEOUS INFORMATION

List honors, awards, extra-curricular activities (school or community), and grades Delta Sigma Pi, Treasurer
Inter-collegiate Business Games team, 1976; Jerry Lewis Telethon volunteer, 1975-77

What part of expenses did you earn during high school?_____ college? 25%
List any hobbies, including sports tennis, water skiing, snow skiing

Draft Status -- _____ Have you been in the United States military service? ☐ Yes ☒ No
If no, explain Not eligible for draft and did not volunteer
_____ Branch of Service _____
Date of entry into active duty -- _____ Date of release from active duty _____
Rank on release from active duty _____ Completion date of Reserve commitment _____

Have you ever been convicted of any criminal action? ☐ Yes ☒ No   If yes, explain _____

List health disabilities none
Are you willing to go to work in any DATA PRODUCTS INTERNATIONAL office in the United States? ☒ Yes ☐ No
List preferences San Francisco, Sacramento, Los Angeles, Seat _ . Denver, Phoenix

Tell something about yourself, including reasons you feel you are qualified for the position.

As the youngest of four children in a military family I have had numerous opportunities
to develop skills in interpersonal relations and personal adjustment. I have had to
make new friends and understand different types of people each time we have moved. I
feel that these experiences would make me more able to assume a selling position. I
have researched the data processing industry in connection with a term paper and
understand the requirements of a sales representative in that industry. I know that
I would be diligent in that rewards are related to performance and the possibility
exists for advancing into a management position.

The information given herein is true and accurate to the best of my knowledge and belief; I understand that all information given
will be verified.

Date 2-2-77   Signature Jean Channell

HIRING COMMITMENT (For Official Use Only)

Interviewer's Comments/Name _____

Department/Office _____ Organization Code _____
Starting Date _____ Expense Allocation Code _____
Bi-weekly Salary _____ Job Title _____
Job Code _____ Date _____
Designated Signature _____ Name (printed) _____

Code 169 Rev. 4/74

Case 14   Data Products International   **131**

Exhibit 2—*continued*

DATA PRODUCTS INTERNATIONAL

EMPLOYMENT APPLICATION

Applicant's Name – *Please Type or Print*

Greenfile	David	Alexander
Last	First	Middle

POSITION APPLIED FOR	REASON FOR APPLYING
Sales	Father's recommendation

an Equal Opportunity Employer who hires without regard to race, religion, sex, color, national origin, or age.

Home Address 16236 San Ysidro
 Number   Street

San Jose   CA   95119
City   State   ZIP Code

Home Phone 219-8385   Business Phone --

Referred By ☒ employee ☐ newspaper ☐ agency

☐ other_____

Social Security Number 4 12 16 – 1 18 – 2 12 17 17

Do you have the right to work in the United States on a permanent basis? ☒ Yes ☐ No

Do you have relatives employed by DPI?
☒ Yes ☐ No   If yes, who? Donald Greenfil
   where? San Jose

Have you ever been employed by DPI?
☐ Yes ☒ No   If yes, when?_____
   where?_____

RECORD OF EMPLOYMENT

Employer Business and Address	Dates FROM (Mo.-Yr.)	Dates TO (Mo.-Yr.)	Salaries BASIC MONTHLY SALARY OR DRAW ACCOUNT	Salaries OVERTIME BONUS COMMISSION	Position and Basic Duties	Reason for Leaving
Safeway, 2336 Cooper San Jose	6/64	9/69	4.65 per hour	none	stock clerk checker	military
San Jose Bee 312 12th street, west	1/73	3/7	4.25/per hour	none	copy assistant	school

Have you any income in addition to your salary? ☒ Yes ☐ No   If yes, explain G.I. benefits

EDUCATION

	Name	Dates Attended From	Dates Attended To	Major	Minor	Degree
HIGH SCHOOL	San Gabriel, San Jose	9/63	6/67	--		graduated
COLLEGE	San Jose State	9/67	6/69	physical education	psychology	--
	San Jose State	9/74	6/77	business	communications	B.A.
OTHER TRAINING						

MISCELLANEOUS INFORMATION

List honors, awards, extra-curricular activities (school or community), and grades __Vet's Club, San Jose State__

What part of expenses did you earn during high school? __25%__ college? __100% inc, GI Bill__

List any hobbies, including sports __flying, jogging,__

Draft Status __served__ Have you been in the United States military service? [X] Yes [ ] No

If no, explain _____

Branch of Service __army__

Date of entry into active duty __12/69__ Date of release from active duty __11/73__

Rank on release from active duty __sp. 4th__ Completion date of Reserve commitment __--__

Have you ever been convicted of any criminal action? [ ] Yes [X] No If yes, explain _____

List health disabilities __none__

Are you willing to go to work in any DATA PRODUCTS INTERNATIONAL office in the United States? [X] Yes [ ] No

List preferences __San Francisco, Portland, San Diego__

Tell something about yourself, including reasons you feel you are qualified for the position.

It has taken me a while to decide what I want to do but now I've decided that I want
to work in the data processing industry. I've completed both school and my military
obligations and am ready to get serious about my career. I know that I can earn a
good living in sales and I'm sure that I would be a good representative of Data
Products International.

The information given herein is true and accurate to the best of my knowledge and belief; I understand that all information given
will be verified.

Date __2/16/77__ Signature __David C. Treenfila__

HIRING COMMITMENT (For Official Use Only)

Interviewer's Comments/Name _____

Department/Office _____ Organization Code _____

Starting Date _____ Expense Allocation Code _____

Bi-weekly Salary _____ Job Title _____

Job Code _____ Date _____

Designated Signature _____ Name (printed) _____

Code 169 Rev 4/74

Exhibit 2—*continued*

DATA PRODUCTS INTERNATIONAL
EMPLOYMENT APPLICATION

Applicant's Name – *Please Type or Print*

PLOWE	EUGENE	J.
Last	First	Middle

POSITION APPLIED FOR	REASON FOR APPLYING

on Equal Opportunity Employer who hires without regard to race, religion, sex, color, national origin, or age.

Home Address 899 Delaware
Number / Street

Vacaville Ca 98275
City / State / ZIP Code

Home Phone 541-5871 Business Phone _____

Referred By ☐ employee ☐ newspaper ☐ agency

☒ other Vocational Counsellor

Social Security Number 4812 - 615 - 78712

Do you have the right to work in the United States on a permanent basis? ☒ Yes ☐ No

Do you have relatives employed by DPI?
☐ Yes ☒ No If yes, who? _____
where? _____

Have you ever been employed by DPI?
☐ Yes ☒ No If yes, when? _____
where? _____

RECORD OF EMPLOYMENT

Employer Business and Address	Dates FROM (Mo.-Yr.)	Dates TO (Mo.-Yr.)	BASIC MONTHLY SALARY OR DRAW ACCOUNT	OVERTIME BONUS COMMISSION	Position and Basic Duties	Reason for Leaving
Galt, Ca. Motor Industries	9/69	8/70	P.T. $3.20/hr.		materials handling	Military Service
Long Beach Long's Drugs	10/73	3/74	$4.00/hr.		Clerk & Stock	Better job on Campus
Long Beach State	6/74	9/75	5.00/hr.		Campus Security	Wanted experience
Liberty Dept Store	9/75		P.T. $1.50/hr. F.T. 2.00/wk		Office Records	

Have you any income in addition to your salary? ☒ Yes ☐ No If yes, explain Dividends on inherited stocks

EDUCATION

	Name	Dates Attended From	Dates Attended To	Major	Minor	Degree
HIGH SCHOOL	Vacaville High	1963	1964			
COLLEGE	Consumnes River	1969	1970			
	Long Beach State	1973	1976	Business	Finance	B.A.
OTHER TRAINING						

MISCELLANEOUS INFORMATION

List honors, awards, extra-curricular activities (school or community), and grades _____

Football letter 11, 12   Jr. Achievement 9,10

What part of expenses did you earn during high school? __NONE_____ college? __50%_____

List any hobbies, including sports __Football, Soccer, Boating_____

Draft Status _____ Have you been in the United States military service? ☒ Yes ☐ No

If no, explain _____

_____ Branch of Service __Army_____

Date of entry into active duty __Aug. 1970_____ Date of release from active duty __7.12.1973___

Rank on release from active duty __Sergeant_____ Completion date of Reserve commitment ___—_____

Have you ever been convicted of any criminal action? ☐ Yes ☒ No   If yes, explain _____

_____

List health disabilities __None_____

Are you willing to go to work in any DATA PRODUCTS INTERNATIONAL office in the United States? ☒ Yes ☐ No

List preferences __California — San Francisco Area or Los Angeles._____

Tell something about yourself, including reasons you feel you are qualified for the position.

I work well with machines and people. I am
interested in modern technology and its potential
for the future. Being unmarried, I am able
to concentrate my energy to the job at hand.
As my college transcript shows, I have received
excellent grades along with continuing outside
employment.

The information given herein is true and accurate to the best of my knowledge and belief; I understand that all information given
will be verified.

Date __2/10/77_____ Signature _____

HIRING COMMITMENT (For Official Use Only)

Interviewer's Comments/Name _____

_____

Department/Office _____ Organization Code _____

Starting Date _____ Expense Allocation Code _____

Bi-weekly Salary _____ Job Title _____

Job Code _____ Date _____

Designated Signature _____ Name (printed) _____

Code 169 Rev 4/74

Exhibit 2—*continued*

DATA PRODUCTS INTERNATIONAL
EMPLOYMENT APPLICATION

Applicant's Name – *Please Type or Print*

Goldner	Alan	Henry
Last	First	Middle

POSITION APPLIED FOR	REASON FOR APPLYING
Selling	good opportunity

an Equal Opportunity Employer who hires without regard to race, religion, sex, color, national origin, or age.

Home Address 3635 E. Parkway, Apt. 16
_____Number_____Street_____

Chico_____CA_____
City_____State_____ZIP Code

Home Phone 232-9098_____ Business Phone __

Referred By ☐ employee ☐ newspaper ☐ agency

☐ other instructor

Social Security Number | 5 | 2 | 5 | — | 1 | 1 | — | 1 | 3 | 3 | 2 |

Do you have the right to work in the United States on a permanent basis? ☒ Yes ☐ No

Do you have relatives employed by DPI?
☐ Yes ☒ No   If yes, who?_____
where?_____

Have you ever been employed by DPI?
☐ Yes ☒ No   If yes, when?_____
where?_____

RECORD OF EMPLOYMENT

Employer Business and Address	Dates FROM (Mo.-Yr.)	Dates TO (Mo.-Yr.)	Salaries BASIC MONTHLY SALARY OR DRAW ACCOUNT	Salaries OVERTIME BONUS COMMISSION	Position and Basic Duties	Reason for Leaving
K-Mart, Chico	6-73	9-73	2.85		clerk	school
Shasta Center Hasting's Menswear	6-75	10-75	3.10		clerk	school

Have you any income in addition to your salary? ☒ Yes ☐ No   If yes, explain scholarship

EDUCATION

	Name	Dates Attended From	Dates Attended To	Major	Minor	Degree
HIGH SCHOOL	Oroville High	9-70	6-73			graduate
COLLEGE	Chico State U.	9-73	6-77	Marketing	Org. Behav.	B.S.
OTHER TRAINING						

MISCELLANEOUS INFORMATION

List honors, awards, extra-curricular activities (school or community), and grades _K-Club scholarship, Chico_

State Varsity Football, 1973-76, Fellowship for Cristian Athletes

What part of expenses did you earn during high school? _0_ college? _10%_

List any hobbies, including sports _Football, track, tennis, golf, model railroads_

Draft Status _1Y_ Have you been in the United States military service? ☐ Yes ☒ No

If no, explain _colorblind_

_____ Branch of Service _____

Date of entry into active duty _____ Date of release from active duty _____

Rank on release from active duty _____ Completion date of Reserve commitment _____

Have you ever been convicted of any criminal action? ☐ Yes ☒ No   If yes, explain _____

List health disabilities _none_

Are you willing to go to work in any DATA PRODUCTS INTERNATIONAL office in the United States? ☒ Yes ☐ No

List preferences _San Francisco, Atlanta, New Orleans_

Tell something about yourself, including reasons you feel you are qualified for the position.

I've spent all of my life in Northern California and am anxious to undertake a position which will allow me to live in a metropolitan community. I think leadership and responsibility are important experiences and I feel that I have had many opportunities to demonstrate these qualities. I have been a athlete and understand the value of a team effort. I think I work well with people. While my selling experience has been limited to retail sales, I know that I will enjoy the opportunity to help people to meet their needs.

The information given herein is true and accurate to the best of my knowledge and belief; I understand that all information given will be verified.

Date _2/10/77_ Signature _Alan Goldner_

HIRING COMMITMENT (For Official Use Only)

Interviewer's Comments/Name _____

Department/Office _____ Organization Code _____

Starting Date _____ Expense Allocation Code _____

Bi-weekly Salary _____ Job Title _____

Job Code _____ Date _____

Designated Signature _____ Name (printed) _____

Code 169 Rev. 4/74

Exhibit 2—*continued*

DATA PRODUCTS INTERNATIONAL

EMPLOYMENT APPLICATION

Applicant's Name – *Please Type or Print*

McNamarra	Brian	Douglas
Last	First	Middle

POSITION APPLIED FOR
Account representative

REASON FOR APPLYING
Sales is the entry level position leading to marketing management.

on Equal Opportunity Employer who hires without regard to race, religion, sex, color, national origin, or age.

Home Address 10404 Bobolink Lane
Number / Street
Walnut Creek CA 94596
City / State / ZIP Code
Home Phone 726-2104 Business Phone _____

Referred By ☐ employee ☐ newspaper ☐ agency
☒ other marketing professor

Social Security Number 21 9 – 6 4 – 6 3 6 2

Do you have the right to work in the United States on a permanent basis? ☒ Yes ☐ No

Do you have relatives employed by DPI?
☐ Yes ☒ No   If yes, who?_____
where?_____

Have you ever been employed by DPI?
☐ Yes ☒ No   If yes, when?_____
where?_____

RECORD OF EMPLOYMENT

Employer Business and Address	Dates FROM (Mo.-Yr.)	Dates TO (Mo.-Yr.)	BASIC MONTHLY SALARY OR DRAW ACCOUNT	OVERTIME BONUS COMMISSION	Position and Basic Duties	Reason for Leaving
C&I construction	Summers 1969-73		$6.25		carpenters assistant	graduation – new job
State of California Dept Motor Vehicles	6-74	9-75	1110	—	staff researcher	graduate school

Have you any income in addition to your salary? ☐ Yes ☐ No   If yes, explain _____

EDUCATION

	Name	Dates Attended From	To	Major	Minor	Degree
HIGH SCHOOL	Walnut Creek	1967	1970	regular program	yes	
COLLEGE	San Francisco St.	1970	1974	business	social science	B.A.
	San Francisco St	1975	1977	Management	Marketing	MBA
OTHER TRAINING	none					

MISCELLANEOUS INFORMATION

List honors, awards, extra-curricular activities (school or community), and grades _____

_____

What part of expenses did you earn during high school? *10%* _____ college? *40%* _____

List any hobbies, including sports _____

_____

_____

Draft Status *1A* _____ Have you been in the United States military service? ☐ Yes ☒ No

If no, explain _____

_____ Branch of Service _____

Date of entry into active duty _____ Date of release from active duty _____

Rank on release from active duty _____ Completion date of Reserve commitment _____

Have you ever been convicted of any criminal action? ☐ Yes ☒ No   If yes, explain _____

_____

List health disabilities *none*

Are you willing to go to work in any DATA PRODUCTS INTERNATIONAL office in the United States? ☒ Yes ☐ No
List preferences *San Francisco, Oakland, Fresno, Stockton*

Tell something about yourself, including reasons you feel you are qualified for the position.
I get along well with people. I used to work for the state and didnt see much opportunity to advance. This would offer more opportunity for me to use my skills and education.

The information given herein is true and accurate to the best of my knowledge and belief; I understand that all information given will be verified.

Date *February 15, 1979* Signature *Brian L. McNamarra*

HIRING COMMITMENT (For Official Use Only)

Interviewer's Comments/Name _____

_____

Department/Office _____ Organization Code _____

Starting Date _____ Expense Allocation Code _____

Bi-weekly Salary _____ Job Title _____

Job Code _____ Date _____

Designated Signature _____ Name (printed) _____

Code 1681 Rev 4/74

Case 14   Data Products International   **139**

fully avoiding taboo topics, such as family plans. When the big week of interviews came, he was ready. (See Exhibit 4.)

The Interviews By Wednesday afternoon Fred was quite pleased. He had seen three of the young men recommended by Jack Cartwright and although there were distinct differences, two of them seemed to be serious about a career in sales with DPI. Brian McNamarra was probably the weakest of the three. He had had little work experience, none of which was in selling. He seemed quite nervous and had no questions

---

Exhibit 3
Managers' Comments on Females in Sales

1. They won't get along with the salesmen.
2. It will turn this place into a party instead of an office.
3. What would the wives think?
4. What would our customers think?
5. What if they cry?
6. Women aren't dependable.
7. Women won't relocate if we try to transfer or promote them.
8. They will get married and have babies.
9. Women aren't interested in machines.
10. We know that men can do the job. Why mess with success?
11. We can't find any with sales experience.
12. They don't like to travel.
13. They won't be able to take care of themselves on the road.
14. Women aren't really serious about careers.

Exhibit 4
Fred Johnson's Interview Plan

Ask:
1. Why are you interested in this type of work?
2. How did you select Data Products International?
3. Why do you feel that you are qualified for this job?
4. Where do you plan to be in your career five years from now?
5. Tell me about something you have done where the results were particularly pleasing to you.
6. How important is money to you?
7. What questions do you have about this position or this company?

Don't Ask:
1. Are you married or do you plan to get married?
2. Does it bother you that all of our salespeople are men?
3. Are you willing to travel?
4. How old are you?
5. How do you handle your home responsibilities and a job?
6. Do you type (HA HA)?

---

to ask when Fred finished describing the job and the company. Although he had a graduate degree, he seemed to place a lot of value on security.

Eugene Plowe seemed like a serious young man with a strong career orientation. He had made an effort to work his way through school in areas related to his field of study. He was full of questions about the company and the job. Fred was impressed that he not only asked questions, but probed for more complete answers. He seemed quite mature and handled himself with confidence.

Alan Goldner seemed a bit less mature than Eugene Plowe, but Fred attributed that to his lack of military experience. A few months in the field would probably buff off any rough edges. His experience in team sports showed through. He was quite easy to converse with and would get along well with the other men and the customers as well. He had asked fewer questions, but seemed very sincere and listened to the answers with care.

On Thursday, Fred faced Joan Channell. She was wearing a three-piece suit. It occurred to Fred that he had never considered what a saleswoman would wear. He wondered what his customers would think if a saleswoman called on them. The interview did not last as long as the others. After he finished his list of questions, he asked if she had any questions or concerns. She asked several questions about the training program. He explained that the company sent each new salesperson to Long Beach for eight two-week training sessions during the first year. He pointed out that the training cost the company a great deal of money and that, in a normal situation, the salesman had started to earn his own way sometime near the end of the second year with the company. Every time he said the word "salesman" he felt uncomfortable, but Joan did not seem to notice. He was glad when the interview was over and congratulated himself on his preparation and avoidance of dangerous subjects.

He was glad when Friday's interview was over, too. David Greenfile was a nice young man, but Fred did not share his idea that he had finally decided what to do with his life. After a few questions, it became obvious that Dave's father had decided for him. He had all the raw materials. He was bright and presentable and understood the requirements of selling. He answered all of the questions appropriately, but did so in a mechanical manner. He showed little enthusiasm for the job. Fred had always felt that a salesperson had to like his work. Fred went home Friday night having made up his mind to offer the positions to Eugene and Alan. He hadn't quite figured out how to justify not hiring Joan, but figured that Jack could send her to interview for a position in another office. She was a bright woman and she would manage.

Bright and early Monday morning Jack called to ask how the interviews had gone. He listened quietly while Fred gave brief descriptions and indicated what he intended to do. Then Jack calmly pointed out that rejection of a qualified minority applicant was a serious move when DPI faced the government-imposed affirmative action requirements. He urged Fred to reconsider his decision.

Questions

1. If you were Fred, what would you do?
2. Given the application materials shown in Exhibit 2 and the case discussion, how would you rank the applicants for a position with DPI?
3. Discuss hiring practices and laws pertaining to hiring "minority" groups. Are they fair? How do such practices and laws affect a company's business?
4. What are some behavioral principles you learned from this case about hiring practices? Explain.

Case 15

Spartan Insurance Company

Helen Trent, the north central regional sales manager for the Spartan Insurance Company, had just finished reading the introduction of a market research study conducted for her firm describing the importance of dyadic interaction in selling. The study noted that personal selling is essentially social behavior, and as such, the outcome of the sales interview is a function of the degree to which the salesperson and prospect (a dyad) have successfully communicated with each other. She considered the findings of many researchers that successful communication was more often achieved when the two parties of a dyad felt that they were similar to each other in many respects. Depending on the studies, these similarities included geographic, demographic, personality, general attitudinal, product specific, and role characteristic congruence variables. Hence, a dyadic interaction (e.g., a sales call) in which the prospect felt similar to the salesperson across a majority of these variables was most likely to result in a sale. Conversely, in selling situations where the prospect perceived large differences in the variables mentioned above, the result was more likely not to be a sale.

Interestingly, the study findings also showed that in the case of an intangible, unsought good (i.e., life insurance), the difference between selling and not selling a prospect was attributed to the quality of the

This case was developed by Professor Edward A. Riordan, Department of Marketing, Wayne State University, Detroit, Michigan.

dyadic interaction about 80 per cent of the time, while only about 20 per cent of the difference was attributed to the prospect's feelings toward the specific product. Trent concluded from the introduction of the study that perceived similarities between the prospect and the insurance agent should play a large part in the determination of the outcome of a sales call. She also wondered how she might put this information to use in her capacity as a sales manager.

Her firm, Spartan Insurance, was a medium-sized life insurance company headquartered in a northern city that sold whole life policies mainly to college seniors, recent graduates, and young professionals. The agencies under her control were located in university towns throughout the six-state north central region (Michigan, Ohio, Indiana, Illinois, Wisconsin, and Minnesota). From 1971 to 1976 each agency in her territory had shown promising year-by-year growth; however, during the years 1977–1980, a leveling off was noticed, with many agency records showing unusual downturns.

Ten-year agent turnover rates had been extremely low, with 75 per cent of her agents originally hired in 1970–1973. During the same time period, prospect pool populations had remained stable and in some university towns had actually increased. The incidence of competitive activity was also about equal to that of ten years ago. In addition, a recent study of twenty to twenty-five year olds by a life insurance trade association noted that about the same attitudes toward buying and owning life insurance prevailed in 1978 as had in 1970. Early in 1980, Spartan Insurance began a comprehensive research study of their agents and prospects in an attempt to obtain some insight into the disturbing sales trend.

Partial Results of the Research Study   Fifteen of her agents and 300 of their prospects (150 sold and 150 unsold) had completed personal interviews and self-report questionnaires for the study. Some early partial results had been furnished to management to indicate progress by the research firm. The data was in a raw form and would have to be hand tabulated. Of the many dyadic interaction variables discussed in the Spartan Insurance research study, one, "role characteristic congruence" was of interest to Trent because it seemed to account for a large percentage of the difference between a "sold" and "unsold" outcome of the sales interview.

Exhibit 1 lists eleven items used in the research instrument employed in the study to measure the prospect's perceptions of both the ideal and actual characteristics of the agent. A seven-point scale with response categories was used to rank each agent role as perceived by the prospect. The questionnaire was administered to the prospects twice; first, to measure the prospects' perception of a life insurance agent's ideal role

Exhibit 1
Role Characteristic Questionnaire Used
to Measure "Ideal" and "Actual"
Perceptions of Agents

Item	Extremely	Somewhat	Slightly	Neutral	Slightly	Somewhat	Extremely	
1. Self-confident	1	2	3	4	5	6	7	Not self-confident
2. Knew my needs	1	2	3	4	5	6	7	Didn't know my needs
3. Well educated	1	2	3.	4	5	6	7	Not well educated
4. Insures people like me	1	2	3	4	5	6	7	Insures people different than me
5. Slow talker	1	2	3	4	5	6	7	Fast talker
6. The type of person I'd introduce to my friends	1	2	3	4	5	6	7	Not the type of person I'd introduce to my friends
7. Expert on insurance	1	2	3	4	5	6	7	Not an expert on insurance
8. Thinks a lot like me	1	2	3	4	5	6	7	Doesn't think like me
9. Explained policy provisions in language I could understand	1	2	3	4	5	6	7	Didn't explain policy provisions in language I could understand
10. The type of person I'd like to know as a friend	1	2	3	4	5	6	7	Not the type of person I'd like to know as a friend
11. Low pressure approach	1	2	3	4	5	6	7	High pressure approach

characteristics; and second, to measure the actual role characteristics of the agent who called on them.

A prospect's perception of the *ideal* life insurance agent could be defined as the total score on the eleven item questionnaire (possible range: 11–77). The *actual* agent perception could be scored in the same manner. It can be noted from the wording of the bipolar adjectives and scale gradients that low numbers typically represent positive or favorable behavioral characteristics, whereas high numbers typically represent negative or unfavorable behavioral characteristics.

The perception of how well an agent fulfilled the prospect's concept of the agent's characteristics was defined as "role characteristic congruence." This term was defined as the absolute difference in score computed by subtracting a prospect's "ideal" score from the "actual" score ($|A - I|$) item by item and/or across the totals. The resulting difference in score (possible range: 0–66) can be regarded as how well (a low score) or how poorly (a high score) an agent's actual performance fulfilled the prospect's perception of the ideal agent. The dyadic interaction research literature considered by Trent would predict that prospects who bought a policy would exhibit high role congruence (low difference in scores) and that prospects that did not buy would exhibit low role congruence (high difference in scores).

Exhibit 2 shows the item-by-item mean scores given by prospects on the "ideal" agent as measured before the sales interview. Exhibit 3 shows the item-by-item mean scores on the same instrument, this time for the agent who had called on the prospect, measured after the sales

Exhibit 2
"Ideal Agent" Ratings[a]

	Prospect			Prospect	
Item	Sold[b]	Unsold[b]	Item	Sold[b]	Unsold[b]
1	1.32	1.43	7	1.09	1.07
2	1.13	1.17	8	1.89	1.73
3	1.42	1.41	9	1.01	1.00
4	1.73	1.70	10	1.79	1.68
5	3.50	3.05	11	2.53	2.07
6	1.77	1.74			

[a]Ratings are mean scores for 150 sold prospects and 150 unsold prospects.
[b]Chi-square tests revealed no significant difference between sold and unsold on any of the eleven items; similarly, a t-test revealed no significant difference between sold and unsold on the entire scale.

Exhibit 3
"Actual Agent" Ratings[a]

	Prospect			Prospect	
Item	Sold[b]	Unsold[b]	Item	Sold[b]	Unsold[b]
1	1.62	2.33	7	2.06	3.95
2	2.00	4.22	8	2.50	5.03
3	2.07	3.75	9	1.49	3.05
4	2.26	4.16	10	2.04	4.52
5	3.86	5.41	11	3.21	5.46
6	2.24	4.47			

[a]Ratings are mean scores for 150 sold prospects and 150 unsold prospects.
[b]Chi-square tests revealed significant differences (p< .001) between sold and unsold on each of the eleven items; similarly a t-test revealed a significant difference (p< .001) between sold and unsold on the entire scale.

interview (the "actual" agent). In addition, agent-by-agent scores linked with their sold and unsold prospects were available for analysis. Trent noted that early partial scores on two other scales "prospect perceptions of the specific product" and "prospect perceptions of the buying situation" showed no significant difference between prospects that bought and those that did not; both groups showed slightly favorable orientatations on both scales.

Questions

1. Using the data shown in Exhibits 2 and 3, construct profiles of sold versus unsold for: (a) ideal ratings, (b) actual ratings. What would these profiles indicate to Trent?

2. Using the data shown in Exhibits 2 and 3, compute the role congruence scores (|actual — ideal|) for: (a) sold, (b) unsold. What implications could Trent draw from this data?

3. How could Trent incorporate the data found in Questions 1 and 2 above in a training program? In an agent evaluation program?

4. In what other ways may important dyadic variables (i.e., demographics, attitudes) be operating in this case?

Case 16

Fast Track to Spin Out

In his office, Bill Edwards smiled to himself, but he was worried. He remembered how red Compton's face had gotten when he told the division director why he did not want the position as internal sales manager. "It's a deadend job; I'd be nothing more than a telephone operator and message center. I prefer to stay in sales; I want to be the sales training manager and eventually the regional marketing manager." Compton was barely able to contain himself; his reply came through clenched teeth: "We'll see about that."

Except for the last six months, Edwards' career with Douglas & Co. had been on a steady rise. Douglas & Co. was a world-wide industrial sales/service company providing consulting and contract sales and service for government and business projects across the U.S. and around the world. Edwards had been associated with the company about eleven years, first, through the Douglas Scholarship and Co-op Program in college, and later after graduation. Now Edwards wondered what had happened to change a promising future.

With just over two years' experience (one year in the field-training program and over a year on his own in the field) Edwards was selected for one of the overseas divisions. Edwards made an outstanding record

This case was prepared by Professors Lawson E. Barclay and Paul C. Thistle-thwaite, both of Western Illinois University. The case was adapted for this book by Professor Darrell R. Hankins of the University of Alabama at Birmingham with the permission of the authors.

for himself in the operational sales and service area. He developed new accounts and expanded the service to present accounts, all with increased sales and profits. He was respected and well liked by his peers and superiors alike. In recognition of his own work and capability to work with others, Edwards was selected to become the sales training manager for the overseas division. (The sales training manager was usually one of the more successful and older field salespeople.) As sales training manager, Edwards was recognized for his outstanding contributions to the training and development of the overseas division sales force.

Then, the transfer to the Midwest Division occurred. The transfer was both a step up and a step down. Edwards was to become a field sales/service representative again; but, the Midwest Division was the "darling" of the company because it was located at company headquarters. As a member of the Midwest Division, one's chances and opportunity to be promoted were greatly enhanced. Thus, it was considered a "mark of distinction" to be selected to join the Midwest Division, but Edwards had mixed emotions about the transfer.

That was almost two years ago. Things had gone from good to bad to worse. Because the operation and clientele of the Midwest Division were "unique," it had its own special training program. After completing a six-month period of supervised field operations, Edwards was allowed to go on his own. As he adapted to the Midwest Division operations and gained independence things improved.

The Midwest Division had two informal groups within its sales and marketing staff, the "old heads" and the "young turks." The "old heads" were the "cadre" who were part of the original Midwest Division staff and the other experienced (and older) personnel who had several years of experience in other Douglas divisions or departments and joined the Midwest Division after it was organized five years ago. The "young turks" were field representatives who had demonstrated outstanding ability or promise in the training program or in their short period of field sales/service experience. The two groups worked and socialized together, yet a dividing line existed. Edwards fell in with the "young turks."

Edwards established a normal routine. His sales and business went well. However, there were problems in the organization. The key positions were staffed by the "old heads." The assistant positions were filled by the "young turks." Whenever a key position was vacated, another "experienced" person was promoted. Edwards wanted to move up in the organization. Salary was not the problem. He knew that he could be more than just a field salesperson, even in the Midwest Division.

Edwards opportunity came when the Market Analysis Division began a special project to re-examine the regional sales potential, sales territory size, and sales force size for the entire company. With his experience in one of the eastern divisions, the overseas division, and now the Midwest Division, Edwards felt he could make a valuable contribution to the project and demonstrate his value as something other than as a field salesperson. Edwards was happy to work on the project, even though he was expected to maintain normal sales coverage of his accounts.

The sales analysis division manager requested that Edwards work a minimum of two, if possible three, days a week on the project. The request was approved by Tom Black, regional marketing manager, with the understanding that Edwards was still responsible for his accounts. Edwards' initial contributions to the project were of immense value. He was able to work on the project two to three days a week, but had trouble adequately covering his accounts in the remaining time, so he began working longer days and on weekends. However, as the project continued, Edwards was only able to work on the project one day a week, sometimes not even that.

Based on data and input from the field, the report dealt with determination of company allocation of manpower and budgets, areas in which Edwards' practical field experience was lightly considered. After three months, the sales analysis division manager advised Black that Edward's lack of commitment in time and interest was of little value to the project. They did not want him anymore.

Edwards' declining performance on the special project combined with the problems of consumer account coverage and general lack of enthusiasm had been noticed by Joe Thompson, the sales manager. Thompson spoke with Edwards about the need to remotivate himself and work to the level of his capabilities. Edwards expressed his frustration and his desire to do more than just field sales.

Shortly after Edwards' and Thompson's meeting, the internal sales manager position became vacant. The internal sales manager was responsible for coordination of manpower, equipment, and other resources with field sales orders and requirements. He was supposed to make decisions concerning special commitments, priority of commitments, and allocation of available resources. Thompson advised Edwards that he could have the position if he wanted it.

No way do I want that job. I know why the last guy left. He could not make a decision without checking with the marketing coordinator and the division director. The one time he did, both of them jumped all over him. No way.

But it gives you an opportunity to correct that 'problem' on the special project with the Sales Analysis Division.

What do you mean 'problem.' They didn't need me over there. I don't care. I don't want that internal sales manager position.

Maybe you had better think it over, both Black and Compton feel you ought to give it a try.

No way.

Since Black is not available, you had better talk to Compton. I'll make an appointment for you this Friday.

And now Edwards was worried. The meeting with Compton had not gone well at all. Edwards still had a sales job at Douglas, but for how long?

Questions

1. Who is at fault? Why?
2. Should Edwards accept the internal sales position? Why?

Case 17

New Manhattan Division Sales Manager

Keith Absher is tired and confused. He is sitting quietly at his desk after three long days spent trying to decide how to handle a complex situation that is now his responsibility. His brief sales management experience and his recently completed MBA courses did not seem to provide answers that would allow him to put the situation in order.

As he struggled with alternatives, his mind drifted back over the three-year period in which he had worked with Lauderdale Foods, Inc. It all started when Absher was recruited during his last year at Delta State. He had never really thought favorably about being a salesperson, but the salary was good and a company car was provided. Absher was also planning to get married and it was important to have a job lined up before graduation. So, he accepted the job until something better came along.

After a two-month training period, Absher appeared to be off to a good start. The job involved calling on supermarkets in a three-county area. Lauderdale Foods, Inc. was a large food processing company that marketed more than 150 products nation-wide. Although salespersons did not deliver the products or stock the shelves, they were responsible for placing orders through regional warehouses, for picking up damaged

This case was developed by Gerald Crawford, Professor of Marketing, University of North Alabama, Florence, Alabama. This case represents an actual situation. Copyright © 1980.

merchandise, and for building displays of the company's highly advertised items.

Absher made real progress under the seasoned leadership of his division sales manager, M. B. Wingfield. He grew to appreciate and respect Wingfield on a personal and professional basis. After one year, however, Absher decided that he did not want to remain in field sales for the rest of his life. He made plans that would, hopefully, bring opportunities for promotion. The first step was to enroll in a night MBA program at Memphis State University.

Things happened faster than anticipated. After a second year in field sales, he was named assistant division manager when the previous ADM was promoted to division manager in another state. Wingfield again trained Absher in his new managerial role. There were fourteen salespeople in the Memphis Division. All were stable, cooperative, and generally effective in their work. Things went very smoothly and no major problems were encountered.

After his third year with Lauderdale Foods, Absher completed the MBA degree and was immediately promoted to DM in the Manhattan, New York Division. Absher and his family were moved to New York and this is when things began to happen.

When Absher reported to work on Monday morning, he met Guy Carter who was his new boss and regional manager over four other sales divisions in the Metro New York area. Absher also met his new ADM who had just been promoted from a sales territory in the Philadelphia area. Carter chatted with both young managers and briefly brought them up-to-date on the division's strengths and weaknesses. Absher immediately recognized that Carter was certainly a different type of manager than his old boss, Wingfield. Carter appeared to be more direct and businesslike than the people Absher was accustomed to back in Memphis. Carter was really not very helpful. To complicate matters, the new ADM had no background in management and had not worked in this division.

Carter suggested that Absher spend one day working with each of his nineteen salespeople. This would be a good way to orient himself in his new assignment. On Tuesday morning Absher met Mike Beasley at his first call. Beasley was thirty-four years of age and had been with the company ten years. He was short and muscular and wore a hairpiece. In the first call, Beasley spoke with the manager and received permission to rotate the Lauderdale Foods products in the dairy case. While Beasley was busy checking dates and putting things in order, Absher noticed that the store manager had opened Beasley's sample case and had taken several product samples and placed them under his checkout counter. After Beasley completed his work in the dairy case, he wrote up the order and had the store manager enter it into his computer order book.

Beasley then proceeded to walk over and very methodically remove the samples from under the counter and put them back in his sample case. He and the manager appeared to say a few harsh words to each other. Later, in the car, Beasley explained that this was not the first time that this had happened and that the manager would "get over it." During the rest of the day several other similar things happened. Absher was not comfortable with the way Beasley handled people even though he had sold a great deal of merchandise during the day.

The next day Absher worked with a highly rated salesperson in the Spanish area. Louis Flores was a handsome young man of Spanish ancestry who frequently spoke to retailers in his native language. In several retail outlets Absher noticed that Flores was "very friendly" with women who worked in the checkout areas and supermarket offices. Although they usually spoke in Spanish, which Absher couldn't understand, it was evident that a good deal of "flirting" was going on. This was against company policy and it did not look very professional. Absher did not say anything about it until he could think it through.

On the third day Absher had arranged to meet George McDonald at his first call. It was a little irritating when McDonald was thirty minutes late. His explanation was that he normally does not make his first call until 9 A.M. anyway. Absher also noted that McDonald took more than one hour for lunch and was ready to end the day thirty minutes before the normal quitting time. McDonald had sold a good deal of merchandise but he surely didn't worry much about company policies. He seemed to do things his own way and this was unusual to Absher.

The new division manager was sitting at his desk thinking through the events of the past three days. Each of the three salespersons that he had worked with were good producers but they handled things in strange ways; they were certainly not like any salespersons he had ever worked with before. It was evident that these people had little respect for company policies and that they had not been trained very well. Absher thought about calling Carter but he knew that it would be a sign of weakness to ask for help so soon. He decided that he would simply have to "confront these salespeople and have an understanding as to what will be expected of them in the future."

Questions

1. How would you advise Absher to handle these men? Why?

Part 5

Motivation, Compensation, and Leadership

Case 18

Whitmore Brick and Block Company

Early in October, 1975, Bill Hollingsworth, marketing manager at Whitmore Brick and Block Company, was reviewing his first draft of the proposed revision in the compensation plan for the company's salespeople. With just under $15 million annual sales, Whitmore was one of the largest brick manufacturers both in North Carolina and in the country. Recently, however, the company had been affected by the general slump in the brick industry and was not experiencing the sales growth it had in the recent past and which was still expected by management. Management felt that the failure of the firm to meet earnings expectations was due only in part to a general industry slump and that much could be done to correct the situation by improving Whitmore's marketing effort. In particular there was some concern that the company's personal selling effort could be improved. Jack Johnson, Whitmore's controller, recently completed a review of sales representatives' salaries and sales performance figures which indicated there was little relationship between the representatives' earnings and their productivity. After discussion between Johnson and company marketing executives, the decision was made to examine whether changes to the existing sales

This case was prepared by Assistant Professor James M. Clapper, Babcock Graduate School of Management, Wake Forest University, as a basis for class discussion rather than to illustrate either effective or ineffective handling of an administrative situation. Originally published in M. Wayne DeRozier and Arch G. Woodside, *Marketing Management: Strategies and Cases*, Columbus, Ohio: Charles E. Merrill Publishing Company, 1978, pp. 530–549.

compensation scheme should be made in an effort to both increase performance and motivation and establish a clearer relationship between performance and compensation. Accordingly, Bill Hollingsworth was given the assignment of reviewing the compensation scheme and making recommendations for changes that would introduce an effective incentive element. Hollingsworth was reviewing his initial work on this project to determine whether he was on the right track.

The Brick Industry

Brick manufacturing is a $360 million a year industry nation-wide. Manufacturers, located throughout the country, are most heavily concentrated in the Southeast. Historically, firms in this capital intensive industry have been small, family-owned and managed operations. This is still largely true today with approximately 65 per cent of the firms having annual sales of less than $3 million. A strong production orientation has been a tradition in the industry with the result that today the industry enjoys perhaps the highest level of production efficiency that can be found among any of the building material industries.

Because of the comparatively high cost of shipping finished brick, manufacturers have found it largely uneconomical to compete for business in markets better served by firms located closer to the market in question. As a result, the brick industry is characterized by high levels of intraregional competition but significantly lower levels of interregional competition.

Brick is widely recognized in the construction industry as a high-quality building material. Available in a wide variety of colors, sizes, and forms and with a variety of performance characteristics, brick has many diverse uses. Despite the recognized quality and versatility of brick products, total demand for brick has not grown at the same pace as has the demand for competitive products. Many people, both within and outside the industry, believe that the cause of this poor competitive performance is the fact that marketing practices in the industry have remained rather primitive compared to those of other industries. According to a report by Arthur D. Little, Inc.:

Few efforts have been made to discover the real needs of the consumer or specifier, and even today the industry is fairly remote from the decision-making process that affects its sales. Although companies have increased their sales force in the recent past and a few use advertising and other promotional methods, the production orientation still predominates. Informal conversations between two or more brick manufacturers are invariably centered upon machine

design, plant labor problems, production costs, and other manufacturing considerations. The industry has long operated, and continues
to operate, in a marketing vacuum and has abdicated its promotional
responsibilities to the dealer and distributor and to the regional and
national association.[1]

Relying on dealers and distributors for marketing and promoting brick
has not been a particularly effective strategy. Building material dealers
and distributors commonly carry a wide variety of competing lines,
serving as outlets not only for brick but also for such commodities as
concrete brick and wood products as well. Thus, dealers do not perceive
their interests as being directly aligned with those of the brick industry.
Further, dealers in the building materials field typically play very pas-
sive, order-taker roles, dispensing technical price information but
making little effort to influence customer choices.

The promotional efforts that have been carried on in the industry
have been directed at contractors and design professionals. These efforts
have taken two basic forms, promotion of the various uses of brick and
promotion of the quality of brick construction. Nonbuilding uses of
brick such as patio paving, have especially been singled out for promotion by the industry. The primary quality themes used include brick's
low maintenance, permanence, and the aesthetic appeal.

Pricing among firms in the industry has been very competitive. When
"in-place" costs are compared, brick also is competitively priced with
most other building materials, the major exception being wood siding.
In the residential housing segment of the market, the competition from
wood siding is an important factor. Costs vary widely from area to area
and fluctuate rapidly over time, but the in-place cost for wood per
square foot of wall area is roughly half that of brick. However, at late
1975 prices, for a home with 2,000 sq ft of floor space, the initial cost
differential between brick and wood siding would be less than $1,800.
In addition, this cost would be more than recovered in maintenance
savings over the life of the house.

The Industry in North Carolina   North Carolina is known as "Brick
Capital of the Nation" because of the state's preeminence in the industry. Twenty-two manufacturers located in the state produce approximately one billion bricks annually for roughly 15 per cent of the entire
nation's output. North Carolina has been the nation's leading brick
producer for over twenty years. Although the industry situation in North
Carolina largely parallels that of the industry at large, there is one

---

[1]*The Brick Industry: An Industry at the Crossroads*, Report C–73958 (Cambridge,
MA: Arthur D. Little, 1972), p. 64.

major difference: North Carolina manufacturers have not relied as heavily on dealers and distributors to sell their product. The twenty-two firms in the state employ among them over one hundred salespeople and secure approximately 90 per cent of their sales as direct sales. This figure compares with the national average of approximately 30 per cent direct sales.

The Company

Whitmore Brick Company, as it was known then, was founded in 1938 by John Whitmore. Whitmore was able to capitalize on his fifteen years experience in the brick industry and progress for the new firm was rapid. By 1957 the Whitmore plant had an annual capacity of 100 million bricks per year.

In 1964, Whitmore Brick bought the Thomasville Block Company at Thomasville in an effort to diversify the holdings of the company and to be able to offer a complete line of masonry products to its customers. At this time the firm's name was changed to its present form. During the 1960s and early 1970s, Whitmore continued to expand both by acquiring other firms and by building new plants. By 1975, Whitmore possessed a total production capacity of 400 million bricks per year and 10 million concrete blocks.

Whitmore's Marketing Effort   Whitmore's primary market area is the Carolinas and south central Virginia. This area accounts for approximately 80 per cent of the company's sales with the remaining 20 per cent distributed throughout the eastern half of the United States.

Whitmore has traditionally been a leader in marketing brick and concrete block in its market area. The firm has one of the most extensive product lines in the business, manufacturing a wide variety of different styles and handling the products of other firms to meet customer needs where there are gaps in the Whitmore line.

In its marketing area, the firm has been a leader in consumer advertising and promotion. Whitmore was the first brick company in the Carolinas to use mass media ads, starting this practice in the late 1950s. Today the firm uses a mix of radio, television, newspaper, and outdoor advertising to make the public aware of the advantages brick has over wood and to sell Whitmore brands of brick. Although Whitmore's consumer marketing effort is among the largest in the industry when measured in dollars, this effort is still small in comparison to the firm's effort to influence the building trades; and the strength of this effort has been the company's sales force.

The Sales Force As indicated in Exhibit 1, the cost of the company's sales organization represents the bulk of Whitmore's marketing expenditures. The firm employs nineteen field sales representatives to cover its direct sale marketing area in the Carolinas and Virginia. One additional sales representative handles what are termed "foreign sales"—sales outside the direct marketing area.

The company's method of absorbing acquisitions resulted in a divisional structure for the firm. Administratively, the nineteen company sales representatives are assigned to the different divisions according to

Exhibit 1
Whitmore Brick and Block Company
Budgeted Sales and
Marketing Expenditures

Advertising	
Agency Fees	$ 2,000
Trade Publications	500
Consumer Magazines	7,000
Newspaper	1,000
Outdoor	10,000
Radio	20,000
Television	25,000
Other	5,000
Total	$ 70,500
Sales Promotion	
Conventions	$ 1,500
Customer Group Functions	3,000
Home Builders Associations	1,000
Novelties	1,000
Samples and Displays	45,000
Other	1,000
Total	$ 52,500
Personal Selling Expense[a]	
Sales Salaries	$420,000
Fringe Benefits	65,000
Sales Meetings	5,000
Travel and Entertainment	100,000
Car Rental	20,000
Total	$610,000
Administrative Expense	
Direct Office Costs	$ 50,000
General Overhead	30,000
Total	$ 80,000
Total Sales and Marketing Expense	$813,000

[a]Includes sales management salaries and fringes.

the scheme outlined in Exhibit 2. However, each salesperson is assigned an exclusive geographic territory and is responsible for sales of all the firm's products within that area, not just the products of the division. The firm's nineteen direct sales territories are indicated in Exhibit 3A–C.

Sales Force Characteristics   Most of Whitmore's salespeople are high school graduates although some have college degrees. They range in age from the mid-20s to early-60s with a median age between 35 and 40 years old. Tenure with the firm varies from four months to eighteen years, with eight years being the median. Turnover is low. In the recent past, the primary cause of turnover has been company dissatisfaction with the sales representatives' performance.

Whitmore traditionally has acquired new salespeople either by promotion of personnel in a division's customer service operation or by hiring people with sales experience gained either with other brick companies or in related industries. Advancement opportunities are available for interested and qualified salespeople. All of the six people currently in sales management with the firm began their service in the sales organization as field sales representatives. In addition, some former salespeople have been promoted to administrative staff positions in other areas of the business.

Job Responsibilities   Salespeople are responsible for sales and field service of accounts. They call on a variety of individuals in their efforts to sell Whitmore brick. As a group, home builders, general contractors, and masons buying their own brick represent the great bulk of actual purchases. However, sales representatives also pay calls on building supply dealers and people who influence the design specifications of buildings or who may have some influence in the actual brand or style of brick to be purchased for a particular building. Such people include engineers and architects, public officials such as building committee members, executives of firms with building plans, and so forth. In order to deal effectively with these people, the salesperson must be totally conversant with the entire Whitmore product line and competitor offerings. Salespeople are not engineers but must be reasonably knowledgeable and able to talk effectively about aesthetics, structural qualities, energy efficiency, price, and life-cycle costs.

Because the business is so competitive, salespeople often encounter potential customers who want to bargain on price. Whitmore sales representatives can and do negotiate price but must receive final approval for concessions from their sales managers.

Closing a sale often requires the efforts of more than one salesperson. As an example, a salesperson may become aware of plans for construc-

Exhibit 2
Partial Organization Chart

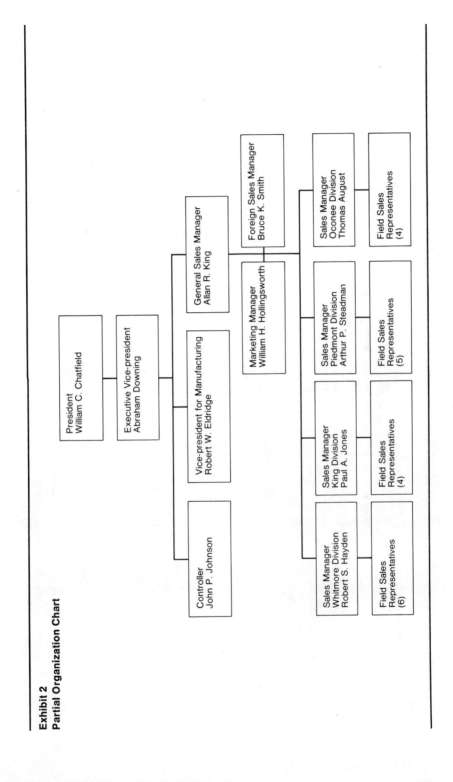

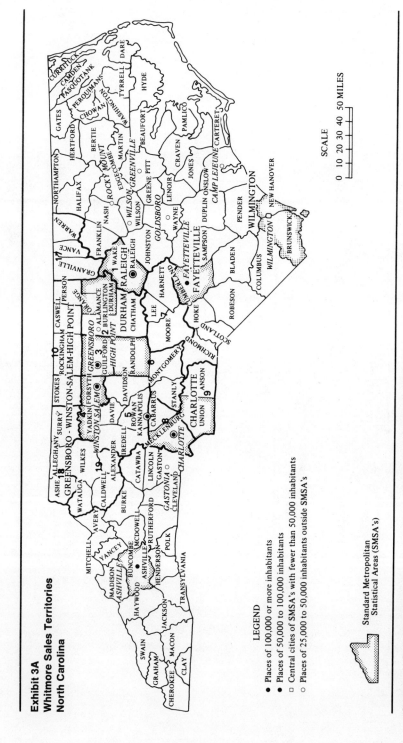

LEGEND

● Places of 100,000 or more inhabitants
● Places of 50,000 to 100,000 inhabitants
□ Central cities of SMSA's with fewer than 50,000 inhabitants
○ Places of 25,000 to 50,000 inhabitants outside SMSA's

Standard Metropolitan
Statistical Areas (SMSA's)

SCALE

0 10 20 30 40 50 MILES

Source: U.S. Department of Commerce Social and Economic Statistics Administration Bureau of the Census.

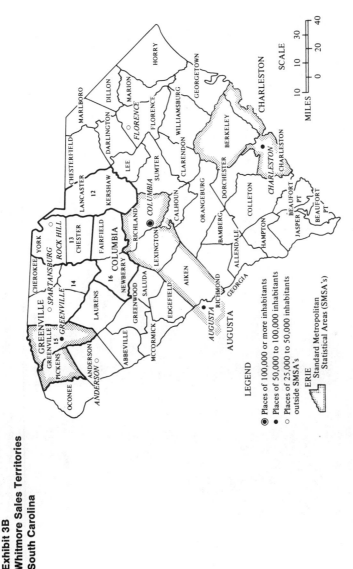

LEGEND

◉ Places of 100,000 or more inhabitants
● Places of 50,000 to 100,000 inhabitants
○ Places of 25,000 to 50,000 inhabitants
  outside SMSA's

ERIE   Standard Metropolitan
       Statistical Areas (SMSA's)

SCALE

MILES

10   0   10   20   30   40

Source: U.S. Department of Commerce Social and Economic Statistics Administration Bureau of the Census.

Exhibit 3C
Whitmore Sales Territories
Virginia

INDEPENDENT CITIES

1 ALEXANDRIA	20 LEXINGTON
2 BEDFORD	21 LYNCHBURG
3 BRISTOL	22 MARTINSVILLE
4 BUENA VISTA	23 NEWPORT NEWS
5 CHARLOTTESVILLE	24 NORFOLK
6 CHESAPEAKE	25 NORTON
7 CLIFTON FORGE	26 PETERSBURG
8 COLONIAL HEIGHTS	27 PORTSMOUTH
9 COVINGTON	28 RADFORD
10 DANVILLE	29 RICHMOND
11 EMPORIA	30 ROANOKE
12 FAIRFAX	31 SALEM
13 FALLS CHURCH	32 SOUTH BOSTON
14 FRANKLIN	33 STAUNTON
15 FREDERICKSBURG	34 SUFFOLK
16 GALAX	35 VIRGINIA BEACH
17 HAMPTON	36 WAYNESBORO
18 HARRISONBURG	37 WILLIAMSBURG
19 HOPEWELL	38 WINCHESTER

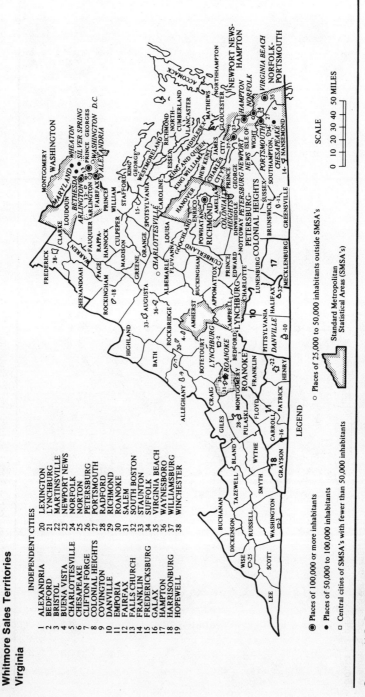

LEGEND

⦿ Places of 100,000 or more inhabitants

● Places of 50,000 to 100,000 inhabitants

□ Central cities of SMSA's with fewer than 50,000 inhabitants

○ Places of 25,000 to 50,000 inhabitants outside SMSA's

Standard Metropolitan Statistical Areas (SMSA's)

SCALE

0 10 20 30 40 50 MILES

Source: U.S. Department of Commerce Social and Economic Statistication Bureau of the Census.

tion of a new building in his territory. He may then ask that another salesperson call on key executives of the firm that will own the building since these executives are physically located in the latter sales representative's territory. Depending on their location, the building's architect and general contractor may be called on by yet another sales representative. Once a sale is made, though, it is the responsibility of the salesperson in whose territory the building is to be located to coordinate with production and shipping to provide the best service possible for that particular job. Brick in existing structures may have to be matched or changes in original quantities and delivery schedules may be requested by the customer, and so forth.

Selection, Training, and Supervision of Sales Representatives

Selection of sales representatives is done on an "as needed" basis. When a vacancy occurs or is anticipated, the sales manager and the marketing manager initiate a search for a new person. Preference is given to qualified employees within the firm who would like to have the job. If no interested and qualified people are found within the firm, the scope of the search is widened by taking out blind employment ads in the large daily newspapers within Whitmore's marketing area and by letting it be known to the trade through the grapevine that the firm has an opening. People with a background in some aspect of building industry sales are preferred although people with sales backgrounds from other industries are also given consideration. The final decision as to who will be hired is made by the sales manager, the marketing manager, and the general sales manager, with the general sales manager having final say if there is some dispute.

Whitmore has no formal sales training program. The company does, however, make extensive use of the training programs and meetings run by the Brick Association of North Carolina and the Brick Institute of America. These programs generally are designed to increase the participant's knowledge of brick and of industry conditions, but the meetings typically contain very little information or guidance on sales technique.

When a new salesperson joins the firm, the first three months are considered a trial period. The sales manager typically will take the representative around the new territory, introducing the firm's regular customers. In addition, the sales manager will spend between four and six days making calls with the new salesperson during the first three months on the job. The sales manager will also solicit information from valued and trusted customers as to their perceptions of the new representative's job performance. Beyond this, the sales representative is evaluated largely by the level of business the territory produces and by the impressions the sales manager gains from normal business-related contact. At the end of the three-month period, a decision is made whether to retain the salesperson on a permanent basis.

The same informal pattern is used to evaluate veteran salespeople. In addition to normal business contact, sales managers occasionally accompany salespeople on calls, primarily at the salesperson's request, either to participate in negotiations with new customers or to lend support on what is anticipated to be a difficult call. In these instances, evaluation is a by-product rather than an objective. For evaluation, more weight is put on the salesperson's performance against quota than on anything else.

Each sales representative has a yearly performance evaluation interview with the manager. At this meeting, the manager discusses impressions of the salesperson's performance and explains the entries made on the performance review sheet (see Exhibit 4). The performance review sheet then is placed in the personnel file and becomes part of the permanent employment record.

As noted above, sales quotas are used in evaluations. Annually, management makes a forecast of company sales by geographic territory. This territorial forecast becomes the quota for the sales representative in that territory who is then expected either to meet or exceed the established quota. A representative is considered to be doing a good job for the company as long as the quota is met consistently. Those people who fail to meet their quota repeatedly are counseled by their sales managers and encouraged to do a better job. Sales managers may spend extra time with those who are having difficulty meeting their quotas and may make sales calls with them. Constructive suggestions for improved performance are usually forthcoming from these contacts.

Sales Representative Compensation   As is almost exclusively the case among the firms in the Carolinas, Whitmore sales representatives are compensated on a straight salary basis and are reimbursed for expenses incurred performing their job. Supplementing their salary is a fringe benefit package worth approximately $2,200 annually. The fringe benefit package is considered better than average in the industry. The average annual salary among company salespeople is $14,200, but there is tremendous variation from person to person with the top earner making $18,900 and the bottom one earning only $10,200 per year. In general, Whitmore's salary levels are competitive with those of other brick companies in the Southeast. In addition to their salary and fringe benefits, each salesperson is provided with a company car that may also be used for personal travel. The sales representatives are expected to pay for the gasoline consumed in personal use of their assigned vehicle, but otherwise are free to use the car for any purpose that will not damage it.

Sales Representative _____   Review Date: _____

Rated By: _____   Distribution: Original—Sales Representative
                                                   Copy—Sales Representative's
                                                   Personnel File

	Excel.	Avg.	Unsat.	Comments (required for all below average ratings)
Territory Management:				
Routing				
Account Coverage				
Call Planning				
Overall Territory Knowledge				
Adherence to Policies & Procedures				
Time & Effort Distribution				
Thoroughness				
Administration & Organization:				
Reporting—Completeness, Accuracy, Etc.				
Record Maintenance				
Expense Control				
Correspondence				
Priority Setting				
Selling:				
Quality of Presentations				
Customer Education				
Account Cooperation				
Special Promotions				
Sales Volume				
Orders vs. Calls				
Knowledge:				
Products				
Competition				

Exhibit 4—*continued*

Customers
Territory Trends
Customer Interests & Needs
Business Practices
Company Policies & Procedures

Personal Characteristics:

Attitude
Enthusiasm
Judgment
Inspirational Abilities
Industry
Resourcefulness
Appearance
Flexibility
Acceptance of Suggestions

Objectives and Recommendations for Performance Improvement:

Sales Rep's Signature _____   Rater's Signature _____

The Problem

The motivation for examining sales compensation was a slowdown in brick sales and the accompanying increase in the per unit cost of sales. This situation prompted Jack Johnson, the company's controller, to examine the firm's sales on a territory by territory basis in an effort to determine key areas in which improvement should be sought. The results of Johnson's investigation were transmitted to Allen King, Whitmore's general sales manager, in memo form on August 20. See Exhibit 5 for Johnson's memo.

After reading Johnson's memo, King called in Bill Hollingsworth to discuss the memo. As marketing manager, Hollingsworth was responsible for a wide variety of sales and marketing administrative functions including market and sales analysis. King felt Hollingsworth would be in the best position to help him evaluate the arguments in Johnson's memo.

After reading the memo, Hollingsworth pointed out to King that the firm's method of reporting sales in a territory where the brick was delivered regardless of who was involved in the sale was in part responsible for the apparent lack of relationship between sales representative productivity and compensation. Some salespeople, notably those in the Raleigh, Durham, and Charlotte areas, had high concentrations of architects and other purchase influencers in their territory and, through calls on these people, were involved in a great many sales for which they received no explicit credit. Hollingsworth also pointed out that to a great extent, the productivity level of the salespeople was determined by the sales potential in the area served. This in turn was influenced in large part by the level of building activity in the area. Sales potential tended to vary greatly from territory to territory and within a single territory varied over time. Hollingsworth did agree, however, that even considering these factors, there did appear to be inequities in compensation when each salesperson's contribution to the firm was considered. Hollingsworth and King had the following exchange.

Hollingsworth: "As you know, Al, each year at annual review time, Bob Haden or Paul Jones is bound to complain that one or two of their good young salespeople are not earning a fair salary for their contributions compared

---

Exhibit 5

To: Al King
From: Jack Johnson
Subject: Sales Productivity Analysis
Date: August 20, 1975

As we all know, overall sales performance year-to-date has been disappointing. Certainly the economic climate has not been as favorable as it was a few years ago, but it is better than last year and yet our sales are lagging. If we continue at the pace set year-to-date, and if foreign sales perform as expected, total sales for this year will be only about $150,000 greater than last year's. This is far short of our target of $400,000 in growth and still leaves us over $1.5 million below our record 1972 sales performance.

In doing some research, I've found very uneven performance among sales representatives. As you can see from the following figures, some people are doing a great job, most are doing what we ask of them, but three sales people are far below quota. More disturbing is that Alquist and Williams are two of our highest paid representatives.

I also checked back as far as 1971 and found that Alquist was marginally under quota in 1971 and just marginally over quota in 1972, our record year. In 1973, like everyone else, he was under quota and in 1974 he exceeded his quota by only fifty dollars. The historical picture for Williams is little better. He did have a good year in 1972 but in 1973 he was below quota and in 1974 he was just

Exhibit 5—*continued*

about even, exceeding his quota by about $1,000. Walters joined the firm in April 1973. In 1974, the first full year of history for him, he was $15,000 below quota. Considering his performance to date, I wonder if Walters wasn't a hiring mistake.

In a capital intensive business like ours, shifts in total sales have a dramatic impact on profitability. As a result, we can't afford to miss any sales opportunities. We've got to make sure we have people in the field who are giving us 100–110 per cent when times are difficult. Look over the following numbers and see if you don't agree we need to make changes.

Salesperson	Territory	1975 7/12 Quota[a]	1975 Sales thru July (7 months)[a]	1974 Sales thru July (7 months)[a]	1975 Salary
Alquist	5	$379	$347	$370	$17,400
Brannen	8	365	363	356	16,000
Douglas	7	373	366	371	12,600
Edwards	18	350	351	347	12,000
Elbertson	15	408	397	396	18,400
Hair	10	379	376	385	13,200
Hughes	3	394	388	386	18,900
Longworth	9	365	356	362	14,900
Mendenhall	14	379	374	376	12,100
Miles	4	385	375	387	14,200
Noseworthy	17	362	354	352	12,400
Parent	19	338	340	n/a (new hire)	10,200
Richards	1	368	371	361	12,400
Solen	12	373	362	364	13,100
Thomas	16	365	357	362	11,400
Tilden	2	379	382	385	13,400
Walters	13	368	349	368	11,400
Williams	11	379	351	373	17,600
Young	6	388	391	389	18,200

[a]Quotas and sales figures to the nearest $1,000.

to some of the older people who have been here longer. They don't think it's fair that the older guys are paid more just because they've been with us longer even though their sales are no better, and in some cases worse, than some of the young guys coming along."

King: "Yes, I know. We do hear that just about every year and every year the answer is the same. To management, longevity counts. Those who have served the firm faithfully deserve to be rewarded. Also, we've got to keep in mind the total salary structure of the company. Some guy who has been working in production in one of the plants for fifteen years is going to be real upset if he sees some young guy who just joined the firm a couple of years ago in sales is making as much as he is. Besides, according to the analysis in Jack's memo, our productivity problems aren't related to the length of service either. It's just that, even allowing for your objections, some people do not appear to be pulling their weight."

Hollingsworth: "Well, you've heard Bob Hayden say we teach people that kind of behavior. Because we pay a man for the time he's been with us more than for the job he's doing, we teach him that extra effort doesn't pay."

King: "Yes, I've heard him but he overstates the case. Anyway, this whole discussion is drifting from the point. I've got to get with Jack to be sure, but it sounds like he wants some drastic action taken. Before I do anything though, I want to be sure of the situation. I'm not going to fire some guy or put him on probation just because he's at the bottom of the productivity list. Hell, there will always be somebody at the bottom, even when everybody is doing well. What I want to know is whether these guys are doing what we expect. If these sales results are due to poor performance, we'll certainly act; but if they're due to external influences beyond the sales representative's control, we'll just have to live with it for now and hope the sales climate improves.

Take Jack's memo back to your office and look it over again. See what you think of his analysis and do whatever analysis of your own you think is appropriate. Get back to me on Friday if you can on this so that we can sit down with Jack and hash this out."

After two weeks of analysis and discussion, the men concluded little other than that changes needed to be made. It was decided to do nothing about the specific individuals cited in Johnson's August 20 memo until some overall plan for coping with the issues of motivation and performance had been devised. Considering some of the arguments they had heard from sales managers over the past few years, it was agreed that the possibility of instituting some sort of incentive compensation scheme as a means of both stimulating performance and insuring some relationship between performance and compensation should be investigated. Accordingly, Bill Hollingsworth was given the task of developing a preliminary plan for review by King and Johnson and eventual presentation to senior management for acceptance and implementation. Hollingsworth was asked to report back by October 16.

Exhibit 6
Whitmore Brick and Block Company
Proposed Incentive Compensation Plan
for Field Sales Representatives

This proposed plan is designed to reward sales representatives for achieving sales objectives and will hold and attract high-producing sales representatives. The plan will reward only those producing a profit for the company.

In designing this proposed compensation plan, the following criteria were taken into consideration:

    a. Must be competitive with other employers in order to attract and hold top quality sales representatives

    b. Easy to understand

    c. Easy to administer

    d. Fair and equitable to individual and company

    e. Provide incentives to reach sales objectives

    f. Place importance on top dollar as well as high brick and block volume

The plan will consist of a base salary and commission on brick and block dollar sales net of discount.

    1. Base salaries will average $8,000 per year. Actual base salaries will be determined individually considering experience, length of service and type of territory or customer mix.

    2. Commissions will be paid at four different rates, depending upon the level of monthly sales, according to the chart below:

Brick and Block Dollar Volume for the Month	Commission Rate for the Month
Less than $50,000	.0085 (.85%)
Between $50,000 and $60,399	.01 (1.0%)
Between $60,400 and $70,833	.0115 (1.15%)
Over $70,833	.0130 (1.3%)

    3. Commissions will be paid on a split basis. One-third of the commission will be paid to the sales representative responsible for specification, one-third to the sales representative responsible for the purchase order, and one-third to the sales representative responsible for servicing the job. In the case where there is no specification involved, the split will be one-half for the sales representative initiating the order and one-half for the sales representative servicing the job. Sales representatives performing multiple tasks on a single sale will receive all the commissions attributable to the activities in which they were involved.

       It will be the responsibility of the sales representative entering the order to make sure that the correct split is entered on the order edit form. Sales managers will provide guidance in the area of exceptional situations.

    4. Commissions will be paid in the middle of the month following actual shipments.

Exhibit 6—*continued*

As an example of how the proposed plan will work, the plan's framework was used to compute commissions that would have been paid on sales during the first nine months of 1975. Total sales in the direct market area during this period were $8,935,740. Field sales representatives' salary and commission would have been $203,357 approximately. Actual salaries paid during the first nine months of 1975 were $206,625.

If the proposed plan is put into effect for 1976 and Whitmore reaches the proposed minimum goal of $12.4 million in sales in the direct market area, total compensation for the nineteen field sales representatives would be approximately $276,000. In this case field representatives' salary compensation will amount to 2.23 per cent of sales.

Two hypothetical examples of individual compensation under the proposed plan are shown on the following chart. As can be seen, the plan insures that a sales representative's level of compensation will be directly related to sales productivity.

In conclusion, the proposed plan is felt to meet all the criteria outlined earlier in the proposal. In particular, it is felt that this plan provides attractive incentives for sales representatives to achieve sales objectives while at the same time insuring a reasonable cost of sales for the company.

Exhibit 6—*continued*
1. John Doe

Month	Actual Month Sales: Brick			Actual Month Sales: Block			$ Volume and Total Commission		
	M Units	Net Price	$	Units	Net Price	$	$	Rate	$
January	704	$52.00	$ 36,608	11,560	.3565	$ 4,121	$ 50,729	.01	$ 346.20
February	660	52.00	34,320	11,560	.3565	4,121	38,441	.0085	326.75
March	800	52.00	41,600	11,560	.3565	4,121	45,721	.0085	388.63
April	968	52.50	50,820	18,480	.3765	6,956	57,776	.01	577.76
May	1,012	52.50	53,130	18,140	.3765	6,830	59,960	.01	699.60
June	1,056	52.50	55,440	20,200	.3765	7,613	63,053	.0115	725.11
July	1,056	53.00	55,968	20,220	.3765	7,613	63,581	.0115	731.18
August	1,056	53.00	55,968	20,220	.3765	7,613	63,581	.0115	731.18
September	1,144	53.00	60,632	20,220	.3765	7,613	68,245	.0115	784.82
October	924	51.50	47,586	20,800	.3565	7,415	55,001	.01	550.01
November	792	51.50	40,788	15,360	.3565	5,476	46,264	.0085	393.24
December	748	51.50	38,522	11,560	.3565	4,121	42,643	.0085	362.47
Total	11,000	$51.94	$571,382	200,000	.3680	$73,613	$644,995	.0101	$6,516.95

Exhibit 6—continued
2. Albert Anyman

	Actual Month Sales: Brick			Actual Month Sales: Block			$ Volume and Total Commission		
Month	M Units	Net Price	$	Units	Net Price	$	$	Rate	$
January	700	$50.00	$ 35,000	20,000	.38	$ 7,600	$ 42,600	.0085	$ 362.10
February	750	50.50	37,875	20,000	.38	7,600	45,475	.0085	386.54
March	800	51.00	40,800	30,000	.38	11,400	52,200	.01	522.00
April	900	51.00	45,900	35,000	.39	13,650	59,550	.01	595.50
May	1,000	51.00	51,000	35,000	.39	13,650	64,650	.0115	743.48
June	1,000	51.50	51,000	40,000	.39	15,600	66,600	.0115	765.90
July	1,000	51.50	51,500	40,000	.40	16,000	67,500	.0115	776.15
August	950	52.00	49,400	35,000	.40	14,000	63,400	.0115	729.10
September	1,050	52.50	55,125	37,000	.40	14,800	69,925	.0115	804.14
October	800	50.00	40,000	30,000	.37	11,100	51,100	.01	511.00
November	800	50.00	40,000	28,000	.37	10,360	50,360	.01	503.60
December	750	50.50	37,875	25,000	.37	9,250	47,125	.0085	400.56
Total	10,500	$51.00	$535,475	375,000	.3867	$145,010	$680,485	.0104	$7,100.62

In the process of developing his proposal, Hollingsworth gave consideration to such issues as the desired income level for good performers, the division of compensation among base salary, individual incentive, and group incentive, and the effect of the proposed plan on total sales costs to the firm. Doing a good job was defined as exceeding quota, and a direct compensation level of $15,000 to $16,000 was felt to be appropriate for this type of performance. It was further decided that base salary should amount to approximately $8,000 per year for the average sales representative. This figure, of course, could be adjusted upward or downward to account for such things as length of service, and to correct for any fundamental inequities resulting from the imbalance of sales territory, or the assignment of additional responsibilities.

Hollingsworth also attempted to design a proposal with which, if it had been in effect during the first nine months of 1975, total compensation expense for the firm would have been no greater than that actually incurred. Also, as sales rose above those 1975 levels, Hollingsworth wanted no more than 1.5 per cent of additional sales to be paid to sales representatives as compensation.

As he sat at his desk this early October morning, Hollingsworth gave one last reading to the report he planned to submit to King and Johnson. Moving to an incentive based salary program represented a radical departure from past practice for the firm, and Hollingsworth was aware that the plan would receive close scrutiny both by King and Johnson and later by senior management. Yet, Hollingsworth was convinced that an incentive program was necessary. He hoped that the program he had devised was favorable to management and salespeople alike, and that in practice it would deliver the promised benefits. The issue was sensitive enough, he felt, that if a false start was made the whole concept of incentive sales compensation might be abandoned. The proposal Hollingsworth intended to present to King and Johnson is contained in Exhibit 6.

Case 19

Ross Paper Division

In September 1973, Robert Davies, vice-president of administration of Ross Paper Division was asked by Daniel Davidson, president of the division, to review the current salesperson compensation plan and to propose any desirable changes.

Traditionally, Ross Paper Division had paid its salespeople a straight salary and an annual bonus. In 1971, however, the company adopted a new compensation plan under which compensation consisted of base income, commissions, and an annual bonus. In the words of Davies, the new plan was designed 1) to encourage increased sales of high-margin paper while maintaining mill volume load, and 2) to provide management with objective means of assessing salespeople's performance and rewarding outstanding contributions to company profits. The new plan went into effect at the beginning of 1972.

Toward the middle of 1973 Ross executives began to question the viability of the new compensation plan. Among other things they felt that the new plan did not take into account the shortage in the paper market occurring at that time. As one executive noted: "At the present time 80 per cent of our grades are on allocation and this will probably increase during the rest of the year and remain in effect through 1974. Thus we must ask what degree of control does a salesperson have over his or her sales volume or product mix?" It was under these circumstances that Davidson asked for a review of the sales compensation plan.

Reprinted with permission from *Cases in Marketing Management* by Jain and Mathur. Orid, Inc., Columbus, Ohio, 1978, pp. 351–372.

Company Background   Ross Paper was a division within the Ross Paper Group which was a part of Ross Corporation. The Ross Corporation was a decentralized, diversified corporation headquarted in Chicago. Its 160 business units, located in thirty-two states and twenty-two countries, were organized into eight operating groups. These groups were: Ross Paper (fine grades of paper); Ross Pulp and Forest Products (pulp, newsprint, and lumber); Ross Paperboard (linerboard, packaging, containers, and board products); Ross Merchant (distribution of paper, plastic, and industrial supplies); Ross Products (school, office, and home paper supplies); Industrial Products (iron castings, coal, soil pipe, and rubber goods); Ross Interiors (home furniture and fabrics); and Advanced Systems (new venture opportunities such as computer technology applied to legal research and printing systems). The Forest Products sector, made up of the Ross Paper, Ross Pulp and Forest Products, and Ross Paperboard groups, had sales of $840,000,000 in 1972. This amounted to 51 per cent of the Ross Corporation's total 1972 sales of $1,526,022,000.

Ross Paper Group   The Ross Paper group was formally made up of four organizations: Ross Paper, Stuart Paper, Gropay (a bark-processing by-product operation producing mulch for gardening and landscaping), and Ross Paper/Specialty. Practically speaking, however, this group was dominated by Ross Paper because this division was the largest in the group and, in fact, was the largest in the entire corporation. Therefore, the policies and practices of the group, including the setting of marketing goals, tended to follow those of the Ross Paper Division.

Ross Paper Division   Ross Paper had four white paper mills located at St. Cloud, Minnesota; Eugene, Oregon; Richmond, Indiana (2); and a coating facility at Yellow Springs, Ohio. The organizational chart of Ross Paper is shown in Exhibit 1. This chart is not precise in that it shows marketing research, distribution, field services, sales training, and communications on the same organizational level as that of the three market managers. From a functional standpoint the former operated as staff to the market managers. The three market managers set the marketing goals for Ross Paper and controlled the activities not only of the marketing function but also of operations and sales.

Distribution Arrangements

About 45 per cent of Ross Paper's products were distributed directly to large end users including convertors (for example, envelope manufac-

Exhibit 1
Ross Paper Division
Partial Organization Chart

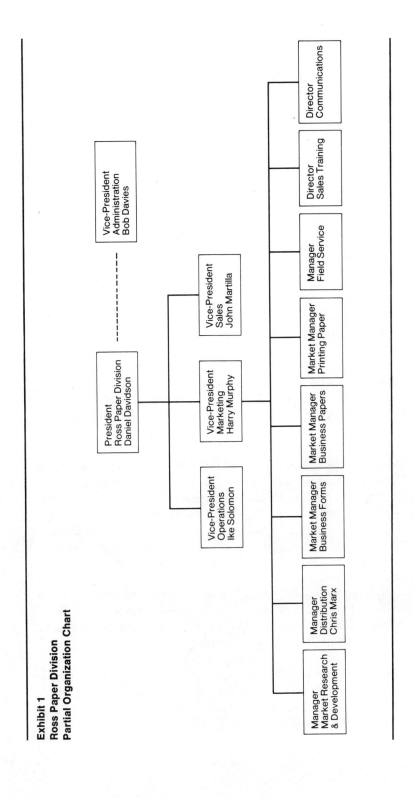

President
Ross Paper Division
Daniel Davidson

Vice-President
Administration
Bob Davies

Vice-President
Operations
Ike Solomon

Vice-President
Marketing
Harry Murphy

Vice-President
Sales
John Martilla

Manager
Market Research
& Development

Manager
Distribution
Chris Marx

Market Manager
Business Forms

Market Manager
Business Papers

Market Manager
Printing Paper

Manager
Field Service

Director
Sales Training

Director
Communications

turers, magazine printers, book publishers, commercial printers, greeting card manufacturers, label manufacturers); original equipment manufacturers (for example, copying machine manufacturers, such as Xerox); in-plant printers; and business forms manufacturers. The remaining 55 per cent were distributed through paper merchants, which in the case of Ross Paper were of two specific types: Ross owned and non-Ross merchants. A paper merchant was a wholesaler who served smaller end users and retailers. Ross had established a number of its own merchants to serve territories that were not being served adequately. In some cases, Ross had acquired the businesses of financially weak merchants. Currently Ross had forty merchants. These were managed by a subsidiary of the parent company called Ross Merchant Group. Ross Paper Division sold about 30 per cent of its products to Ross owned merchants. The balance of 25 per cent was sold to non-Ross merchants. The Ross owned merchants also bought paper from other manufacturers, almost like non-Ross merchants did. Likewise, they sold to end users and retailers like non-Ross merchants, and thus sometimes competed against Ross Paper's direct sales effort to end users. Exhibit 2 depicts Ross Paper's channel arrangements.

Current Sales Compensation Plan   Under the current sales compensation plan, the salespeople had two opportunities to add to their earnings. First, their monthly income could increase as the earnings from their sales increased. Second, they could earn a year-end bonus for profit improvements achieved.

Monthly Income   A salesperson's monthly income was made up of a fixed and a variable portion. To provide an incentive for each member of the sales force to develop his or her markets and increase the contribution to Ross profits, the company paid a monthly commission on sales. However, recognizing that salespeople did not always have direct contact with the end user, but must often work through merchant accounts and their sales forces, the company also guaranteed each salesperson a fixed base income.

Base income accounted for the major portion of monthly cash compensation and protected salespeople against wide swings in sales levels beyond their control. The expected base income for the average sales territory was about 70 per cent of monthly cash compensation, with commission earnings accounting for the remaining 30 per cent. However, because the variable commission earnings could increase with improved performance, while the base income remained fixed for the period, the exact split between the monthly base income and commissions varied from person to person, territory to territory, and period to period.

Exhibit 2
Ross Paper Division
Channels of Distribution

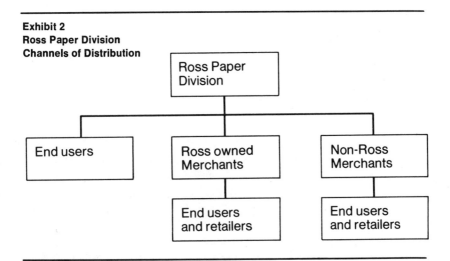

Each salesperson's base income depended on the size of his or her territory (the dollar volume of accounts and their margin contribution) and the overall level of performance. As a salesperson handled the territory and built up the volume and margin, his or her base income increased. Adjustments in base income levels were based on an annual review of performance and territory assignments. At the start of each operating period, regional managers reviewed each salesperson's performance and base income with him or her. The income of established salespeople was protected when market growth and penetration made it necessary to redefine territory responsibility at the start of an operating period (See Appendix A).

No changes in territory assignments were made in the course of the operating year. If a salesperson left, his or her accounts were temporarily assigned to other salespeople. The earnings for the territory were accumulated until the end of the year, when they were divided among the salespeople involved on the basis of account volume and average mix.

The base income established for the operating period was paid on the last day of each calendar month.

The remainder of a salesperson's monthly compensation came from commission earnings. This was a variable income and fluctuated in direct proportion to the volume, product mix, and net selling price of the shipments credited to a salesperson during the preceding month.

The commissions earned on a sale depended in part on the average profitability of the items sold. Each grade of paper had been assigned a profit code based on its average contribution to Ross profits. For each profit code (0 through 10), a commission rate had been set that directly reflected the profitability of the items assigned. Exhibit 3 illustrates the

Code	Commission Rate	Paper Grade
	($ per ton)	
0	.05	Tablet (3F)
1	.15	Fastfold (1F); Envelope (3E); Recycled Offset (31); Recycled Bond (1X); Maderite Offset (3B)
2	.30	Form Bond (1E); Papeteries (1H); Coated Cover (2Q) #5 Coated Offset (2L); #5 Coated Gravure (2N); CIS Sheets (20A); #5 Coated Letterpress (2M)
3	.42	Safety Paper (1B); Maderite Bond (1D); Special Opaque (1V); CIS Label Stock (20B); CIS Gravure (20E); Publishers Offset (3C); OEM Bond-CD (1W)
4	.55	#4 Coated Letterpress (Process Plate (21))
5	.65	Ross Bond (1A); Ross Opaque (1Q); #4 Coated Matte (2K); Ross Web (2R); Cockle Bond (1Q); Letterpress (3D)
6	.80	Moistrite Bond (1C); #4 Coated Offset (M.O.E.) (2J)
7	.90	Trans/rite (1T); #1 Coated (Black & White) (2D); #1 Offset (Moistrite) (3A)
8	1.20	Rossbrite (1N); Cast Coated (2A)
9	1.70	Offset Masters (1G); AcroArt
X	.60	Test Market Items (Trials). Once marketability is assured and volume and costs can be anticipated, the resulting margin will classify the product in Codes 0–9. Test Market; Transform (1K); Trials (1P); Coated Trials (2P)

current assignments of paper grades to the profit codes and the associated commission rates in dollars per ton.

Because more profitable grades had higher commission rates, a salesperson could increase his or her commission earnings by improving the sales mix. Thus, the compensation plan was designed to encourage each salesperson to be selective in his or her selling efforts.

An important aspect of Ross profitability was not selling price. For example, a 10 per cent reduction in the net selling price of a grade typically meant a 30 per cent reduction in its profit contribution. Because each salesperson had an opportunity to influence the net selling price he or she achieved, the determination of commission earnings included an adjustment for price results.

Price performance was measured by determining the ratio of current net selling price to the historical price for the grade, i.e., the prices obtained during the period since the last price increase. The performance factor was expressed as a percentage. Of course, if a price increase were announced during the operating period, the historical net selling price for that grade was adjusted accordingly one month after the price adjustment. New product introduction had a price factor of 100 per cent for the first year while base period data was accumulated.

Commission earnings were determined by applying the appropriate commission rate to the shipments for the period and adjusting for the price performance factor. Thus, net commissions equaled tons shipped times commission rate times price factor. If, for example, a salesperson's net selling price decreased 10 per cent in a given period, the potential commissions (tons times commission rate) were multiplied by 90 per per cent to determine the amount of commission earnings for that grade.

Exhibit 4 is a sample of the earnings statement that was given to each salesperson every month. All commissions were credited on the basis of tons shipped and calculated to the nearest ten cents and 1 per cent of price. For example, a shipment of 125 tons of paper grade that paid $.90 per ton as commission, for which the net sales price was 5 per cent below historical levels, would result in commission earnings of

$$125 \times .90 \times .95 = \$106.87$$

Exhibit 5 describes the computation of the price adjustment factor.

Under the current sales compensation program, each ton sold yielded a commission. Therefore, every salesperson was virtually assured of an opportunity to earn more than his base monthly income. Appendix B details how commissions were paid for specification sales.

Commission earnings and commission statements were mailed to arrive in the regional office approximately three weeks after the close of each cost period. Thus, a check received in the latter part of July represented payment for June's commissions.

In addition to monthly base income and commission earnings possibilities, the compensation program provided an attractive year-end bonus opportunity for improved profit contribution.

Each salesperson faced different opportunities in his or her territory and should have been striving to capitalize on these opportunities to improve results each year. In addition, sales forecasts were set annually that reflected the results Ross Paper considered reasonable performance in each territory. To reinforce these improvement efforts and reward outstanding results, the compensation plan included a year-end profit improvement bonus opportunity.

The year-end profit improvement bonus was based on increases in commission income. Commission income in the Ross program was an

Exhibit 4
Ross Paper Division
Salesperson Commission Statement

Salesperson _____ No. _____

Period ending _____ 19 _____

Eligibility (E) Tons _____

Commissions $ _____

Forecast (F) Tons _____

Commissions $ _____

FACSIMILE

ACTUAL REPORT WAS A COMPUTER PRINTOUT

Product Grade		Commission Code	Tons Shipped		% of E	Commissions		Price Adjust- ment Factor	Commission		% of E	Commission Rates Per Ton Shipped
No.	Description		Current Period	To Date		Current Month	To Date		Current Month	To Date		
1A	Ross bond	5										
1B	Safety paper	3										
1C	Moistrite	6										
1D	Maderite	3										
1E	Form bond	2										
1F	Fast fold	0										
	Sub-totals											
2A	Cast coated	8										
2D	#1 coated	7										
2I	#4 coat. LP	5										
2J	#4 ct. offset	6										
	Sub-totals											
3A	#1 offset	7										
3B	Other offset	2										
3C	Pub. offset	3										
3D	Letterpress	5										
3E	Envelope	1										
3F	Tablet	0										
	Sub-totals											
	Grand Totals											

Exhibit 5
Ross Paper Division
Price Adjustment Factor

Realizing that price improvements or decreases had an amplified effect on margins, this adjustment was made to commission earnings to reflect the change in profits

$$\text{Factor} = 1 + \left(\frac{\text{Actual price - base price}}{\text{base price}} \right)$$

Example A
(Positive)   Actual price \$256/ton, base price \$241/ton

$$\text{Factor} = 1 + \left(\frac{\$256 - \$241}{\$241} \right)$$

$$= 1 + \left(\frac{\$15}{\$241} \right)$$

$$= 1 + (.0622)$$

$$= 1.0622 \times \text{commissions}$$

Example B
(Negative)   Actual price \$237/ton, base price \$241/ton

$$\text{Factor} = 1 + \left(\frac{\$237 - \$241}{\$241} \right)$$

$$= \left(\frac{-\$4}{1 - \$241} \right)$$

$$= 1 + (-.0165)$$

$$= 1 - .0165$$

$$= .9835 \times \text{commissions}$$

accurate index of the profit contributed by a salesperson because commission rates directly reflected the profitability of each grade of paper and commission earnings included adjustments for price performance. For example, a salesperson with \$3,000 in commission earnings had brought in half the profit of a person whose commissions totaled \$6,000 for the same period.

In addition, the average commission rate was a valuable relative measure of profit mix. For example, a salesperson with a commission average of \$1.10 per ton was selling a product mix that was 10 per cent more profitable than was a person whose average was \$1.00 per ton.

A profit improvement bonus (PIB), paid yearly, could be earned when commission results exceeded a bonus eligibility (E) point. To calculate the E point, the tons sold in the previous year were multiplied by the current commission rates and a price performance factor of 100 per cent. Current commission rates were used so that a salesperson was not unduly penalized or rewarded if commission rates were changed to reflect current profitability of a grade of paper. A price performance factor of 100 per cent was used so that a salesperson did not earn a bonus for just equaling last year's price if mix and volume remained the same.

To provide a meaningful reward, the year-end bonus was set at twice the amount the commission earnings increased beyond the E point. Thus, a salesperson received three dollars for every one dollar increase in commissions, i.e., one dollar in added commission earnings plus two dollars in profit improvement bonus.

As a general rule, management did not adjust the E point from the previous year's results. The base year was reconstructed only under rare circumstances such as a revision of the territory, shut down of a machine, discontinuance of a product line, etc. Appendix A describes in detail the mechanisms for volume transfer. In addition, a management decision was needed to determine whether adjustments were required in situations such as the following:

1. Acquisitions: Customer firms might be acquired or merged with other organizations and substantial volume could be lost or gained as a result.
2. Reorganization: Customer firms might consolidate, relocate, or reorganize their buying functions so that volume was moved from one territory to another or from field sales to house account classification.
3. Catastrophes: Fires, windstorms, and strikes might put a customer out of business temporarily or permanently, causing significant volume losses.

Adjustments in eligibility level were limited to circumstances that had a continuing impact of major significance. No attempts were made to adjust on the basis of performance of individual accounts, a single order or bid, or short-term business swings.

This profit improvement bonus rewarded each salesperson for the balanced development of his territory. Because commission earnings were a combination of volume, mix, and price performance, a salesperson could earn a bonus by improving price and mix performance even if he lost volume. Of course, in times of general business downturn, commission earnings could be affected, and few salespeople might be able to demonstrate the improved performance necessary for the year-end bonus. However, the lower eligibility point that would apply the following year offered an attractive bonus reward for regaining past performance levels.

Additional year-end bonus could be earned by exceeding the forecast performance (F) point. Each fall, the tonnage forecasts prepared in conjunction with Ross' sales planning were converted into forecast commission earnings by multiplying by the appropriate commission rate. If the forecast was exceeded, the amount of commissions over forecast was multiplied by four to calculate the additional year-end bonus earned as recognition of the outstanding contribution represented by such performance. As a general rule, once a forecast was established, it was not adjusted during the operating period.

There was no limit to the amount of bonus that could be earned for improved contribution to Ross profits. As indicated, once a salesperson exceeded his base commission levels, his bonus accrued at twice the commission increase in reserve for year-end award until forecast was reached. When commissions exceeded forecast levels, the bonus reserve increased at four times the increase in commissions. Exhibit 6 illustrates the bonus calculation mechanism. Management reserved the right to review the results to make certain that a salesperson had not been unduly penalized or assisted by factors beyond his control.

Bonus awards were paid as quickly as possible after the close of the year. Checks accompanied by a bonus calculation summary were normally mailed to arrive in January.

Exhibit 7 summarized how sales compensation was derived under the current plan.

The current plan had been implemented over a two-year period. The first year, Ross Paper guaranteed, for each salesperson and regional manager, a compensation equal to at least his 1971 salary. If compensation (commissions and/or bonus) earned under the plan exceeded

---

Exhibit 6
Ross Paper Division
Profit Improvement Bonus
For Salespeople

Commissions	Total for 1972	$6985				
	Forecast for 1972	$6600				
	Actual for 1971 (assumed to be eligibility commissions)	$6150				

Commission improvement						
1971 to 1972 forecast		$ 450	×	2	=	$ 900
1972 forecast to actual		385	×	4	=	$ 1540
		$ 835				$ 2440
	Added commission					_Profit improvement bonus_
Total increased earnings						$ 3275

Exhibit 7
Ross Paper Division
Computation of Sales Compensation

$$\text{Monthly earnings} = \text{Base income} + \left(\text{Tons shipped} \times \text{Commission rate} \times \text{Price factor}\right)$$

Example = $1,275.00 + (1,020 × $.62/ton × 428/409)

= $1,275.00 + $661.78 = $1,936.78 for the month

$$\text{Year-end bonus} = 2\left(\text{Forecast commissions} - \text{eligibility commissions}\right) + 2\left(\text{actual commissions} - \text{forecast commissions}\right)$$

Example = 2 ($7,652.00 − $7,111.00) + 4 ($7,941.36 − $7,652.00)

= 2 ($541.00) + 4 ($289.36)

= $1,082 + $1,157.44 = $2,239.44 for the year

current salary levels, Ross Paper paid the additional income earned, but there was no penalty for performance below the 1971 level. Commission statements, however, were issued as though the plan was in full force.

Introducing the current plan, the vice-president of marketing had said:

This proposed compensation program incorporates many of the positive features of both salary and commission programs. It does not expose the salesperson to wide swings in income that can result under a pure commission program. On the other hand, it offers each salesperson an excellent opportunity to increase his or her income by improving performance. In addition, it reinforces the Ross Paper's business plan by using forecasts, and it ties incentive income to profit economics.

Criticism of the Current Sales Compensation Plan   The current compensation plan was introduced in January 1972. By the third quarter of 1972 it was fully in operation. The vice-president of administration, Davies, felt that everyone concerned knew the major ingredients of the plan, how a salesperson could increase his or her benefits, what might be the impact of a given product mix on commissions and margins, and so on. In Davies' opinion, a breakthrough had been achieved in designing a dynamic sales compensation plan. It provided the best of the two worlds; it offered sales personnel the best benefits and at the same time maximized company profits. Davies' optimism was understandable because he was instrumental in designing the plan and in successfully selling it to the top management of the division. He was in his early fifties and had been with the company for twenty-eight years, all of them associated with Ross Paper Division. In the words of Daniel Davidson, president of the division, "Bob was the brain behind many strategic moves the division made." In his opinion, Davies would find a solution for any problem that none of them could solve. The younger employees, however, considered Davies to be a theoretician without a formal degree, who happened to be there by virtue of being an old associate of top management.

Reaction of the Vice-President of Sales The first person to take issue with the current compensation plan was John Martilla, vice-president of sales. Although he enthusiastically backed the plan when it was introduced in 1972, continued complaints from the salespeople, channeled to him by various market managers, made him wonder whether the plan was any good.

In a sales meeting at which both vice-president of administration and vice-president of sales were present, the regional sales managers voiced gross dissatisfaction with the compensation plan. They were so disturbed by the plan that when the vice-president of administration tried to answer some of their criticism against the plan, they overruled him and would not allow him to talk. Finally, Martilla called off the meeting assuring the regional sales managers that the plan would not be continued beyond 1973 in the present form.

Listed below are the major weaknesses of the current plan, as envisioned by Martilla based on his communication with market managers and salespeople.

1. There was an underlying assumption that if during a given year, two salespeople increased their earnings by like amounts it was a result of like improvement in performance; however, such was not the case. It seemed possible that there could develop a disparity between salespeople assigned to Ross owned merchants and those assigned to non-Ross merchants. If the division elected to force tonnage through Ross owned merchants it seemed apparent that a salesperson assigned to an independent merchant had to sustain a greater sales effort than did a salesperson assigned to a Ross owned merchant.

2. When the original program was first proposed there was an excess capacity, thus volume improvement was one of the underlying objectives. However, such was not the case in today's market nor would it be in the near future. Although management recognized this problem by eliminating commissions on those grades put on allocation, the attempt only magnified some of the inequalities. Salespeople in the business forms unit essentially have only two grades that qualified for commission (Trans/Rite and Trans/Form) while merchant and publishing sales personnel had a greater range of opportunities.

In September 1973, 80 per cent of paper grades were on allocation and thus would probably increase during the rest of the year and remain in effect through 1974. Of course, there was still an opportunity for mix improvement for certain salespeople; however, the question of what degree of control a salesperson had over his or her total product mix remained.

3. Another apparent weakness in the program, which several salespeople mentioned during a meeting at which the current program was presented to selected field representatives, was that it was impossible to offer all sales personnel the same financial opportunity because of the nature of the paper industry. This meant the assigning of major accounts; and because of their sheer size, there were many levels of management servicing these accounts other than the salespeople.

4. One area that could cause potential problems was the neglect of management to deal straightforwardly with the salespeople. Some of the material that had gone out to the field had been written in such a way that the salespeople realized their eventual earnings were based on both arbitrary and subjective decisions in many cases.

Martilla made the following comments for improving the sales compensation plan:

1. Each type of channel of distribution should be treated as an individual business unit for sales incentive purposes.

2. There should be an emphasis on margin contribution rather than an emphasis on volume.

3. The concept of commissions should be eliminated.

4. The program should be developed around a salary plus bonus.

Others' Reactions The question of sales compensation became a controversial topic in the entire organization. Everybody seemed to know about it, talked about it freely, and had suggestions to make for improvement. Shown here is a memorandum that the manager of distribution had written to Harry Murphy, vice-president of marketing.

September 24, 1973

TO: Harry Murphy, Vice-President Marketing
FROM: Chris Marx, Manager/Distribution
SUBJECT: 1974 Sales Compensation Program

Harry, during the managers' meeting this past week a great deal of discussion was centered around the 1974 compensation plan. It was felt for a number of reasons that the current plan should be eliminated during 1974 because it is basically a volume-oriented plan. We would like to return the salespeople to a 100 per cent salary level and then pay them a bonus at year-end with payment based on a number of criteria. Some of the suggestions were as follows:

1. Average margin per ton,
2. Key account planning,
3. Performance against budget,
4. Outside education interests,
5. Performing the normal sales administrative duties as well as complying with the regional manager's and head office's requests.

The total bonus would be divided among the inside salespeople, outside salespeople, and the regional managers, paid on a percentage basis determined by this office, yourself, and John Martilla.

One way of allocating the money among the groups would again rest at our level, but as a "rule of thumb" we could take the amount of dollars available divided by the number of salespeople in the plan. At year-end the regional managers would recommend to this office the bonus per salesperson based on performance. This would not be based on current salary level or tenure, but solely on performance.

Another idea for determining the amount of the bonus is that it could be based on the division's profit level, improvement over the previous year, a strategic installation such as a new machine, and so on.

Harry, I feel the basic philosophy of the compensation program is agreed upon throughout the sales force. Salary plus bonus and the bonuses paid to the sales force should equal the total bonus paid this year or whatever is the allowable amount under the governmental controls.

I would appreciate your comments and Bob's regarding the initial discussions and your recommendations.

Thank you.

                                        Chris Marx

As many as twenty similar letters were exchanged in the organization questioning the worth of the current compensation plan. Finally the matter reached the president, Daniel Davidson. Davidson asked Davies to review the sales compensation plan, in the light of growing dissatisfaction in the organization, and to arrive at an alternative plan. Davies was asked to prepare a definite compensation plan with immediate effects so that the salespeople could be told before Christmas how they would be paid in 1974.

After having a series of meetings with various executives in the organization and with the help of a consultant, a professor of marketing at the local university, Davies made substantial changes in the compensation plan. The highlights of the new plan are discussed below.

New Sales Compensation Plan   The sales compensation plan for 1974 was modified from the plan in effect for 1973. While it still consisted of a base salary plus commissions plus bonus, it had been revised substantially.

The compensation consisted of three parts; a base salary, commissions earned, and a year-end bonus. The base salary and commissions earned were to be paid on a monthly basis while the bonus was to be paid at year-end.

1. Base Salary.   There was to be a base salary established for each salesperson by the end of 1973. This base was established in conjunction with the regional manager and reflected both commissions anticipated to be earned in 1974 up to "E" point and any merit increases that were awarded.

    This base salary was to be paid in twelve monthly installments on the last day of each month. It would be adjusted during the year if necessary due to transfer, promotion, merit increases, or other reasons.

2. Commissions.   Commissions, based on the margin contribution, were established for each grade. It was the intent to establish the commission rate per ton so that the base salary plus commissions to equal the "E" (Eligibility) point came out on average, to be only 10 per cent of total compensation (base + commissions). This was considerably lower than it had been in previous years and took into account the oversold allocated marketing situation existing at that time in the paper industry. Thus, the base represented the bulk of the monthly payment in 1974.

    The commission rates established for each grade were applied against the grades and tonnages purchased by merchants and/or direct customers in a territory in 1973. These total commission dollars constituted a salesperson's commission target for 1974 and established his "E" (Eligibility) point.

Commission rates applied to all grades sold in 1973 except for those grades that had been discontinued or dropped. In addition, all customers that had been *dropped* in 1973, due to Ross sales policies, were removed from the 1974 commission eligibility point.

All commissions were paid as earned in 1974. A check covering commissions earned in the previous month was distributed by the middle of the succeeding month.

3. Bonus.   The major change in the compensation plan was the bonus portion. Whereas in the past the commissions earned constituted a major incentive portion payout, the establishment of the commissions as a lower percentage of total compensation meant that the major incentive or additional payout feature of the plan was in the form of the bonus.

In the previous plan the commissions earned over "E" point were multiplied by a factor of 2 to arrive at the bonus payout. This was changed and the bonus mainly reflected an overall evaluation of each salesperson's performance measured against that of every other salesperson.

Exhibit 8 titled "Salesperson Evaluation Form," lists the various categories against which each salesperson was evaluated. This evaluation form was initially completed by a regional manager, but reviewed with the vice-president of sales and others to ensure that several individuals had inputs and there was a consensus concerning a salesperson's performance.

The main features of the personal performance portion of the bonus system were established as:

- Points were awarded in each of the several categories:
    10 = outstanding
     8 = excellent
     5 = average
     2 = poor
     0 = unsatisfactory

- These points were totaled and bonus dollars were awarded in direct proportion to these points. Therefore, the salesperson with the highest number of points received the highest dollar bonus award and so on.

Exhibit 8
Ross Paper Division
Salesperson Evaluation Form

Performance Criteria	Point Award[a]				
	10 Out-standing	**8** Excel-lent	**5** Aver-age	**2** Poor	**0** Unsatis-factory
(1) Personal Habits (Appearance, absentee record, punctuality, etc.)					
(2) Administrative management (Timeliness, thoroughness, promptness with correspondence and other details involving customers and company. Does he or she plan time wisely?)					
(3) Attitude (Overall, to company and to others. Is he or she leader type?)					
(4) Continuing education (Effort toward a better understanding of the business, its technology, the business environment, etc., as evidenced by continuing education efforts both within and outside the company)					
(5) Outside activities (Within the business such as graphic arts organizations, salesperson's associations, and/or community or other affairs that relate to his or her standing and importance within the industry or community and enhance both his or her image and Ross's)					
(6) Customer feedback (What do the customers say about the salesperson—has he or she impressed them sufficiently to warrant a compliment? While unsolicited, they are of most value. The regional manager will probably want to solicit feedback where it is not forthcoming.)					
(7) Care of company property and finances (What is the record with regard to company cars, expenditures on expense account; the settlement of R&As, etc.)					

Exhibit 8—*continued*

Performance Criteria	Point Award[a]				
	10 Out- standing	8 Excel- lent	5 Aver- age	2 Poor	0 Unsatis- factory
(8) Sales training, customer education, etc. (What is the track record at sales meetings, number and effectiveness; what education or training has he or she inaugurated for customers; how effective is he or she before these groups; manner and content of presentation)					
(9) Specifications effort (What is the extent and effectiveness of the salesperson's specifications efforts. Is he or she spending time conscientiously and aggressively in this area? If possible, measure results)					
(10) Market development (Addition of new merchants or customers; improvements in existing)					
(11) Merchandising ability (The extent and creativity with which he or she uses advertising, promotional and public relations tools, and products developed within Ross; or those that he or she has developed alone or in conjunction with a merchant or customer)					

[a]Eleven award categories were established with points that ranged from 0 to 10. That meant it was possible to achieve 110 points. If $30 a point was awarded as bonus, an average performance warranted 55 points × $30 = $1,650 as bonus award, while an outstanding rated $3,300. In order to further award the top performers, there was an additional cash award to the top 5 or 10 people, i.e.,

```
#1 - $3,000
#2 - $2,000
#3 - $1,500
#4 - $1,000
#5 - $  500
```

- The exact amount of the dollar bonus for each point awarded in the performance evaluation was established based on the earnings of the division (and the limitations of the pay board). It was not dropped any lower than $30.00 a point which meant that if a person achieved only an average performance in all respects he or she achieved a personal performance bonus of at least $1,650. In addition, his or her compensation was also enhanced by commissions earned and any bonus dollars earned for exceeding "E" point.
- It was possible for a salesperson to earn bonus dollars by exceeding the "E" point on commissions earned. All commissions earned over "E" point were multiplied by 0.5 (or 1.0) and this dollar total was paid in the form of a bonus reward. However, in view of the reduced commissions that could be earned under the 1974 plan, the potential for bonus dollars, by exceeding "E" point, was smaller and the bulk of the bonus payout was in the form of the performance bonus.
- All bonus dollars earned were paid out no later than February 15 of the succeeding year.

Summary The Ross Paper Division of the Ross Corporation initiated a new sales compensation plan in 1972. The plan consisted of a fixed base income, monthly commissions, and an annual profit improvement bonus. The fixed base income was about 70 per cent of monthly compensation while commission earnings accounted for the remaining 30 per cent. The earned commissions of a salesperson depended on the product mix sold because each grade of paper had been assigned a commission rate that directly reflected its profitability and the net selling price at which the salesperson made different sales. The bonus was determined based on commission earnings. A bonus eligibility (E) point was established, and the bonus received was twice the amount the commission earnings increased beyond the "E" point.

In about a year's time the sales force, the regional sales managers, and the line executives at the head office found the compensation plan to be highly inadequate in many respects. The matter eventually reached the president of the Ross Paper Division.

The president asked the vice-president of administration, who had played a key role in designing the compensation plan, to review it and suggest any changes that might be desirable. After a thorough examination he proposed a revised compensation plan.

In the revised plan, while the underlying mechanics of determining sales compensation remained the same, the commission earnings accounted for only 10 per cent of monthly compensation. The major change in the compensation plan was the bonus portion; that is, the additional payout feature of the plan was in the form of a bonus. The bonus was determined based on an evaluation of the salesperson.

Appendix A
Volume Transfer Procedures

As the market grew and Ross sales penetration increased in each territory, there would be a continuing need to reevaluate the size and make-up of the sales territories. Territorial realignments made on the basis of these evaluations could lead to changes in a salesperson's volume potential.

1. If realignments increased the size of the territory, the salesperson had the opportunity for a large base income and more commissions.
2. In instances in which territories decline, the Ross sales compensation program protected a salesperson's income until he or she could build back the earnings lost in the transfer. This feature of the program was called "volume transfer awards."

When a salesperson's territory was decreased, the resulting loss of income was calculated and used as the basis for volume transfer awards. Included in this figure were both the loss in monthly base income and monthly commission earnings. The amount of monthly commission earnings lost was calculated by multiplying the volume given up by the preceding year's commission average.

The volume transfer award was handled as follows:

- The first year: maximum of 100 per cent paid to the salesperson losing the volume.
- The second year—maximum of 67 per cent paid.
- The third year—maximum of 33 per cent paid.

The volume transfer award thus provided a declining income protection over a period of three years. These awards were paid quarterly so that this income was not confused with the regular monthly sales income (base plus commissions). The salesperson also had an opportunity to earn a larger year-end bonus, because his eligibility point was lower.

Of course, as the volume was replaced over the next three years, the salesperson's base income increased in line with the volume increase. When a salesperson's monthly income (base and commissions) reached the level he earned before the volume transfer, the volume transfer award was terminated. During the year when this point was reached, it was possible for the quarterly payments to exceed the protection needed. In this case, payments in excess of the original earnings level were deducted from the profit improvement bonus paid at year-end.

The purpose of this volume transfer award was to make it easy for an experienced aggressive salesperson to do additional sales development without jeopardizing his or her income. The award was not intended for application when volume had to be reduced due to physical incapacity, semiretirement, and the like. It was intended for growth situations where expanding markets and increasing penetration had to be supported by additional sales efforts.

Appendix B
Specification Sales by Field Salesperson

An important way for an account salesperson to increase his or her commission earnings through selective selling was to develop new accounts (national accounts in his territory and the customers of merchants) through specification sales. If this specification work resulted in orders for assigned accounts, he or she automatically received the commission earnings for the improved volume and mix. However, if the specification work resulted in a national contract or shipments in another territory, the salesperson responsible for the sale received credit only if his or her efforts were specifically identified. Therefore, each regional manager had to verify the specification sales identified by his salespeople that were shipped into another territory to ensure that his salespeople received proper credit.

The actual commissions paid for the grade of paper involved in these specification sales were added to accumulated commission earnings and counted toward reaching E and F points. However, after reaching "bonus" territory, these specification commission earnings were multiplied by 2 after E point and by 4 after F point.

Any commissions earned through specifications were not used in the setting of E and F points for the next year.

The commissions for specification work were paid out in the month after they were earned, while bonus payments were made at year-end.

Case 20

Outdoor Sporting Products, Inc.

The annual sales volume of Outdoor Sporting Products, Inc. for the
past six years had ranged between $2,400,000 and $2,550,000.
Although profits continued to be satisfactory, Hudson McDonald,
president and chief operating officer, was concerned because sales had
not increased appreciably from year to year. Consequently, he asked
a consultant in New York City and the officers of the company to
submit proposals for improving the sales personnel's compensation plan,
which he believed was the basic weakness in the firm's marketing
operations.

The Products Outdoor's factory and warehouse were located in
Albany, New York, where the company manufactured and distributed
sporting equipment, clothing, and accessories. Hudson McDonald
had organized it in 1946, when he felt the market for sporting goods
would grow because of the predicted increase in leisure time and the
rising level of income in the United States.

Products of the company, approximately 700 items, were grouped
into three lines: (1) fishing supplies, (2) hunting supplies, and (3)
accessories. The fishing supplies line, which accounted for approximately 40 per cent of the company's annual sales, included nearly every

Adapted from a case prepared by Professor Zarrel V. Lambert, Auburn University
and Dr. Fred Kniffin, University of Connecticut. Used with permission.

item a fisherman would need, such as fishing jackets, vests, caps, rods and reels of all types, lines, flies, lures, landing nets, and creels. The hunting supplies line contributed 30 per cent of annual sales; it consisted of hunting clothing of all types, safety garments, shell holders, whistles, calls, and gun cases. The accessories line, which made up the balance of the company's annual sales volume, included items such as compasses, cooking kits, lanterns, hunting and fishing knives, hand warmers, and novelty gifts.

Although the sales of the hunting and fishing lines were very seasonal, they tended to complement each other. The January–April period accounted for the bulk of the company's annual volume in fishing items, and most sales of hunting supplies were made during the months of May through August. Typically, the company's sales of all products reached their lows for the year during the month of December.

Outdoor's sales volume is $2,509,935 for the current year, with products manufactured accounting for 35 per cent of this total. Imported products, which came principally from Japan, comprised 50 per cent of the company's volume. Items manufactured by other domestic producers and distributed by Outdoor accounted for the remaining 15 per cent of total sales.

McDonald reported that wholesale prices to retailers were established by adding a markup of 50 to 100 per cent to Outdoor's cost for the item. This practice was followed on products manufactured by Outdoor as well as on items purchased from other manufacturers. The resulting average markup across all products was 70 per cent on cost. Outdoor's market area consisted of the New England states, New York, Pennsylvania, Ohio, Michigan, Wisconsin, Indiana, Illinois, Kentucky, Tennessee, West Virginia, Virginia, Maryland, Delaware, and New Jersey. The area over which Outdoor could effectively compete was limited to some extent by shipping costs, since all orders were shipped from the factory and warehouse in Albany.

Outdoor's salespeople sold to approximately 6,000 retail stores in small- and medium-sized cities in its market area. Analysis of sales records showed that the firm's customer coverage was very poor in the large metropolitan areas. Typically, each account was a one- or two-store operation. McDonald stated that he knew for a fact that Outdoor's share of the market was very low, perhaps 2 to 3 per cent; and for all practical purposes he felt the company's sales potential was unlimited. McDonald believed that, with few exceptions, Outdoor's customers had little or no brand preference, and in the vast majority of cases they bought hunting and fishing supplies from several suppliers.

It was McDonald's opinion that the pattern of retail distribution for hunting and fishing products had been changing during the past ten years as a result of the growth of discount stores. He thought that the proportion of retail sales for hunting and fishing supplies made by small and medium-sized sporting goods outlets had been declining as compared to the percentage sold by discounters and chain stores. An analysis of company records revealed that Outdoor had not developed business among the discounters, with the exception of a few small discount stores. Some of Outdoor's executives felt that the lack of business with discounters might have been due in part to the company's pricing policy and in part to the pressures that current customers had exerted on company salespeople to keep them from calling on the discounters.

Outdoor's sales force for the current year totaled eleven men full time. Their ages ranged from twenty-three to sixty-seven, and their tenure with the company from one to ten years.

The company's sales force played the major role in its marketing efforts, since Outdoor did not use magazine, newspaper, or radio advertising to reach either the retail trade or consumers. One advertising piece that supplemented the work of the salespeople was Outdoor's merchandise catalog. It contained a complete listing of all the company's products and was mailed to retailers who were either current accounts or prospective accounts. Typically, store buyers used the catalog for purposes of reordering.

Most accounts were contacted by a salesperson two or three times a year. The salespeople planned their activities so that each store would be called on at the beginning of the fishing season and again prior to the hunting season. Certain key accounts were contacted more often.

The Compensation Plan The salespeople were paid straight commissions on their dollar sales volume for the calendar year. The commission rate was 5 per cent on the first $225,000, 6 per cent on the next $75,000, and 7 per cent on all sales over $300,000 for the year. Each week, a salesperson could draw all or a portion of his accumulated commissions. McDonald encouraged the salespeople to draw commissions as they accumulated, because he felt the men were motivated to work harder when they had a very small or zero balance in their commission accounts. These accounts were closed at the end of the year, so each salesperson began the new year with nothing in his account.

The salespeople provided their own automobiles and paid their traveling expenses, of which all or a portion were reimbursed per diem. Under the per diem plan, each salesperson received $45 per day for Monday through Thursday and $21 for Friday, or a total of $201 for the normal workweek. No per diem was paid for Saturday or Sunday nights in the territory.

In addition to the commission and per diem, a salesperson could earn cash awards under two sales incentive plans that were begun two years earlier. Under one, called the Annual Sales Increase Awards plan, a total of $7,800 was paid to the five salespeople who had the largest percentage increase in dollar sales volume over the previous year. To be eligible for these awards, a salesperson had to show a sales increase over the previous year. These awards were made at the January sales meeting, and the winners were determined by dividing the dollar amount of each salesperson's increase by his volume for the previous year, with the percentage increases ranked in descending order.

Under the second incentive plan, each salesperson could win a Weekly Sales Increase Award for every week in which his dollar volume in the current year exceeded his sales for the corresponding week in the previous year. Beginning with an award of $3 for the first week, the amount of the award increased by $3 for each week in which the salesperson surpassed his sales for the comparable week in the previous year. If a salesperson produced higher sales during each of the fifty weeks in the current year, he received $3 for the first week, $6 for the second week and $150 for the fiftieth week, or a total of $3,825 for the year. The salesperson had to be employed by the company during the previous year to be eligible for these awards. A check for the total amount of the awards accrued during the year was presented to the salespeople at the sales meeting held in January.

The company frequently used "spiffs" to promote sales of special items. The salesperson was paid a spiff, which usually was six dollars, for each order he obtained for the designated items in the promotion.

For the past three years, in recruiting salespeople, McDonald had guaranteed the more qualified applicants a weekly income while they learned the business and developed their respective territories. During the current year, five salespeople: Allen, Duvall, Edwards, Hammond, and Logan, had a guarantee of $300 a week, which they drew against their commissions. If the year's cumulative commissions for any of these salespeople were less than their cumulative weekly drawing accounts, they received no commissions. The commission and drawing accounts were closed on December 31, so each salesperson began the new year with a zero balance in each account.

The company did not have a stated or written policy specifying the maximum length of time a salesperson could receive a guarantee if his commissions continued to be less than his draw. McDonald held the opinion that the five salespeople who currently had guarantees would quit if these guarantees were withdrawn before their commissions reached $15,000 per year.

McDonald stated that he was convinced the annual earnings of Outdoor's salespeople had fallen behind earnings for comparable selling positions, particularly in the past six years. As a result, he felt that the company's ability to attract and hold high caliber professional salespeople was being adversely affected. He strongly expressed the opinion that each salesperson should be earning $30,000 annually.

In December of the current year, McDonald met with his comptroller and production manager, who were the only other executives of the company, and solicited their ideas concerning changes in the company's compensation plan for salespeople.

The comptroller pointed out that the salespeople who had guarantees were not producing the sales that had been expected from their territories. He was concerned that the annual commissions earned by four of the five salespersons on guarantees were approximately half or less than their drawing accounts.

Furthermore, according to the comptroller, several of the salespeople who did not have guarantees were producing a relatively low volume of sales year after year. For example, annual sales remained at low levels for Gatewood, O'Bryan, and Wates, who had been working four to five years in their respective territories.

The comptroller proposed that guarantees be reduced to $150 per week, plus commissions at the regular rate on all sales. The $150 would not be drawn against commissions, as was done under the existing plan, but would be in addition to any commissions earned. In the comptroller's opinion, this plan would motivate the sales force to rapidly increase sales, because incomes would rise directly with sales.

From a sample check of recent shipments, the production manager had concluded that the salespeople tended to overwork accounts located within a fifty-mile radius of their homes. Sales coverage was extremely light in a sixty to one-hundred-mile radius of the salespeople's homes. The coverage seemed to result from the desire of the salespeople to spend most evenings during the week at home with their families.

He proposed that the per diem be increased from $45 to $54 per day for Monday through Thursday, $21 for Friday, and $54 for Sunday if the salespeople spent Sunday evening away from their homes. He reasoned that the per diem of $54 for Sunday would act as a strong incentive for the salespeople to drive to the perimeters of their territories on Sunday evenings rather than use Monday morning for traveling. Further, he believed that the increase in per diem would result in a more uniform coverage of the sales territories and an overall increase in sales volume.

The consultant from New York City recommended that the guarantees and per diem be retained on the present basis, and he proposed that Outdoor adopt what he called a Ten Percent Self-Improvement Plan. Under the consultant's plan, each salesperson would be paid, in addition to the regular commission, a monthly bonus commission of 10 per cent on all dollar volume over his sales in the comparable month of the previous year. For example, if a salesperson sold $30,000 worth of merchandise in January of the current year and $27,000 in January of the previous year, he would receive a $200 bonus check in February. For salespeople on guarantees, bonuses would be in addition to earnings. The consultant reasoned that the bonus commission would motivate the salespeople, both those with and those without guarantees, to increase their sales.

He further recommended discontinuing the two sales incentive plans currently in effect. He felt the savings from these plans would nearly cover the costs of his proposal.

Questions

1. What plan should the company use to compensate its salespeople? Why?

Case 21

Levi Strauss and Company

The sales executives of Levi Strauss and Company, a San Francisco clothing manufacturer, are considering the possibility of setting up a sales contest for the company's field salespeople. These people, currently supervised by nine regional sales managers, contact retailers directly throughout the nation and account for most of the company's domestic sales.

Levi Strauss and Company was founded in 1850. Levi's overall, the company's rugged, tight-fitting blue jean, was the mainstay of the company for many years and is still a very important part of the firm's product line. In 1928 Western wear, including stockman pants and Western shirts, became the first of several additions to the company's assortment. The introduction of Western wear was followed with wool shirts in 1949, casual wear—including pants, slacks, shorts, and coordinated jackets—in 1952, double knee jeans in 1954, and matched work sets of pants and shirts in 1956. In 1953 part of the Western wear line was separated out into a more style-promoted line called ladies' California Ranch Pants, including pants and shorts for women and girls. Colored Levi's jeans made from cotton twill were introduced

*Data and at times management opinions and decisions have been altered in preparing this case in order to protect confidential information and/or to focus the case problem along a particular line. This case was prepared by Harry E. Allison for the University of California at Berkeley as a basis for class discussion. It is not designed to present either a correct or incorrect illustration of the handling of administrative problems.

as a part of the Levi's jean line in 1959. In the decade of the sixties these product lines were restructured, and they are currently organized into five product divisions: Jean Division, Sportswear division, Boy's Division, Levi's For Gals Division which includes all of the company's apparel items for women, and Levi Strauss International which handles all overseas markets.

All Levi Strauss salespeople are paid on a straight commission plus expenses basis. This is a common method of compensation in the clothing industry and, in the opinion of company management, the best way to insure incentive. Levi Strauss and Company lines, particularly the Levi's jeans and casual wear, have good consumer acceptance; thus, company salespeople typically receive attractive annual incomes.

Performance and morale are generally high within each of the nine sales regions. With its growth in stature and its greater geographic outreach, the company has both expanded its lines and added items within lines so that in recent years the salespeople have found themselves in the extremely desirable situation of facing increasing sales within contracting sales territories. The resulting higher incomes, fewer days away from home, and greater advancement opportunities arising from the creation of new sales positions have all contributed toward creating a highly motivated and generally satisfied sales force.

Under such conditions the sales staff is considering a sales contest not because of the need to shake the sales force out of its doldrums or to give new life to declining products, but rather as a means of further stimulating an already favorable situation. The national sales manager, in particular, sees several possible contributions that a sales contest may make in the company's current sales situation. First, a contest may be used to increase casual wear sales in the off season. Although the sales of this line have grown substantially, recent plant expansion provides an opportunity for increased off season sales. It is rather common for manufacturers of casual wear items to adjust to their seasonal sales by reducing their output level for two or three months out of the year. The top management of Levi Strauss, however, has traditionally stressed uniform year round employment because they feel a strong moral obligation to provide their employees with continuous work. In addition, reducing output for sixty to ninety days causes a certain number of employees to shift to other jobs so that recruiting and training costs are increased. The latter is particularly significant in the case of Levi Strauss because the company puts heavy emphasis on turning out a top-quality garment and a high turnover of employees makes quality control difficult to achieve. In the past the output of casual wear plants has largely been stabilized by producing for inventory during the off season. This solution, however, is becoming less and less feasible. Growth of the company's casual wear production facilities means that inventories of rather substantial absolute size have to be accumulated in order to keep the regular labor force busy throughout the year, while the increased emphasis on style and fashion in casual wear in recent years has made the holding of such large inventories at the start of the season extremely risky. A sales contest might alleviate this situation either by increasing the off season shipments of casual wear, even though total casual wear sales are not appreciably increased, or by increasing sales of the company's matched sets of work pants and shirts. The latter are manufactured on the same equipment and by the same factory labor force as the casual wear line and can be readily produced and held in inventory during the off season because the style of the work sets is quite stable from year to year.[1]

Second, although the Levi Strauss sales force has always been an aggressive, high-producing unit, the national sales manager feels that it is very possible that his employees can do even better if put to the challenge. He notes that every organization, the best as well as the worst, has some degree of reserve capacity and that it is almost impossible to assess the amount of such capacity accurately without actually putting the organization to the test. A sales contest covering all lines, for example, may well carry the sales force to a new level of attainment and by so doing have the salespeople accept the new higher level of performance as a normal expectation for their day-to-day output.

Third, the national sales manager thinks that a sales contest may provide a base for creating excitement within the total sales force and at the same time serve as a vehicle to help put across material on sales pointers. A periodic general review of sales approaches seems necessary simply to keep the sales organization up to par; yet, management has to be careful to make these exposures and re-exposures as palatable as possible. Regional sales meetings and direct mail releases for a contest can readily incorporate good sales practices and discussions of sales problems. Here a sales contest is being viewed not so much as a means to lift the sales organization to new levels of performance, but rather as a means of ensuring that morale and performance remain at their present high level.

Several individuals in the company's top management have objected to sales contests offering merchandise, money, or travel awards because they feel that such awards amount to paying the salespeople a second time for doing the job they are supposed to do, and because they fear that the salespeople may come to expect such additional compensation as a part of their regular income. Also the national sales manager is well aware that a sales contest may not succeed and, furthermore,

---

[1]Because of differences in plant equipment and construction techniques there is no production flexibility between Levi's jeans and casual wear.

may even have a negative impact. For example, concentration on the casual line may only serve to unbalance the sales effort, or the competitive excitement of an internal contest may move beyond friendly, morale-building rivalry into the area of jealousy and hard feelings between individual salespeople. Furthermore, the salespeople may decide that the whole contest is "kid stuff" largely dreamed up by management to get more work out of them. Poorly designed contests which each person does not feel he or she has a reasonable chance of winning are particularly likely to have one of the latter effects. In addition, contests can frequently result in undesirable selling practices such as overstocking, accepting orders from poor credit risks, splitting commissions with the buyer, and neglecting service. These can, in turn, be harmful to long-run sales. Finally, an offsetting sales slump may follow a successful contest simply because of an after contest letdown by the sales force.

Because the company has had no recent experience with internal sales contests, there are no internal data to guide the sales staff in its consideration of such programs. Thus, the national sales manager has asked one of his assistants to study the question of the company sponsoring an internal sales program and to prepare a well-supported recommendation on the matter. He notes that such a recommendation can not be systematically arrived at without first extensively reviewing the published materials on sales contests and designing what appears to be the best possible contest for the company to sponsor. The report is first to define the individual elements of the proposed contest and then to arrive at a recommendation for or against the use of a sales contest by the company, taking into account the expected contribution of the contest to the general marketing program and comparing it to other possible uses for the same funds.

As a minimum, the national sales manager wants the proposal to specify the particular objective or objectives of the contest, its length, how many would win, how performance would be measured, the extent of attempts to involve salespeople's families, the number and type of awards that would be given, and the cost of the program. The national sales manager notes that in sales contests the individual salespeople typically compete for awards against other salespeople or against their own past records. In the former case the top awards go to those having the best sales performance as measured in terms of total dollar volume, units of product, number of new accounts, number of displays, etc., or in terms of each salesperson's relative increase in such values over some office assigned quota or over the salesperson's own performance in some base period. In the cases where the salesperson competes against himself or herself, every salesperson achieving some individual level of performance in total dollar volume, number of new accounts, number of displays, etc., or making a required percentage increase in such performance factors over either past performance or quota, receives an award. The value of these awards, whether merchandise or money, generally varies with the amount by which the base is exceeded. Competition among salespeople is sometimes combined with "self-competition" and awards are given to every salesperson meeting certain absolute or relative performance levels, while additional awards are given to the salespeople who exceed their specified goals by the widest margins.

In some cases, the salespeople are not placed in a competitive situation either with themselves or with others, but are awarded for performance on a per unit rate much as might be the case under a regular compensation plan. They, in effect, receive so much money or so many merchandise credits for every unit of performance. The units of performance may be defined in dollars of sales, units of a specific product, amount of calls, number of new accounts, number of special displays, etc. In still other special programs, both the per unit award and contest approaches are combined so that all participants receive an award for performance at some predetermined per unit rate with further awards or prizes going to those turning in the top performance as evaluated according to some contest criteria. Finally, some programs either include elements of group competition in addition to individual competition, or are based entirely on group or team performance.

The national sales manager points out that merchandise, money, travel, or honor awards may be used either separately or in some combination in any proposed contest, and says that he will send his assistant a report he has in his files on the relative merits of these different awards. He also notes that if merchandise awards are included, consideration should be given to the possible use of a sales incentive house as a source of the merchandise items. By using such an agency, Levi Strauss can offer a choice of award items and, at the same time, avoid merchandise handling problems because the winners can be paid off in points that would be redeemed through the prize catalogs of the incentive agency. He adds that several trading stamp companies have entered the sales incentive field. Under their plans the sponsor awards trading stamps to the contest winners, and these stamps are then redeemed at local redemption centers or through the usual stamp catalog procedures. The stamp companies claim that their programs are both easier to administer and more effective in involving the salesperson's spouse than are the point-type programs.[2]

2"Two Can Save Stamps Faster Than One," *Business Week*, 16 June 1962, pp. 140 and 142.

Before making a decision the sales manager reviewed the merits of merchandise, money, travel, and honor awards. See Appendix A.

Questions

1. Design what you consider to be the best internal sales contest for Levi Strauss and Company to sponsor, defend the major elements of your design, and then develop a recommendation on whether or not the company should put your sales contest into effect.

Appendix A
Merchandise, Money, Travel, and Honor Awards

Merchandise awards have the advantages that:

1. Small awards, particularly those under twenty dollars, or even under fifty, look much more impressive in merchandise than in cash. In such cases the dollar and cents amount may look too piddling to evoke any positive response, and may even create a negative reaction if individuals consider that what they are being asked to do has benefits to the company that far exceed the value of the award.

2. Merchandise awards are purchased at wholesale or near wholesale prices, but tend to be evaluated by the recipient at retail prices. Use of merchandise, in effect, expands the particular incentive budget. Coupling this with the point that small awards appear more impressive in merchandise form, it becomes possible to offer many more awards, although smaller in value, for the same incentive budget through use of merchandise. This, in turn, permits a broader distribution of the awards and, as a result, creates a more effective incentive response.

3. Merchandise awards can be semi-luxury and luxury items that the recipient would not feel free to purchase from his own funds. Such items include relatively inexpensive things as well as more expensive ones.

4. Merchandise awards can be promoted, i.e., glamorized, more readily than money. The result of such promotion is greater interest and excitement and increased active participation in the program.

5. Merchandise awards become something tangible and lasting to remind the participant and other family members of the positive

results of his or her extra effort. They serve as durable individual and family good will builders for the company. Money awards all too often never get home to begin with and, if they do, they frequently disappear into the nothingness of the general family budget leaving no continuing reminder of the award. This latter observation holds particularly in the case of low or medium value awards.

6. The tangibility of merchandise awards is reflected in yet another way. These awards are frequently readily visible, or can be shown with good taste, to others outside the family. Explanations of why an award was received result in recognition and pride of accomplishment for the recipient beyond that secured through a citation of the award to his or her coworkers. In the case of small monetary awards, the amounts seem too insignificant to mention to others, while for large monetary awards it would frequently be considered bad taste to call them to the attention of outsiders.

7. Merchandise awards are often items for spouses or children, or for general family use; thus, they make the most of a participant's motivation to do something for a specific loved one or for the family in general. With this also goes the expectation of becoming the family hero for having secured the award for them.

8. Merchandise incentive schemes can be announced more gracefully to the participant's family than can money schemes. This increases the possibility of capitalizing on the motivation that arises both from family support and family push. Some programs may go so far as to try to draw the spouses into participating by offering performance credits, or a separate award, for such things as letters on how they plan to help their spouse achieve an award or for indicating which prize they would like to have their spouse receive. Some discretion needs to be exercised in working through the family, as some individuals feel that it is an invasion of their privacy and that, while the company may have a right to put pressure on them, they should not have to face the same thing, at the company's instigation, from their spouse and/or children at home.

9. Merchandise awards may create both a stronger initial incentive and a more sustained effort than other awards. The goal of the participant is frequently more definite in that he or she is striving for a specific award item. The possibilities of receiving some award are greater due to the larger number of awards that may be offered over a cash program, and earning only half of a toaster, bicycle, bowling ball, etc. is meaningless. This should be noted particularly in sales or safety incentive programs in which everyone can receive an award if his or her performance is good enough.

10. Merchandise awards have little danger of being viewed as a regular part of the recipient's pay. All money awards, regardless of the basis on which they are awarded, if they are awarded too frequently, involve the risk of becoming considered a permanent and regular part of the individual's income. When this happens, the award ceases to create any incentive; and furthermore, if it is discontinued, this can have an appreciable negative impact on incentive.

Cash awards have the primary advantage of universal appeal. Merchandise awards have the problem that the specific award items offered may be items that the individual already has. Along with this goes the problem of what to do about individuals who qualify a repeated number of times for the award, but have little use for multiple units of the award item. Money, furthermore, can be put where it yields the most benefit or satisfaction to the receiver, e.g., for outstanding bills, the mortgage, or merchandise. Money, therefore, can be particularly effective in motivating low paid individuals or almost all individuals at times, such as Christmas, when most are in need of extra cash.

Finally, money has an advantage in that it is relatively easy to award in do-it-yourself programs. There is no problem of selecting specific award items, no purchasing to transact, no inventory to worry about, no delivery of award items to arrange, and no merchandise complaints to handle. Using a merchandise incentive house, a direct shipping manufacturer, or gift certificates from local wholesale or retail sources are, of course, other ways of solving these problems. Similar problems in the case of travel awards can be avoided by use of merchandise incentive agencies or regular travel agencies.

Travel awards also involve most of the advantages cited for merchandise awards. They can be semi-luxury and luxury affairs that the receiver could not, or would not, purchase with his or her own funds. They are very promotable in that they are particularly easy to glamorize. They are strong company good will builders as they can be something tangible and lasting for the recipient and those who accompany him or her through their memories of the many experiences of the trip, photographs taken on the trip, and souvenirs purchased at the places that were visited. Recognition from others is no problem with the travel award, as the trip is something friends are aware of, may well be envious of, and can be told about in detail afterwards.

When family members are included in the trip, there is ample motivation to do something for another family member, and a "family hero" feeling is created if the award is achieved. Family travel awards are particularly effective in getting the spouse's support and push. Furthermore, they will usually bring forth a strong initial effort and a sustained effort. Vacations are generally on an annual basis; thus, the incentive toward earning one can readily be extended to cover a period of ten to twelve months. Trips also are especially adaptable to continued efforts to step up performance throughout the incentive period by enticing the individual to strive for a better trip, a longer stay, more side trips and special events, or the right to take more members of the family.

Travel awards have the merit over both money and merchandise awards that, if the travel is done on a group basis with one or more business meetings, e.g., sales meetings, being held during the trip, federal income tax does not have to be paid on the award. Income taxes must be paid on both money and merchandise awards, the latter are valued at a "fair" market value, however, rather than at list price. Some companies do pay the tax on any money and merchandise awarded as part of their incentive program, but the recipient must still pay the tax on the tax money. Avoidance of the tax on incentive awards through the use of trips incorporating business sessions increases the value of the award to the recipient at no cost to the company's incentive budget, and at the same time provides a captive but generally ready and receptive audience for the business sessions.

Travel awards have the weaknesses that they take the receiver of the award away from his job for the duration of the trip; that the idea of receiving a planned, paid for vacation may move into the category of being viewed as a permanent and regular part of the recipient's annual income if awarded too frequently; and that they have a high cost. Furthermore, travel awards do present some problems in flexibility. Individuals may not be willing or able to travel due to their own distaste for travel, family circumstances, health, etc., or may not be able, or want, to go with a group, at the required time and/or to the specified place. Also, as with merchandise awards, an individual may qualify for multiples of the same award when he has no use for them. These objections can be partially offset, as in the case of merchandise awards, by offering a wide selection of alternative trips on an individual basis (this eliminates the possible tax advantage of a travel award) with differences in locations, distances, lengths of stays, number of individuals covered by the award, etc. The greater variety does not, however, in this case, answer the problem of the individual who either does not want or can not travel. Thus, there is a need to offer merchandise or money alternatives with travel awards in order to cover such situations.[1]

---

[1] It is generally felt that it is a poor policy to have a cash alternative for small to medium-value merchandise awards as the amount of cash only tends to depreciate the award.

Honor awards include a wide variety of things ranging from both public and private congratulations from high-ranking officials to publicity in house organs, trade papers, and local newspapers; titles, such as salesperson or group of the month or year; certificates of merit; and membership in achievement clubs on through pins, plaques, and trophies to award dinners and expense-paid convention trips for recipients and their spouses.[2] All of these have the common characteristic of being relatively inexpensive with the possible exception of the expense-paid convention trips.

Low cost is the primary merit of honor awards over money or merchandise awards. In addition they have the asset that they are particularly adaptable to group awards based on group production, safety, or sales performance. Honor can be subdivided among the members of the group with little depreciation effect on the individual shares. A group money or merchandise award, on the other hand, dwindles into insignificance quite rapidly as it is subdivided into more and more individual shares. Group competition in sales performance can be quite effective in motivating individual performance and in developing an *ésprit de corps*.

The position of those holding a negative view of the effectiveness of honor awards is typically summarized by the words, "you can not eat honor awards" or "honor awards will not pay the rent," while the opposite view is characterized by the statement, "man does not live by bread alone, he has psychological as well as physiological needs." Phelps and Westing go on from the latter consideration to point out that in the case of sales contests, "Management has often been surprised at the interest and enthusiasm which developed when non-monetary awards were the *only* ones offered in a contest."[3]

Honor awards are automatically incorporated into any incentive program in which the top performers receive public recognition. Because the cost of honor awards relative to their potential for motivating performance is low, every merchandise, money, or travel award program should be deliberately designed to capitalize on honor awards rather than merely on accruing some of their benefits largely by chance. Award dinners, articles in house organs, notices on company bulletin boards, and coverage in the trade and/or local press are some of the ways to bring this about.

---

[2] When the emphasis is on side trips and non-convention activities with company appropriated time playing a relatively insignificant role, the latter is better classified as a travel award rather than as an honor award.

[3] D. Maynard Phelps and J. Howard Westing, *Marketing Management*, Rev. ed. (Homewood, Illinois: Richard D. Irwin, 1960), p. 699.

Case 22

The Shopping News

The *Shopping News* was organized in response to the needs of a group of businesspeople in the Pleasant Grove area of Dallas for some type of newspaper that would be strictly a sales tool to help them sell their products. Using his newspaper experience with the *Wall Street Journal*, the Dallas *Morning News*, and the Dallas *Times Herald*, Joe Harty began publication of the paper in 1955. The paper was mainly composed of display advertising and some classified advertising, but news or anything of that nature was not included.

Over twenty-four years, the *Shopping News* has increased its circulation from about 2,000 copies distributed by an independent distribution company to three editions and a circulation of about 98,000 copies handled by its own distribution company. One edition covers Pleasant Grove, another covers Lake Highlands and White Rock, and still another covers Garland. All of these areas are east or northeast of Dallas. The paper itself now covers some neighborhood news, but for the most part maintains its original function as an advertising tool. It is circulated as a free paper and as such, derives all of its operating revenues from selling its services to advertisers, with operations being handled by a full-time group of forty employees.

The major philosophy of the *Shopping News* is to provide the very best media in order to get the best response for a customer. In addition to this, a secondary philosophy is to handle the advertiser's account in a way that is acceptable to him or her. This philosophy has been

This case was written by William Noland under the supervision of Charles A. Futrell, Texas A&M University.

successful from the standpoint that advertisers have received better results by advertising on a local level through the *Shopping News* than they have through using the larger daily newspapers.

Robert Harty   During the first fifteen years of its existence, the *Shopping News* grew under the leadership of the founder, Joe Harty. However, organization within the company was not extensive as most of the effort exerted by Harty and other top managers went towards developing new business. In 1970, Joe Harty persuaded his son, Robert Harty, to take over the business as president while he went into semi-retirement and assumed the responsibilities of chairman of the board. Robert Harty's initial purpose as president was to observe the operations of the *Shopping News* in order to organize it more efficiently and effectively.

When he joined the company, Robert knew very little about the newspaper business even though his father was in this type of work. He was a graduate of North Texas State University where he majored in art design and minored in business. After graduation from North Texas, he earned a Master's degree in Religious Education. However, studies in Religious Education did involve organizational and managerial principles meant to prepare people for working in church organizations.

Upon completing his formal education, Robert became involved in full-time church work in West Texas. After a few years, he accepted a position with the Baptist Publishing House in Nashville, Tennessee. There he worked designing and publishing periodicals, as well as supervising a staff working under him. He spent five years in Nashville before assuming the responsibilities of president of the *Shopping News*.

Instead of gradually working his way into the business, Robert was quickly given responsibility for the paper at an important time in the company's life. The paper had grown in overall size, but the organizational structure had not kept pace and was antiquated. Robert arrived at a time when decisions had to be made that would either allow the business to continue moving forward or cause it to regress. He set out to reorganize the company, drawing on his experience and expertise in management and organization. Some jealousies and resistance to change occurred, but these eventually worked themselves out, with people either leaving on their own volition or staying to become loyal employees.

One of the first modifications made by Robert was to segment the work into departments and assign a supervisor to handle the people in each department. The supervisors would then report directly to the president. Job descriptions and procedures were written up to make the responsibilities of each employee more specific. Other minor changes were also made to permit a smoother and more efficient workflow between departments. Resistance to these changes occurred, but gradually died as employees became accustomed to them and trust developd between the employees and the president.

Display Sales: Background

As a part of the reorganization, ad sales were divided into two departments: (1) classified sales and (2) display sales. Classified sales consist mostly of ads placed by individuals over the telephone and accounts for about 25 per cent of the company's revenues. Display sales is where the money is, accounting for about 75 per cent of revenues on the average. The display sales are the larger advertisements run by businesses, or by advertising agencies for businesses.

In the eight years after the present sales organization was instituted, the display sales department had three different sales managers. The first was an excellent salesperson but did not turn out to be a good manager. He left the *Shopping News* and went into sales for another newspaper. The second sales manager had advertising experience with other newspapers as well as with the *Shopping News*. He remained as sales manager for a while but his abilities and skills made him more valuable in another area of the company. Hence, he was transferred and relieved of his sales management duties. The last sales manager proved to be more concerned about himself than about the company when conducting business, and was eventually persuaded to leave. At this juncture, Robert decided against hiring another sales manager and instead assumed the responsibilities himself for supervising the sales force. As a result, sales increased and a mutual understanding was developed between Robert and the sales personnel.

Display Sales: Present

Presently, the display sales force is composed of six salespeople. Their primary responsibility is to telephone and visit clients in order to sell ads and to advise them on what should be placed in the ads. Each salesperson is assigned a territory and is expected to work the accounts within that territory. For a time, sales personnel were spending very little time selling. Robert then instituted a daily report system in which each salesperson reported the number of calls and visits made, as well as on any remarks made by the clients. This improved sales activity while at the same time affording Robert a better view of the accounts.

Compensation is based totally on commissions. Each salesperson receives 15 per cent of everything he or she sells in addition to a weekly salary. Yearly salaries can range anywhere from $13,000 to $40,000, depending on how much effort a salesperson is willing to put forth. In addition, bonus incentives are offered for such things as each new account brought in and for achieving total sales goals which have been set based on previous year's performance. Robert takes a very active role in helping salespeople develop goals for performance. Another motivational tool has been the use of outside speakers, but in most cases the salespeople have not needed that kind of motivation, with the exception of Ned Saunders. As Robert put it, "Ned can come up with a thousand and one ways to spend the company's money. He seems more interested in spending company money than in making money."

Ned Saunders Harty continued his discussion of Ned Saunders: "When he came to the company, he was given the best sales territory. It was the affluent White Rock-Lake Highlands area and sales ranged from $3,500 to $4,500 per week. I did this because he had more experience in sales than any other person we had had. He did well for nine to twelve months, but then sales started dropping. He has been with us for three years and each year sales have been dropping in his territory."

"He is a friend but I am still his boss. Yet, he resents anything that helps me to know what he is doing with his sales, such as filling out reports. He even resents filling out the slips that must be turned in for payroll each week. Almost every three months or even more frequently, I have had to sit down with him for an evaluation, and to switch his accounts because he has not been keeping them up. The problem is he resents supervision and my trying to help him discover what is wrong with his sales because they have dropped by $3,000 in a three-year period."

"I have tried to discuss what is wrong, whether it has been a supervisional problem or a problem he is having with his accounts. In most cases it has come down to the fact that I have talked with the individuals he has been calling on and have found out that he is bothersome. I have discovered this, too, because I cannot carry on a conversation with him. He continues to remain after we talk, wanting to sit around and shoot the breeze. I feel that this is the way he is behaving with his customers and most of these people are business people. They only have time to tell it like it is, and then go on and do something else. They can not stand around chatting. Ned also stands around and talks to the other salespeople, taking up their time because they do not want to be rude. As a principle, I have discussed these problems with him personally. They have been written up, with one copy going to him and another copy to his personnel file. Usually within two weeks of these meetings, his sales have gone up, but I have had to police the situation and keep tabs on him."

Robert continued, "I have discovered that he is spending time in other types of businesses. He is selling insurance, vitamins and food supplements, and some other type of product. Ned has always been an idea person; always going to hit the jackpot just around the corner. He is in his fifties, but he has not hit it yet. He is not realistic. His problems are not so much with me and the company, but that he is not giving the job 100 per cent. He likes to let people know that he is a "professional" salesperson, and yet people who do not have the training or background he has have been able to outsell him in the last few years."

"He must be supervised very closely, yet he rebels under close supervision. I have really spent more time in the last three years with him than with any other person I have supervised before. I am really not sure where I can go from here with him."

Questions

1. How would you describe the management and leadership style of Robert Harty? Could it be improved? How?
2. If you were Robert, what actions would you take concerning Ned's performance? Why?

Case 23

Teletronic Electronics

Chris White was New Orleans' district sales manager. He was fifty-one years old and had been with Teletronic Electronics (TE) for twenty-two years. TE was a distributor of several thousand different types of small electrical parts, such as fuses, batteries, and wiring. In 1977 a company recruiter hired Judy Luby as a salesperson and assigned her to White. This made a total of nine salespeople White was responsible for, with accounts in Louisiana, Arkansas, and Mississippi.

The First Female Salesperson Luby graduated from Texas A&M University, majoring in industrial distribution. She was active in campus organizations, while maintaining her 3.86 grade point average. Luby had worked in her father's business an electronic distributorship like TE, located in Dallas, the last three summers. Luby wanted to be on her own, so she turned down her father's offer of a job after graduation. She was excited about her job and felt that she had a lot to offer. Even though she was the first woman to work for White, and one of only six women employed by TE, Luby felt that she could do the job as well as any man.

Sales Training Luby attended a three-week training program, learning about products, policies, competition, and selling. Each week

This case was developed by Professor Charles M. Futrell and is based on several conversations with the person called Judy Luby. The name of the firm has been changed.

trainees were tested. Luby scored top in her class with a 97 per cent average. Trainers rated her exceptionally high on her personality, motivation, ability to get along with others, self-discipline, and selling ability. She made several suggestions on sales techniques based on what she had learned while working at her father's business that were eventually used throughout the company.

When White received a summary of Luby's excellent training scores and comments from the trainers, he remembered a young man several years ago who wanted to tell him how to run his sales job. He thought "Why me? Why do I get stuck with these generous ones who know it all? And a female! Why, I'm old enough to be her father!"

White Drops by   Luby was assigned the New Orleans sales territory and rented a very nice apartment. About three months after she began work, White dropped by Luby's apartment to drop off some business forms she had requested. She was going out of town Monday and would not receive them by mail in time. White saw Luby talking to several people by the swimming pool in her building. She seemed very glad to see him. Luby was in her bathing suit, as were two of the four people, two male and two female, she was with, and whom she introduced to White. White discovered they worked for two of their largest customers. Luby asked White whether he would like to go for a swim, but he said "No," left the forms, and went back to his office steaming. The next week a letter went out to all salespeople reminding them to work a full day. That Friday Luby stopped by the office and said she had sold them both a large order. White said it was not professional for a young woman to conduct business in that manner. Luby became so mad she began to cry.

White Won't Pay   Expense vouchers are sent to White for approval. Several small items, not normally approved, had been paid for by Luby herself. For example, she had sent flowers to several buyers who had been in the hospital, and had sent expensive birthday cards to several of her customers. Recently, however, she submitted vouchers for several dinner and entertainment expenses that were not approved. When Luby asked White to pay for two season tickets to the New Orleans Saints home games, he blew up. Luby explained that she had taken several customers to the games, and felt that it had turned into business entertainment. White said "No" and told her he would pay for standard expenses in the future.

It was not a week later when the wife of a buyer for one of their largest customers called the office requesting Luby's address. White took the call and was glad he did. The woman was upset because Luby had taken her husband to a football game and he had come home late that night quite intoxicated. The buyer told his wife he had been out with a salesman from TE. His wife found out it was a saleswoman and she was furious. White called Luby that night and explained the situation. She apologized and said it would not happen again.

At that time Luby asked White whether the company would pay for her to take courses at a local university. White said "No" and told her he was not in favor of that because it would take away from her job. After all, he didn't even have a college degree and has been successful. Luby said she had already enrolled in an evening graduate level sales management course that would count toward a MBA. For her class project she had collected sales data from the other salespeople in the district and developed a plan to geographically restructure sales territories and their accounts. Luby said the professor would have it graded in three weeks, and she would like to take his comments and present the final plan to White. "However," Luby said, "we'll have to meet at the university one morning because I have the data on their computer. There are some things I'd like to show you." White said he was not interested, and told her she needed his approval to collect such information. He suggested she reconsider taking evening courses.

Job Performance   At the end of her first year on the job, Luby was number 4 out of 295 salespeople in terms of percentage of sales increase. Corporate management wanted to move women into management, and asked White whether Luby would be a good candidate. He said it was too soon to know, and also commented that he personally had doubts that she could fit in and work as part of a team. White said that she likes to do things on her own and that he didn't think she could hold up under pressure.

Luby's Suggestion Goes to the Home Office   Two weeks later White received a telephone call from the national sales manager, Sam Moore. Moore said he had received Luby's report on realigning sales territories and felt it was excellent. In fact, he wanted to fly down next month and talk with White and Luby about realigning sales territories for the entire sales force using Luby's suggestions. Moore asked White whether he had read the report. White said "No, because Luby has only been with us one year and I don't feel she has the background to make such a suggestion."

After White hung up the telephone he went into a rage. "That, that know it all has gone too far. She has by-passed me and made me look bad. I have put up with all of this I can stand. I am the boss and I don't care what Moore says, she and I are going to have it out." White told his secretary to call Luby and have her at the office at 9:00 the next morning.

Questions

1. Why is White behaving this way?
2. Why is Luby behaving this way?
3. What will White do at the meeting? Is it the right thing to do?
4. Ideally, what should White do?

Case 24

The Peet Corporation

The Peet Corporation is a $3 billion firm selling various products found in retail grocery stores. Its health and beauty division employs 325 salespeople nation-wide. The sales force has eleven regional sales managers reporting to the national sales manager. Each regional manager has an assistant regional manager. Reporting to him are four to six district sales managers.

The Industry The firm is in a highly competitive industry. The industry leader is Procter & Gamble selling such products as Crest, Gleem, Head and Shoulders, and Prell. Other competing companies include Lever Brothers, Bristol-Myers, Warner-Lambert, and Johnson and Johnson.

In 1977 the industry experienced 6 per cent growth and, in 1978, 8 per cent growth. The industry is relatively resistant to downward movement in the economy, and so is expected to continue to grow. Firms in the industry realize this and spend millions of dollars on marketing their products.

John Adams—His Career Path John Adams had been hired after completing his MBA at Dartmouth, as an assistant product manager

This case was developed by Professor Charles M. Futrell. The names of the company and the names of the people involved have been changed.

in the toiletries division. After two years he was promoted to product manager, where for five years he was extremely successful managing several of the firm's important product lines. Abe Coleman, the national sales manager, was impressed with Adams' performance. He persuaded Adams to become his administrative assistant with the promise that Adams would move into sales management. With several years of experience, Coleman felt Adams could replace him when he retired in eight years. With Adams' ability, he could progress quickly into top corporate management, and it was Coleman's plan to groom Adams for upper management.

Adams was Coleman's assistant for three years. In this job he helped formulate objectives and strategies for the entire sales force. He analyzed the performance of the sales regions and suggested ways to improve it while reducing costs. It was an important job, especially because Coleman had been under intense pressure to increase sales. The corporation's goal was to reach $4 billion in sales as quickly as possible. Coleman felt that Adams was of great help in suggesting ways to improve sales force performance.

The Midwest Sales Region   To Coleman, the Midwest sales region appeared to be an ideal region for Adams to take over, and Adams agreed. After several visits, Adams concluded that the senior office secretary and the four district managers ran the operations of the region. It had a country club atmosphere, with no pressure on people to increase sales. Sales for this region had been the lowest in the company for six out of the last seven years. Sales had increased 3 per cent each year, but this was far under the company's overall 9 per cent increase and the industry's 8 per cent increase in sales.

Once when Adams and Jim Barrows, the Midwest regional sales manager, were talking, Barrows commented that the company was spending millions on promotion, which was an excellent way of selling company products. "All my men do is take orders. The products sell themselves, so why should we get our blood pressure up trying to sell large promotional quantities to our accounts? People are going to buy our products because of our advertising, heavy sampling, and all of those cents-off coupons sent out by our product managers."

John Adams—Regional Sales Manager   When Adams took over as regional sales manager, he was given full support by Abe Coleman. Coleman made it very clear to everyone that Adams had his full backing in all operational matters.

The Midwest region is responsible for approximately $300 million in sales and has a $2.09 million operating budget. Adam's responsibilities also include developing regional and district sales objectives and strategies, including the leadership and motivation of four district managers and thirty salespeople.

Adams did not waste any time. He had been used to making recommendations to Coleman on regional sales operations. Now he could implement his ideas. He began by reorganizing all office procedures. He added two secretaries and an office assistant. These three people received and analyzed all data from field sales personnel. Previously the district managers had this responsibility. A mini-computer was installed to help in analyzing the data. When a big sale was made, or a salesperson went over his or her monthly sales quota, Adams would personally call and congratulate the person involved. He began to publish a monthly bulletin and mail reports on all salespeople's progress in meeting their quotas. He increased his budget for sales meetings to include such things as live entertainment, excellent food and drink, and resort locations. Twice a year he tried to work with each salesperson. Once a district manager found someone to hire, Adams flew them to his office for an interview. He gave the final approval because he felt that recruiting and hiring was one of the most important parts of his job. Six months after they started the job, he visited with the new salespeople in their territories for four days and trained them "the right way."

Adams Gets Results By the end of Adams' first year on the job, operations and sales were improving. By the end of his second year, his region won second place in the regional awards at the national sales meeting. This meant larger bonuses for all sales personnel. (Salespeople were paid a straight salary, and they had opportunities to win various sales contests throughout the year.) They received a quarterly cash bonus based on the sales region's performance. All salespeople received the same amount. Adams and the district managers also received a cash bonus which was usually 20 per cent larger than that received by the salespeople.

In January of Adam's third year he underwent a series of tests to determine the cause of a recurring health problem. When all of the results were compiled, his doctor discovered that he was suffering from a terminal illness. There was no precise estimate of his life expectancy, but he was given a few years at best.

Problems Begin Since Adams had become regional manager, turnover had gone from 3 per cent to an average of 20 per cent a year. Two district managers had resigned. One of them left the company and the other took over a sales territory. Another district manager had been terminated. After learning of his illness, Adam's dominant personality became domineering. His attitude of "do it my way or else" was intensified. In September the national sales manager began getting letters and telephone calls from district managers expressing dissatisfaction with Adams. One manager cited the fact that in April Adams showed up at the district sales meeting unannounced and completely took it over. The meeting was a disaster because Adams had done little planning. Adams treated the manager as if he were his butler, not a sales manager. The other district managers heard about it and became furious. A few of the salespeople hated Adams because of the pressure he put on them when he worked with them. However, most of the salespeople appeared to like him. They were in favor of being sales leaders in the company and wanted to be the number one sales region.

However, the district managers were ready to quit. They feel they are supervisors not managers. One manager said, "He takes over my responsibilities. I really have very little to do. My salespeople look to Adams for direction, not to me." One manager said Adams became so upset at him because a routine report was late that he thought Adams was going to hit him. "Adams flew sixty miles to my house to pick it up and when he arrived he exploded."

Coleman's Comments "I am aware of the fact that the district managers feel Adams' personality is becoming unbearable. We have become alarmed at the high turnover rate. However, he had a lot of 'dead wood' that had to be eliminated. Adams felt he needed to take complete charge to shape up the region. As far as I know, there were only two or three very minor complaints about Adams during his first two years. I gave him complete authority over the region. He has done a very good job of improving sales and decreasing costs. We are well aware of his health problems. He is assuming more authority than we intended. However, there has been no clear decision on how to approach him. I'm not sure he is at fault. He is excited about the prospect of being the manager of the top sales region this year, and he may make it. He has also been developing a plan to restructure the region, eliminating one or two of the district manager's positions and up to ten salespeople. He wants to stop calling on small accounts and says he does not need four district managers. He says this will help him better service customers. For Adams, customers come before anything else."

Eddie Hall's Comments Eddie Hall has been with the company for four years and was promoted by Adams to district manager nine months ago. Hall described Adams in the following manner:

"He has a good performance record, and is extremely demanding of himself as well as of others. He has difficulty delegating. He spends thousands of dollars sending us motivational literature, and is always reading material with titles like "How to Discover the Real You" or "Look Out for Number One." At any time he may go into a long oral report on something he just finished reading. Why we see Vince Lombardi's motivational film 'The Second Effort' at the beginning and end of all of our sales meetings. In back of his desk on a four by four foot sign he has written:

The Second Effort

1. Mental Toughness Is Essential to Success
2. Control the Ball
3. Fatigue Makes Cowards of Us All
4. Operate on Lombardi Time
5. Make the Second Effort.

On another wall is a sign that says:

Three Levels of Effort

1. I'll Try
2. I'll Do My Best
3. I'll Do Whatever It Takes.

He often combines psychoanalytic theory and information from some sales motivation material he has just read into his own theory of sales management. I still do not know what Freud, Jung, or Horney have to do with motivating salespeople.

"Adams is a handsome guy who can control any business or social conversation. When recruiting, he can be charming. He can discuss in great depth current events, politics, art, music, and can really impress you with his knowledge of wine, how it is grown, made, etc. Sports, why he can tell you about history, averages, and his future predictions for football, basketball, baseball, you name it, college or professional, and especially the Ivy League universities.

"Few people live up to his expectations as high achievers. Adams' own name is really the only one on the list. He determines the rules of the game, and they have to be followed. He loves his job, and he gets results. His illness is the only thing holding him back from a promotion into the home office now. He said last week that his doctors did not know what they were talking about. He could overcome his sickness with the right diet, exercise, and a positive mental attitude.

"I wish Coleman and the other regional managers could hear how Adams runs them down and how he could do it better. He probably could, too. He can tell you in a minute who is selling what, in what quantities, to what customers, in almost all sales territories. If you need an answer to a question, he can give you one instantly. His time is so well organized and planned that you would not believe it. I guess I'm as close to him as anyone. I'm glad I had this experience working for Adams; however, I couldn't stand it much longer."

Questions

1. Using Exhibit 1, what would Adams' profile as a manager be?
2. What leadership style did Adams assume? Was it justified?
3. Would you fire a man who has done what he was hired to do?
4. Should consideration be given to Adams' health problems?
5. How do you take back authority from Adams?
6. Can you make any suggestions that might ease the tensions that exist between Adams and his district managers?
7. If Adams is replaced, what problems will the new regional manager face?

Exhibit 1
John Adams' Profile

Factor		Rating		Your Score
1. The situation Adams faced when becoming manager was:				
	Favorable 3	Average 2	Unfavorable 1	
2. Adams could be rated as follows:				
a. Concern for people and their problems	High 3	Average 2	Low 1	
b. Concern for getting things done	High 3	Average 2	Low 1	
c. Knowledge of human relations	High 3	Average 2	Low 1	
d. Knowledge of motivational skills	High 3	Average 2	Low 1	
e. Concern for company interests	High 3	Average 2	Low 1	
f. Concern for customer interests	High 3	Average 2	Low 1	
g. People are self-motivated	High 3	Average 2	Low 1	
h. People must be motivated	High 3	Average 2	Low 1	
i. People are self-motivated but at times must also be motivated	High 3	Average 2	Low 1	
3. Adams' relationship with others can be rated as:				
a. With superiors	Good 3	Average 2	Poor 1	
b. With his managers	Good 3	Average 2	Poor 1	

Exhibit 1—*continued*

Factor	Rating			Your Score
c. With region's salespeople	Good 3	Average 2	Poor 1	
4. How much power does Adams have?	High 3	Average 2	Low 1	
5. Adams' personal needs are: a. Physiological	High 3	Average 2	Low 1	
b. Safety	High 3	Average 2	Low 1	
c. Social	High 3	Average 2	Low 1	
d. Ego	High 3	Average 2	Low 1	
e. Self-actualization	High 3	Average 2	Low 1	
f. Affiliation with others	High 3	Average 2	Low 1	
g. Personal achievement	High 3	Average 2	Low 1	
h. Personal power	High 3	Average 2	Low 1	

Part 6
General Cases in Sales Management

Case 25

Home Tractor, Inc.

Home Tractor, Inc. manufactures six major product lines: push lawn mowers, power lawn mowers, riding mowers, garden tillers, lawn tractors, and garden tractors. The company is divided into five geographical regions. As shown in Exhibit 1, annual sales have steadily increased to $362.6 million as of 1980. In fact, sales have increased at a more rapid rate than industry demand, and the company's market share has been increasing.

Jim Tanner, national sales manager, takes great pride in these figures and has always felt his group was working at their maximum potential.

Market Information System At the beginning of 1980 a market information system (MIS) was installed to provide a continuous audit of the firm's marketing operation. It was hoped that the MIS would aid in the allocation of time and dollars in such a way as to generate higher sales volume and net profits by concentrating market effort in the most profitable areas. The company wanted to examine market segments and determine which were producing the majority of sales and profits so management could divide the total marketing resources in the most efficient manner. Because different net profits and sales are often contributed by different product lines, price lines, and geographical areas, management wanted to direct the majority of marketing expenditures at those areas in which the profit, sales, or a profit-sales ratio's return per marketing dollar spent was the highest. As one

Exhibit 1
Home Tractor, Inc. Sales

Year	Company Sales Volume (Millions)	Industry Demand (Millions)	Share of Market (%)
1972	265.1	16,150.1	1.64
1973	280.0	17,200.0	1.63
1974	287.0	17,289.2	1.66
1975	294.4	17,420.2	1.69
1976	303.4	18,059.6	1.68
1977	315.2	18,541.2	1.70
1978	337.4	19,736.2	1.71
1979	340.8	19,929.8	1.71
1980	362.6	20,839.0	1.74

manager said, "We must allocate our funds where we get the most bang for the buck." It was felt that MIS could aid in such things as sales forecasting, evaluating market position, production planning, inventory control, sales force planning, and appraising pricing, advertising, sales promotion, and distribution strategies.

An important part of MIS is the computer-generated data used to assist the sales analyst. Corporate management wanted to examine the extent to which the so-called "80-20 principle" was operating. They realized that a major part of the company's sales and profits may directly result from a small number of customers, products, or geographical areas. It was felt that some marginal or unprofitable products, geographical areas, or customers should be carried in order to complement the existing product line and encourage sales volume in the more profitable areas. Furthermore, MIS could be used to examine the effect that averaging, summarizing, and aggregating data has on the true sales or profit picture. Management did not want to assume that, just because sales were increasing, this meant that the company's operations could not be improved.

Financial Analyses   One of the first reports generated by MIS was the income statement shown in Exhibit 2. The contribution margin approach, rather than the full cost approach, was used to prepare the income statement. As shown, variables costs (those that fluctuate with net sales volume), including marketing and manufacturing costs, are first subtracted from net sales for each segment. This contribution margin is the amount that each respective segment contributes to company overhead and to net profits. Nonassignable costs and fixed costs are not allocated to the segments. The contribution margins serve as measures of relative profitability. Tanner noted that the Western

Exhibit 2
Home Tractor, Inc.
Income Statement,
Contribution Margin Approach

	Entire Company (000)	Southwest (000)	Southern (000)	Eastern (000)	Western (000)	Midwest (000)
Net Sales	$362,600	$68,898	$68,756	$78,522	$74,274	$72,150
Less Variable Costs:						
Manufacturing Costs	238,606	44,094	45,244	52,610	50,506	46,152
Marketing Costs:						
Sales Commissions	11,536	2,342	2,062	2,506	2,674	1,952
Transportation & Shipping	2,418	602	472	334	426	584
Warehousing	806	152	148	172	134	200
Credit & Collection	1,814	374	352	386	280	422
Assignable Costs:						
Salaries: Salespeople	36,920	7,398	6,608	7,272	7,446	8,196
Salaries: Marketing Manager	2,308	400	446	474	462	526
Advertising	6,804	1,396	1,362	1,486	1,272	1,288
Sales Promotion	2,872	576	560	636	554	546
Total Variable and Assignable Costs:	304,084	57,334	57,254	65,876	63,754	59,866
Contribution Margin	58,516	11,564	11,502	12,646	10,520	12,284
Nonassignable Costs:						
Institutional advertising	810					
Fixed Costs:						
General Administration	4,054					
Manufacturing	46,092					
Net Income (before taxes)	7,560					

region was the lowest in terms of profitability. He also observed that, if regions were ranked in terms of profitability, the Eastern region would be the most profitable.

Management was pleased to see that every region was making a positive contribution to net profits and overhead. Several managers suggested that there was no need to continue the analysis. However, Tanner asked that this contribution margin approach be extended to product line (see Exhibit 3). He was somewhat surprised to see that the lawn tractor line was unprofitable. It appears from certain territorial analyses that the very profitable garden tractor line may be compensating for the lawn tractor line's losses. He could not tell from this analysis alone the reason for the poor performance of the lawn tractor line. Industry demand for lawn tractors may have declined and the firm may not have anticipated this economic fact; or the new model of lawn tractor may have mechanical defects or poor aesthetic features. "We don't know, but what I am sure of is that management should take appropriate measures to find out what the problem may be. Maybe MIS is better than I first felt it was because, without this analysis, the success of our other product lines may have hidden this from us," stated Tanner.

Regional Sales Analysis   Tanner requested a regional breakdown of company sales volume. Last year he had developed a retail sales index to serve as a relative measure of the dollar volume of retail sales that normally occur in each region. Based on that index he had established quotas for the sales regions, districts, and individual territories. As shown in Exhibit 4 all except the Western region were meeting quotas. Tanner did not know why sales were down. He called John Anderson, the Western regional sales manager, and asked him to look into the matter and report back to him in two weeks. Anderson knew sales were slow; however, he had not been that concerned until now.

Western Sales Region   To examine the $478,000 loss Tanner used the district sales breakdown shown in Exhibit 5. It was very apparent that the Northern California sales district was experiencing problems. He called Kurt McNeal, the district manager, and asked him why sales were down. Kurt said "John, I was just about to call you. I'm getting ready to fire Leslie Stark. His sales are down. You know he is in the process of getting a divorce and his personal life must be getting in the way of business." "Have you talked to him?" asked Tanner. "Yes, he claims competition is using that area as a test market for a new line of garden tractors. However, I suspect he is not working very hard and the competition is stealing our business. You know we have some large retail chain accounts there and we can not afford to lose that

Exhibit 3
Home Tractor, Inc. Income Statement,
Contribution Margin Approach
(by product line)

	Company (000)	Push Mowers (000)	Power Mowers (000)	Riding Mowers (000)	Garden Tillers (000)	Lawn Tractors (000)	Garden Tractors (000)
Net Sales	$362,620	$66,900	$44,734	$70,342	$17,352	$44,114	$119,168
Less Variable Costs:							
Manufacturing	238,606	47,662	29,792	45,454	11,260	39,668	64,770
Marketing	16,564	2,916	2,652	3,162	532	2,848	4,464
Assignable Costs	48,904	8,150	7,654	8,776	2,000	6,446	15,860
Total Variable and Assignable Costs:	304,084	58,728	40,098	57,932	13,792	48,980	85,094
Contribution Margin	58,516	8,172	4,636	12,960	3,560	(4,886)	34,074
Nonassignable Costs	810						
Fixed Costs	50,146						
Net Income (before taxes)	7,560						

Exhibit 4
Home Tractor, Inc.
Regional Breakdown of Sales

Region	Retail Sales Index	Expected Sales (000)	Actual Sales (000)	Dollar Deviation
Midwest	99	$71,848	$72,100	+ 252
Southwest	95	68,946	68,948	+ 2
Southern	9	64,592	68,756	+ 4,164
Eastern	105	76,204	78,522	+ 2,318
Western	103	74,752	74,274	− 478

Exhibit 5
Home Tractor, Inc.
Western Region Sales

District	Expected Sales (000)	Actual Sales (000)	Dollar Deviation
Washington	$ 8,970	$ 8,994	+ 24
Idaho-Oregon	7,850	7,842	− 8
Northern California	21,602	21,014	− 588
Southern California	36,330	36,424	+ 94

business. So let's replace him." "Before you do, Kurt, look over some of the data I'm mailing you, then talk to Leslie. After this, if you still feel you should let him go, you have my permission. I'm not sure he's doing so badly compared to the rest of you."

Up until this time McNeal had been working with total sales figures and figures that salespeople developed on their own so it was difficult for him to break out sales data. In fact, he really did not want to do it. He felt it was the company's job, and not his responsibility. If sales were down they would let him know. Up until recently he had always meet his overall sales quota. Several days after the conversation with Tanner, McNeal received the data shown in Exhibits 6, 7, and 8. It was amazing to him to see this much detail in the data. When he saw that Stark was the only person selling below quota and in fact making the district's performance look bad, he made up his mind to fire Stark.

Questions

1. What do you feel is the main purpose of a firm's marketing information system? Do you feel Home Tractor has an adequate MIS?
2. Do you agree with McNeal's decision to fire Stark? Why?
3. What action, if any, should John Anderson take? For example, should he let McNeal handle the problem of low sales in the district?

Exhibit 6
Home Tractor, Inc.
Western Region,
N. California District Sales

Sales-person	Expected Sales (000)	Actual Sales (000)	Differ-ence	Perfor-mance Index[a]
J. Boles	$5,696	$5,792	+ 96	101
L. Stark	5,584	4,842	− 742	86
J. Dozzier	6,012	6,046	+ 34	100
A. Penny	4,310	4,334	+ 24	100

[a](Actual Sales/Quota) × 100.

Exhibit 7
Salespeople's Dollar Gain or
Loss Over Expected Sales

	Salesperson							
	J. Boles		L. Stark		J. Dozzier		A. Penny	
Products	Expected Sales (000)	Actual Sales (000)	Expected Sales (000)	Actual Sales (000)	Expected Sales (000)	Actual Sales (000)	Expected Sales (000)	Actual Sales (000)
Push Mowers	$ 939	$1,009	$1,032	$1,044	$ 999	$1,008	$ 588	$ 605
Power Mowers	630	609	544	540	971	980	686	702
Riding Mowers	207	160	208	234	896	900	848	851
Garden Tillers	1,072	1,112	1,098	1,096	1,291	1,295	873	858
Lawn Tractors	1,670	1,702	1,526	1,616	733	735	635	652
Garden Tractors	1,178	1,200	1,176	312	1,122	1,128	680	666
TOTALS	5,696	5,792	5,584	4,842	6,012	6,046	4,310	4,334

Exhibit 8
Salespeople's Percentage Gain or Loss

	Percentage Gain or Loss Over Last Year		
	Territory	District	Region
J. Boles			
Push Mowers	7.0	8.9	7.6
Power Mowers	− 3.4	− 1.5	3.7
Riding Mowers	− 1.7	41.4	3.8
Garden Tillers	3.6	−14.8	− 4.2
Lawn Tractors	1.9	8.2	11.5
Garden Tractors	10.1	−18.6	− 9.1
L. Stark			
Push Mowers	11.0	8.9	7.6
Power Mowers	− 2.2	− 1.5	3.7
Riding Mowers	.4	41.4	3.8
Garden Tillers	− 8.2	−14.8	− 4.2
Lawn Tractors	15.2	8.2	11.5
Garden Tractors	−46.3	−18.6	− 9.1
J. Dozzier			
Push Mowers	9.0	8.9	7.6
Power Mowers	1.0	− 1.5	3.7
Riding Mowers	1.7	−41.4	3.8
Garden Tillers	5.2	−14.8	− 4.2
Lawn Tractors	1.6	8.2	11.5
Garden Tractors	21.6	−18.6	− 9.1
A. Penny			
Push Mowers	8.6	8.9	7.6
Power Mowers	3.1	− 1.5	3.7
Riding Mowers	.8	41.4	3.8
Garden Tillers	−15.4	−14.8	− 4.2
Lawn Tractors	−10.5	8.2	11.5
Garden Tractors	− 4.0	−18.6	− 9.1

Case 26

Davis Furniture Company

John Ryan, the sales manager for the Davis Furniture Company, was contemplating his sales force on a cold day in December of 1979. It was at this time each year that he evaluated the performance of each salesperson, determined quotas, reduced or established new sales territories, and determined the need for more or fewer salespeople.

Ryan knew that his ability to manage his sales force would have a great impact on the actual sales of the firm. In the past, he had had numerous other responsibilities which had restricted the amount of time he had to devote to the sales force. Now, due to the creation of a new management post, he had been relieved of these extra duties and was able to spend adequate time on the sales force.

The Company

The Davis Furniture Company was a manufacturer of contemporary household furniture, covering the complete range of products from main pieces to accessories. The company, which had been started in the 1940s by two brothers, had grown from a relatively small operation to one of the largest in the furniture field. The firm maintained five production plants that were spread geographically across the country.

This case was developed by Mr. George Stevens for his MBA under the supervision of Professor Charles M. Futrell. Copyright © 1980.

The furniture industry, which was highly competitive, recognized Davis furniture as a moderately priced, quality product. Because of the size of the firm, Davis was considered to be a trend setter in new designs and furniture ideas.

The firm was always highly visible at the nine semi-annual furniture shows held across the country. Through effective advertising and promotion, Davis Furniture Company had been able to establish itself as the manufacturer of a quality product that the average family could afford and enjoy.

Sales Force Issues   Davis Furniture Company was one of the few furniture companies that was able to maintain its own sales force. Currently, the company had ten sales territories that were serviced by one salesperson and an assistant each. The salesperson was the one who actually went to furniture retailers and attempted either to make an initial sale, or make additional sales if Davis was already covered. Currently, there were over 29,000 furniture retailers in the country. The assistant was responsible for processing any orders the salesperson made. The assistant was also responsible for maintaining the company furniture showroom for the sales territory. The showroom was open on a daily basis and was available to retailers and decorators who wished to review the Davis line. If a retailer wished to place an order, the assistant would have the salesperson, who would make the sale, call the retailer.

The present compensation for a salesperson includes a $15,000 base salary, a 5 per cent commission on sales over 80 per cent of quota, and a 10 per cent commission on sales over 100 per cent of the quota. Assistants were given a straight salary of $12,000. Ryan estimated quotas by taking into account: 1. historical trends, 2. sales force composite, and 3. executive opinion. Most salespeople agreed that the established quotas were fair. However, some problems existed. The primary problem was that, because Davis Furniture sales were growing so rapidly, sales potential in a territory outgrew the sales capabilities. For example, a territory might be projected at having a sales potential of $5,000,000, but a salesperson working ten or twelve hours a day could only make $3 million in sales. If the quota was set at $5 million for the territory, it would appear that the salesperson was not working as hard as he or she actually was. Consequently, a new salesperson would be hired for the territory or a new territory established. Secondly, Ryan was not able to ascertain the amount of time salespeople were spending servicing existing accounts versus establishing new accounts. He felt this was necessary in order to ascertain the sales potential of a particular area.

Previously, Ryan had had a problem replacing a salesperson who had quit unexpectedly. After a frantic search, he fortunately found a furniture sales representative who was willing to come over to Davis. This man had a good deal of experience and was able to perform adequately in a short period of time.

The position of salesperson required a great deal of knowledge about the items in the Davis line, as well as knowledge of the area.

Ryan realized that if by some chance he was forced to fire or replace an established salesperson in one of the territories, he would be faced with a difficult situation. He knew that it would be necessary to establish some sort of recruitment and training program that could be implemented in the event of a sales position opening.

Davis Furniture Company had reached its present place of prominence in the furniture industry in a number of ways:

1. The company had been one of the first to affiliate its product with several chain department stores.
2. The quality had not diminished as sales had increased.
3. Advertising and promotion techniques had been extremely effective in making the Davis Furniture well known.

In order to retain this prominence, Ryan was endeavoring to maintain the sales force at a high level. Some of the data that Ryan had compiled on some of his sales territories is included below. Before calculating the quotas for each sales territory, he decided to analyze the data he had available. As an additional aid, he had contacted each of his salespeople and asked them to estimate the amount of time they spent on servicing their old, established accounts.

Davis Furniture Company Sales

1960	3,000,000
1970	10,000,000
1976	25,000,000
1977	27,000,000
1978	28,000,000
1979	30,000,000
1980	32,000,000 (Estimate)

Sales Territory #1: includes Maine, New Hampshire, Vermont, Massachusetts, Connecticut, Rhode Island. Showroom located in Boston. Salesperson: Jim Green.

	Quota	Sales
1977	$2,000,000	$2,050,000
1978	2,200,000	2,200,000
1979	2,300,000	2,400,000
1980	2,400,000	2,550,000 (Est.)

Time spent on servicing old accounts—80 per cent.

Sales Territory #2: includes New York, Pennsylvania, New Jersey. Showroom located in New York City. Salesperson: Lou Black.

	Quota	Sales
1977	$3,000,000	$3,100,000
1978	3,500,000	3,300,000
1979	3,800,000	3,350,000
1980	4,000,000	3,350,000 (Est.)

Time spent servicing old accounts—70 per cent.

Sales Territory #3: includes North Carolina, South Carolina, Georgia, Florida, Alabama, Mississippi. Showroom located in Highpoint, North Carolina. Salesperson: George Stevens.

	Quota	Sales
1977	$1,500,000	$1,700,000
1978	2,000,000	2,100,000
1979	2,200,000	2,300,000
1980	2,400,000	2,600,000 (Est.)

Time spent servicing old accounts—70 per cent.

Sales Territory #4: includes Texas, Oklahoma, and New Mexico. Showroom located in Dallas. Salesperson: Joe Sherman.

	Quota	Sales
1977	$2,000,000	$1,800,000
1978	2,100,000	1,850,000
1979	2,300,000	1,800,000
1980	2,300,000	1,800,000 (Est.)

Time spent servicing old accounts—60 per cent.

Sales Territory #5: includes California. Showroom located in Los Angeles. Salesperson: Scott Abbott.

	Quota	Sales
1977	$2,500,000	$2,800,000
1978	3,000,000	3,300,000
1979	3,500,000	3,800,000
1980	4,000,000	4,200,000 (Est.)

Time spent servicing old accounts—75 per cent.

Questions

1. What is the main problem in this case?
2. What is your evaluation of each salesperson?
3. What suggestions do you have for John Ryan to improve the total management procedures of his sales force?

Case 27

Amos-Owens Corporation

The Amos-Owens company was incorporated under Delaware law in 1914, as a successor to a New Jersey chemical corporation established in 1898. Through the years it has acquired companies manufacturing such diverse products as ethical pharmaceuticals, medical and surgical supplies, biologicals and diagnostic products, and consumer goods such as candy, chewing gum, mouthwashes, and vitamins. Amos-Owens is a research-oriented scientific corporation with products that are developed, manufactured, and marketed around the world by approximately 40,000 people in more than 120 countries. Corporate sales in 1980 reached $3.4 billion, which reflects a five-year compounded annual growth rate of 12 per cent. The five-year compounded net income growth rate was slightly less at 9 per cent; however, net income of $267,000,000 was considered quite healthy. Per share earnings were 16 per cent higher in 1980 than in 1979.

Corporate management's goal was to continue, and if possible increase, this trend. Due to the firm's large amount of international business, world economics have a direct effect on corporate earnings. With inflation, increasing gold prices, political unrest, and the weakening of the U.S. dollar it was felt that it may be difficult to increase per share earnings at the present rate. To meet the corporate goal,

This case was developed by Professor Charles M. Futrell. The names of the company and the people involved have been changed.

management asked all operating divisions to recommend ways to reduce costs without sacrificing sales. Because the principal products of the corporation are in the ethical health care area, the pharmaceutical division came under close scrutiny.

The Pharmaceutical Salesperson

The pharmaceutical manufacturer's representative is commonly called a "detail man." He may also be referred to as a "pharmaceutical salesperson" or a "medical service representative." The function of a detail man is to promote the use of and sell ethical drugs and other pharmaceutical products to physicians, dentists, hospitals, and retail and wholesales drug establishments by utilizing his or her knowledge of medical practices, drugs, and medicines. He informs customers about new drugs, and explains their characteristics describing clinical studies conducted with the drugs. He also discusses dosage, use, and effect of new drugs and medical preparations.

Amos-Owen's salespeople are responsible for selling company products and disseminating information to all customers in their particular geographical area or sales territory. The salesperson is in constant contact with those individuals whose decisions influence sales in the area. The person who has the primary influence on drug sales is the medical doctor. Pharmacists, nurses, and hospital staff personnel can also influence the sales of prescription drugs. The chain of events that results in the sale of drugs can take three paths: the salesperson can directly sell injectable or oral medication to the physicians; the salesperson can persuade the doctor to write a prescription for the medication. The patient then takes the prescription to the drug store and has it filled. Finally, physician orders of medication in the hospital result in product sales. The principal channel of distribution is through wholesale druggists who sell to retail and hospital pharmacies. In addition, the companies sell on contract to the federal government, which makes products available through its distribution network.

Amos-Owens' management feels much of their success has been due to providing the medical community with useful, authoritative product information. They select their salespeople from applicants having varied educational backgrounds. For example, Exhibit 1 shows a breakdown of the salespeople's educational training, and Exhibit 2 lists the levels of education the salespeople have attained. Ninety per cent are college graduates and the remaining 10 per cent are individuals who have been with the company many years and were hired at a time when a college degree was not a job requirement. Predominately, salespeople

Exhibit 1
Salesperson's Educational Background

College Major	Relative Frequency (Per cent)
Physical Science	29.5
Business	25.0
Social Sciences	17.9
Education	9.7
Pharmacy	7.5
Engineering	1.7
Other[a]	8.7

[a]"Other" represents sales personnel with education or training obtained in the armed services or in such specialized areas as laboratory technicians, X-ray technicians, and physical therapy.

Exhibit 2
Salespeople's Educational Levels

Educational Level	Relative Frequency (Per cent)	Cumulative Frequency (Per cent)
High School	1.0	1.0
Some College	7.3	8.3
College Graduate	64.8	72.9
Some Graduate School	23.0	95.9
Master's Degree	3.9	100.0

have majored in the physical and social sciences and business. The company feels that a good educational background is desirable due to the technical aspects of their products and the educational backgrounds of their customers.

To be able to intelligently discuss the company's products with members of the health professions, the pharmaceutical salesperson must be well trained. Salespeople must possess information on competitive products as well as on their own. Consequently, each salesperson undergoes a four-week initial training program before being assigned to a sales territory. After the salesperson has been initially trained and begins to make sales calls on customers, he or she continues to receive updated product information. Once a month salespeople participate in sales meetings at which they are introduced to an occasional new product, given information on present products, and exposed to sales techniques that are designed to increase job effectiveness. Thus, product knowledge and sales techniques are the primary selling tools of the salesperson.

Organization Structure

Each of the corporation's sales organizations consists of a district manager and about nine to twelve salespeople. A single regional manager may be responsible for five to six district managers. Seven regional managers throughout the country report to the national sales manager, who in turn reports to the director of marketing. Staff members include a sales training manager, a sales promotion manager, a specialist in sales communications, and a marketing research manager. This organization, then, has the responsibility of administering the sales program.

The sales program's success stems from the sales obtained in the individual salesperson's territory. This sales area is a given geographical area that contains a certain group of physicians, hospitals, and wholesalers. The salesperson is required to make sales calls only on the members of the health profession and on accounts in the area. Thus, the sales generated by the salesperson are a function of a combination of factors such as medical personnel (physicians, dentists), retail pharmacies, hospital pharmacies, drug wholesalers, purchasing agents, the population in the territory, the promotional efforts of the company, federal and state regulations, seasonal factors, disease problems, and the ability of the salesperson.

Performance Appraisal The problem of appraising the performance of the individual salesperson can (because of the above factors) cause management difficulty. Because there is no sure way of knowing the degree to which sales in one territory or district benefit from detailing activities in another, performance evaluation is not based solely upon sales figures for the salesperson's territory. The salespeople's immediate supervisor evaluates their total job performance. Actual sales increase or decrease does enter into the evaluation process. However, it is somewhat subjective due to the many factors influencing sales. As shown in Exhibit 4, there are nine major areas of the job that are appraised each year. The salesperson's ability to meet overall sales quotas, and individual product quotas have always received major importance in performance appraisals. The other performance factors are the "means" to obtaining sales. They are used to develop a profile of why a salesperson's sales are increasing or decreasing. As shown in Exhibit 4 all of the major factors involved in selling pharmaceutical products are emphasized to salespeople because they are included in the yearly appraisal and stressed to the salespeople. Salespeople are expected to contact all customers and their key personnel in order to aid in selling.

Exhibit 3
Sales Force Organizational Structure

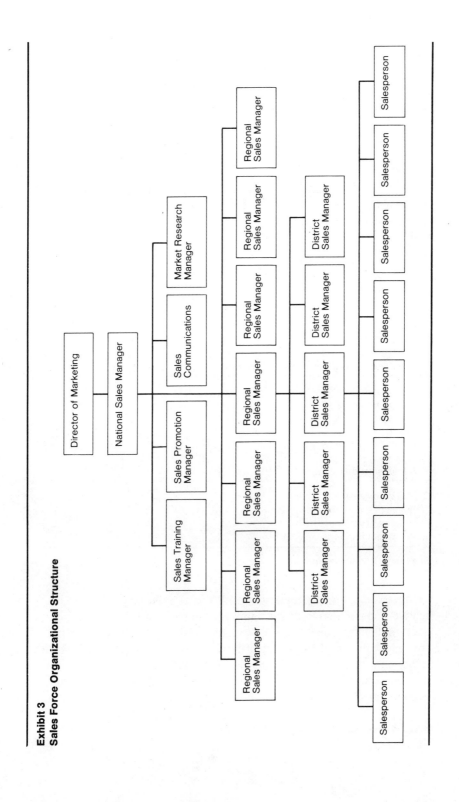

Exhibit 4
District Sales Manager's Yearly Appraisal

Name of Rep.:_____   Territory:_____

Skills	Outstanding	Satisfactory	Unsatisfactory
Product Knowledge			
1. Company products	[ ]	[ ]	[ ]
2. Competitive	[ ]	[ ]	[ ]
3. Medical vocabulary	[ ]	[ ]	[ ]
Overall Planning			
1. Preplanning sales presentation	[ ]	[ ]	[ ]
2. Customer call programs	[ ]	[ ]	[ ]
3. Call backs	[ ]	[ ]	[ ]
4. Use of daily written plan	[ ]	[ ]	[ ]
Overall Sales Skills			
1. Listening skills	[ ]	[ ]	[ ]
2. Doctor participation	[ ]	[ ]	[ ]
3. Ability to sell without pressure	[ ]	[ ]	[ ]
4. Ability to overcome objections	[ ]	[ ]	[ ]
5. Ability to ask for the business	[ ]	[ ]	[ ]
6. Clear, well-developed presentation	[ ]	[ ]	[ ]
Overall Hospital/Medical School/ Nursing Home			
1. Displays	[ ]	[ ]	[ ]
2. Key nurses	[ ]	[ ]	[ ]
3. Cultivates residents/interns	[ ]	[ ]	[ ]
4. Pharmacy relations	[ ]	[ ]	[ ]
5. Administration relations	[ ]	[ ]	[ ]
Overall Wholesaler Relations			
1. Speaks at monthly meetings	[ ]	[ ]	[ ]
2. Obtains promotions	[ ]	[ ]	[ ]
3. Personnel relations	[ ]	[ ]	[ ]

Summary Comments Here and on Reverse Side

Compensation   Salespeople are paid a straight salary, plus an incentive bonus determined on relative attainment of their district's sales quota. All salespeople receive the same amount, which is typically equivalent to 5 to 10 per cent of their salary. They are furnished with a car, and reimbursed for expenses. The company pays 100 per cent of their family health and life insurance. A sum equal to 8 per cent of their salary is paid by the company to a pension plan.

Sales Force Information System   Given the importance of sales, the corporation has developed an information system that keeps con-

Date:	DSM Name:		
Skills	**Outstanding**	**Satisfactory**	**Unsatisfactory**

Retail Calls

	Outstanding	Satisfactory	Unsatisfactory
1. Preplanning	[ ]	[ ]	[ ]
2. Rapport	[ ]	[ ]	[ ]
3. Knows people	[ ]	[ ]	[ ]
4. Checks, rotates stock	[ ]	[ ]	[ ]
5. Aggressively sells deals	[ ]	[ ]	[ ]
6. Details pharmacists	[ ]	[ ]	[ ]
7. Good shelf space	[ ]	[ ]	[ ]
8. Obtains promotions	[ ]	[ ]	[ ]

Personal Traits

	Outstanding	Satisfactory	Unsatisfactory
1. Attitude	[ ]	[ ]	[ ]
2. Ego	[ ]	[ ]	[ ]
3. Empathy	[ ]	[ ]	[ ]
4. Appearance	[ ]	[ ]	[ ]
5. Conference participation	[ ]	[ ]	[ ]
6. Self-improvement	[ ]	[ ]	[ ]
7. Human relations	[ ]	[ ]	[ ]
8. Management potential	[ ]	[ ]	[ ]
9. Paper work	[ ]	[ ]	[ ]

Sales
1. Sales potential: [ ] Growing   [ ] Static   [ ] Losing
2. Actual sales: $_____ _____ This year; $_____ Last year
3. Percentage improvement: _____% This year; _____% Last year
4. Meeting individual product quota: _____No. Quotas; _____No. Met

General
1. Is the person working at potential? _____Yes _____No Why?_____
2. Is the person devoting time necessary to maintain and improve sales
   territory? _____Yes _____No Why?_____

stant track of sales and gives each salesperson and manager totals for individual product sales in the geographic area. Daily, each regional office sends the sales communication office the sales totals on all products. Product sales are tabulated on a weekly, monthly, quarterly, and yearly basis and distributed to all sales personnel. For example, each week sales personnel received a report on the sales of products being emphasized by the sales force for the one month promotion period, and an update on total monthly sales. Product and territory sales quotas are based on past sales for the territory. Past sales of the territory, relative to the salesperson's district's sales, are the basis for developing the territory's sales potential. Only 5 per cent of the products account for 70 per cent of total sales. These products receive major promotional emphasis by the sales force during the twelve sales periods in the year. Quarterly and at the end of the year each salesperson also receives a sales report comparing last year's individual product sales to this year's individual product sales.

Furthermore, salespeople receive a monthly accounts receivable statement on all customers. It shows the customer's current amount owed, along with all or any part of that balance that is thirty, sixty, or ninety days past due. In addition, salespeople receive the account's sales to date, and a year-to-date summary of the dates and times each customer was contacted. This is developed from the daily customer computer call cards sent to the district manager by the salespeople. The district manager forwards these to the sales communication manager who uses the computer to develop these reports for all appropriate sales personnel.

Hospital and Medical School Specialist

In recent years all of the larger pharmaceutical companies have created a "hospital" sales force. The salespeople in these groups are responsible for the large hospitals and medical schools in a territory. They do not call upon retail or wholesale customers. Large hospitals, for example above 400 beds, represent large sales. Furthermore, medical schools contain many of the nation's leading authorities on drug usage. The medical doctors teach medical students the advantages and disadvantages of using one drug over another. Consequently they are opinion leaders in the medical community. Their positive opinion about a product can influence its use by the other physicians. These customers need an experienced, well-trained salesperson responsible for conveying complex, technical product information to these medical experts. John Richards, president of Amos-Owens has asked Scott Wiley, the national marketing manager, to develop a plan for the creation of a hospital sales force that would operate in each region and be responsible to its own national sales manager.

Pharmaceutical Companies Amos-Owen's two largest companies are Eli-Owens and Smith-Stone; both sell pharmaceuticals. Between the two companies they sell approximately 1,100 items, including different products and different sizes of the same product. Basically the two companies sell completely different products, but each has the type of sales organization structure shown in Exhibit 3. Each firm has a sales force of approximately 400 salespeople who often call on the same customers.

To corporate management, the merger of these two sales organizations seemed a long-run method of reducing selling costs without sacrificing the excellent promotion of products by their sales personnel. Yet there would be numerous problems and possible high short-run costs involved in such a major reorganization.

Questions

1. Describe the various factors that would be involved in merging the two pharmaceutical companies.
2. Discuss the salesperson's roles in selling pharmaceutical products. How is performance evaluated? Is the compensation program sound? Why?
3. Develop a single sales organization plan for presentation to Amos-Owen's corporate management.

Case 28

David Namer: An Interview with a Professional Salesperson

In February, 1975, Dr. Jeffrey A. Barach and two graduate business students were researching the ethics of salesmanship. In the course of their research, they met and interviewed David Namer, a professional salesperson for fourteen years, vice-president of a marketing research organization, and author of a manuscript called "The People Business."

In his manuscript, Namer was deeply concerned with salesmanship as a profession. He wanted to change the image of the salesperson and provide what he felt were the basic tenets of salesmanship.

The following is an edited transcript of the interview, wherein Namer is called upon to answer specific questions as to how his manuscript relates to the many "gray areas" encountered in the day-to-day pursuit of the professional salesperson. In several instances, passages from Namer's manuscript have been included to clarify his responses.

The appendixes include two "pitches" provided by Namer, in which he illustrates common sales techniques used in door-to-door encyclopedia sales.

Question: Mr. Namer, your book "The People Business" puts the sales profession on a very high plane. It appears that you

This case was prepared by Ladd Cutter and Brad McKean under the direction of Professor Jeffrey A. Barach, Tulane University, as a basis for classroom discussion and not to illustrate either effective or ineffective handling of an administrative situation. The case was revised for this text, with permission of the copyright holder, by Darrell Hankins, University of Alabama in Birmingham.

are saying salesmanship is practiced to some degree by everyone.

Namer: Everyone is involved in the people business. What is the people business? Nothing less than the day-to-day contact and involvement of people, which I call selling. From the first days of Adam and Eve, man has been trying to sell others his own ideas, beliefs, viewpoints or services.

Man is resistant to change, he will resist change, and will fight change all the way down the line. He must be sold, sold on an idea, sold on a product, sold on a service. This is why the salesperson is so important in society today and has been since the beginning of time.

Question: Do you mean that the consumer is too dumb to know what is good for him?

Namer: I don't mean that they're dumb in the sense of not being educated or not knowing what's going on around them. What I am saying is that they're ignorant about the *new things* going on around them, to the changes being made.

Question: Something disturbs me here, and that is the targeting of your book.

Namer: When I sat down to write the book, I reflected on my thirteen years in sales; I really like sales. During that time, I was constantly thinking of ways to improve the occupation, or upgrade it, of making it more professional. I wanted to bring salesmanship out of the "drummer" image and to spread that professionalism to all salespeople regardless of what they are selling. That is why I named my book "The People Business."

Originally, the book was to be targeted at salespeople; however, as it developed it turned out to be applicable in all phases of life. My main contention is that everyone is selling in their day-to-day interactions with other people. I'm selling my ideas to you and vice versa. Whether or not I get my ideas across to you determines the success of my presentation, whether or not I make the sale.

Question: Do you feel that salesmanship is inherent? Are there born salespeople?

Namer: There are no, or at least very few, born salespeople. To be an efficient, successful salesperson you must be trained. The concepts of selling are universal; they must be formulated, nurtured and grasped—then the means will fall into place, just like a puzzle.

Question: What selling experiences have you had?

Namer: I've sold just about everything: encyclopedias, magazines, coffee; recently I've been selling commodities including flour, rice, wheat, cement, lemon oil, etc., all in bulk lots.

Question: What about product knowledge? I think it would be difficult to sell cement without specific knowledge of its applicability.

Namer: Absolutely; the salesperson must have working knowledge of his product; he must have all the answers for anticipated questions.

Question: What about the sales pitch itself? There are some encyclopedia companies that entice a customer by promising a "free" set of encyclopedias as a neighborhood demonstration unit. The only catch to this is that the customer must furnish a letter extolling the virtues of the encyclopedia to the company and must keep the encyclopedia up-to-date for ten years with yearbooks, which add up to the full cost of the encyclopedia.

Namer: I can continue that! You know, Mr. Jones, that works out to less than half the price of a pack of cigarettes a day for a year. Now you know, seventy dollars a year for ten years, that's kind of ridiculous. Sending a check out every year, that's time-consuming for both of us. Tell you what I'm going to do. If you will agree to pay the $720, or $20 a month over a period of three years, we will give you, tonight, this beautiful book case, unlimited research service on the subjects of your choice, and so on. Isn't that fair?

Question: That's what I had in mind. Is it successful?

Namer: Absolutely, it's a beautiful pitch. It and its many variations are highly successful.

Question: Are people dumb or ignorant? Why do they fall for it?

Namer: I don't think people are dumb, I don't think they're ignorant either. I think people are unaware. They are ignorant in that they're not exposed to the business atmosphere. They don't know how things are done. In other words, a salesperson can enter the home and create the illusion that you're getting something for nothing. There is a little bit of larceny in everyone.

Question: Well, do you think that this is fair play? Would you use that pitch?

Namer: No, that is not fair in the sense that you are taking advantage of people who are unaware or are less aware than you are.

Question: Could you possibly provide us with an example of what you consider to be an unscrupulous sales pitch?

Namer: Certainly.

(THE PITCH, AS SUPPLIED BY NAMER, IS INCLUDED IN ITS ENTIRETY AS APPENDIX A.)

Question: You agree with what you wrote in your book. You stress honesty.

Namer: Yes, honesty and straightforwardness. To be truthful, however, I have used this pitch in my early selling days with both encyclopedias and magazines. I like to consider those early days tinged with deception and dishonesty as being my learning period. The latter portion of my career has been dedicated to honesty and legitimacy.

Question: Now, can you draw a line as to what is good and evil, black and white, so to say? The pitch that we've been talking about is obviously over the line, but you are not going to go completely the other way—for example, here are the issues, here are the pluses and minuses. That would constitute a judicial approach—your approach would seem to be more advocative.

Namer: I don't think you can draw a line. Each case must be approached individually. It depends on the product you are selling and the needs of the people to whom you are selling. Suppose I was selling quality encyclopedias to a family who could afford it. Assume that their children need and want the set. In this case I would apply pressure to an extent that I wouldn't normally use. I wouldn't take the approach that the children would grow up ignorant, that they will fail in society, that they won't complete high school, or will never get into college, etc. What I would say is that the children would not have the advantages of their peers.

Question: Can you give an example of what you consider to be within the bounds of ethical behavior? Something to demonstrate how you would handle the sale of a set of encyclopedias today?

Namer: That's not difficult. Instead of a canned approach, let me give you a scenario that will demonstrate quite graphically the dynamics of the sale, the events leading up to it, how I would handle objections, and several closes which I would use.

(THE SCENARIO AS GIVEN BY NAMER IS IN-CLUDED IN APPENDIX B.)

Question: Do you have to have absolute faith in your product before you step in the door? Have you sold items you didn't believe in?

Namer: At one time, when I was a lot younger, I was able to sell something I wholeheartedly didn't believe in, or that I thought was inferior. I think, and my ego confirms this, that I can sell anything to anyone because I'm a very good salesperson. Now morally I wouldn't sell if I didn't per-ceive a genuine benefit to the purchaser.

Question: On another track, there are times when a salesperson has built up the customer to the point of purchase—you say you can sell anything, disregarding ethical practices—at that point, to what extent is the customer begging the sales-person to help make the purchase decision? Is the fact that the customer was dumb enough to set himself up reason to rip him off like the tennis player who refuses to come to the net asks to be "chopped" at?

Namer: I don't think that people should be taken advantage of, unless they are aware of the rules. Tennis is a win-lose situation; when you enter the court you intend to take advantage of every weakness your opponent possesses, sub-ject to strict and unbending rules.

Question: You have stated in your book that life is a game, that America is competitive as is selling. How far towards the tennis court do you feel the salesperson should go?

Namer: You are right, but the rules and boundaries must be clearly stated to all contestants. You must be sure that all contes-tants play by the same set of rules. This is one of my major points. It's all right to take advantage—this might be a quirk of my thinking—of someone to whom you have clearly stated the rules. If you use a rule or fine print, but you've made him aware that the fine print exists, he has the equal opportunity of using that against you.

Question: Give me an example.

Namer: Take a company purchasing agent and a salesperson. When a contract is written it clearly states the rules according to which the product is delivered and under what conditions. Generally there are penalty clauses. The purchasing agent specifies a delivery date, the seller accepts knowing that he cannot deliver on time, but he needs that contract. The buyer has covered himself, knowing that the penalty clause will cover his company and ensure speedy delivery. Each has taken advantage of the other.

Question: Who is responsible for the sucker? What about the guy who has got to have something for nothing? Does this give license to the salesperson to teach him a lesson?

Namer: It is not the duty or place of a salesperson to teach the customer a lesson. The sole function of the salesperson is to sell his product, period. He may, by his function as product advocate, teach the customer a lesson but subsequent bad publicity may be detrimental to him and to his product.

Question: What about the obligation of the buyer?

Namer: The buyer has no obligation to the salesperson. The obligations of the sale rest solely on the shoulders of the salesperson.

Question: When industrial sales are made, big-ticket items are moved. Corporate salespeople do a great deal of entertaining, some involving large gifts, call girls, and the like. Do the ends justify the means using these sales techniques? Do kickback fall within the same category?

Namer: I would say that kickbacks do fall within the same category. My contention, as I've stated before, is that the buyer's role is to get what he wants at the lowest possible price. Any means that he has of achieving that is completely justified on the part of the buyer. The salesperson is the professional. It is his business to distinguish what constitutes a legitimate buyer from a phoney or unqualified buyer. If he can not, he doesn't belong in the business.

Question: Have you ever encountered a situation in which a buyer has indicated that he wanted you to furnish him with the company of a woman? How does the guy get his point across? How do you know?

Namer: There are many different ways. First, you will know through the grapevine that a particular buyer has an affinity for women, and salespeople who have provided him with what he wants have been awarded contracts. He might hint directly or indirectly to you that he wants a woman.

I wouldn't do this. I don't think any salesperson should. I think that only a very weak salesperson would resort to those tactics in order to make a sale. This includes excessive entertaining, kickbacks, whatever. I would rather not make this type of sale. This comes up to a lesser degree in encyclopedia sales. Sometimes, in order to close a sale, salespeople kick back part of their commissions. I have not done this in seven years of selling door-to-door. I would refuse to do it. Another ploy is to give away a premium such as a globe or a dictionary to get in the door.

Question: What if the salesperson encounters evidence of collusion or price fixing? What if, in a client's office, he spots a competing bid on the desk that indicates price collusion?

Namer: That is of no concern to the salesperson. That is a top management affair.

Question: What about cribbing information on your customer? When I used to sell, I would look across the client's desk and, if I saw competing bids, I would try to read the quotes.

Namer: That's not unethical, you have to know what other people are doing in order to compete. It's a dog-eat-dog world out there, they're doing it to you. You also need to know about your competitors so as to judge your own product.

Question: Many firms consider salespeople to be their intelligence-gathering force. What about the ethics of divulging privileged information?

Namer: It's the duty of the salesperson to scout out his competition. If you see something on my desk, it is public because I made no effort to hide it. If you rifle my desk, or if I tell you that something is off the record, it would be unethical of you to divulge it. However, the salesperson is almost morally obligated to utilize any information obtained ethically to his benefit. Observance is not dishonest, nor is it unethical.

Question: How about handling receptionists and secretaries? Is it ethical to woo them or to bribe them from time to time with little gifts?

Namer: When you go into a firm the first person you meet is a secretary or a receptionist. You must woo this woman to get her on your side. She helps you with your sale by making the buyer more accessible. I don't believe that is unethical or immoral. You are selling yourself and that is a very good quality.

Question: Let's consider retail selling for a moment. When a customer is trying to decide between two items, what is the salesperson's role here, and how does he avoid losing the sale because the customer can't make up his mind?

Namer: Three things come into play here. First, the salesperson must be an astute listener. He must sense which way the customer is leaning. Second, he must give the customer greater confidence to make up his own mind. In order to do this, the salesperson must be able to adapt to the customer's needs.

Question: Can you expand on the role of adaptability in selling?

Namer: I have found that adaptability is a trait that all salespeople must possess. The salesperson must always be ready to confront new selling situations and be able to cope with them. He must realize that he can not change people, that people change only when they want to, that he must change himself first, and that he must always be positive in his mental outlook.

Question: How does self-confidence fit in?

Namer: The basic principle on which the world of selling is founded is confidence or trust. Therefore, it is the salesperson's job not only to exude these qualities, but also to create a trusting relationship with his customer.

Question: In other words, you are saying that adapting to the customer's viewpoint is part of the process of building his confidence in his decision. That's an important point.

Namer: Often the buyer approaches the salesperson with a need or want before it is expressed in terms of a specific product or service. Through conversation the salesperson can assist the buyer in exploring and focusing on his need and can also explore his own capacity in terms of goods or services to satisfy this need. This interchange of ideas leads to a clarification of the buyer's problem and also to an understanding of how the salesperson can help solve it.

Question: Should a salesperson push a sale in light of obvious dysfunction? How hard should a salesperson push a higher ticket item despite the fact that it appears incongruous with the customer's appearance?

Namer: Yes, the sole function of the salesperson is to make a sale, within the ethics and morality of sound business practice. Anything he does to make that sale benefits his function in life. A customer that comes in and wants to spend his money should be able to, and if the salesperson can coax him to spend more than intended, that's fine. This really is a gray area of ethical behavior. Usually, if the salesperson can convince the customer to buy, that is sufficient justification that the customer wants the product. It's the customer's, not the salesperson's taste that matters. Sometimes, of course, it is more important in the long-run for the salesperson to be sure that the customer gets what he really needs. This is particularly true in industrial selling, where the salesperson is trying to solve the buyer's problem, and if he doesn't do it, he will lose the business to the salesperson who can.

Question: Okay, let's continue that train of thought. I'm concerned with the buyer's right to control his destiny when he walks into a store. Generally, the buyer's aim is to get the best possible deal. If, for instance, I went to a camera store selling many brands and ask for advice, suppose the salesperson recommends a certain brand of camera because he is paid "push money" by that manufacturer. Is "push money" ethical?

Namer: I would say that this would be an ethical approach to sales, if taken in the light that, even though the store sells many brands, it tends to specialize in one. Furthermore, if a person enters a store, asks for a specific model item, is satisfied with the price as quoted, you, the salesperson, are justified in making that sale regardless of the underlying motivations inherent in that sale.

Question: Okay, here is the final question. If, for instance, I am not mentally ready, not all fired up to lead a marketing class case discussion, what is lost? When I do my damnedest to present a case, what is the value-added in the difference between low-pressure, judicial teaching and high-pressure, advocative teaching, am I really selling?

Namer: Yes, I think you are. You're selling yourself and your ideas. What you're interjecting into the situation is a touch of realism, humanity, and warmth. You're getting away from the mechanistic process where you say this is A, B, C, etc.; choose any one, all or none. Just because the facts are stated in black and white doesn't mean there isn't a human element in there somewhere. You're placing yourself in the role of human being by expressing this humaneness, this enthusiasm. By doing so, you are conveying your thoughts; you are imputing to your listeners your excitement and enthusiasm; and you are drawing them out of their apathy, their blaséness. They get excited—maybe not to the point of agreeing with you, but even if you get them to the point that they disagree, you will have brought out their spirit. You have them thinking, you have them using what makes them unique, God's gift—their brains.

Questions

1. What responsibility does the salesperson have towards the prospect?
2. What is the role of salespeople in our economy?

Appendix A
David Namer: Encyclopedia as
Advertising Premium Pitch

AT DOOR

(KNOCK ON DOOR)   Hello! I'm Dave Namer with the Marketing
Division of Intercontinental Encyclopedias, Inc.[1] What is the family
name here? (GET NAME)

Mr. (or Mrs., depending on who answers the door) _____,
I'm not here to sell you anything. In fact, I am part of an advertising
and promotional campaign making a survey of *your* neighborhood's
ideas on education. If I may step in, I can better explain to both you
and your _____ (wife or husband) what this is all about. (STEP
TOWARD THE DOOR. IF ONLY ONE SPOUSE IS PRESENT,
RE-SCHEDULE TO COME BACK WHEN BOTH ARE THERE.)

INSIDE   (POSITION YOURSELF SO THAT YOU ARE
SEATED NEXT TO YOUR PROSPECTS; MAKE SURE THAT
T.V. AND STEREO ARE OFF, THEN PROCEED.)

Mr. & Mrs. _____, as I previously stated, I am taking a survey
of your neighborhood. The purpose of this survey is to select one
qualified family to participate in a rather unusual offer.

You see—Intercontinental has just come out with a new edition of
its educational library. After many years of planning and an investment
of over $30 million, we are now ready to market and sell our library.
In order to make the salesman's job a lot easier, we have decided to
place our library in the home of a selected family. This is done at
no cost or obligation to the qualified family.

(SHOW A PICTURE OF SET AND EXPLAIN.)   Now I know
what you must be thinking. No one comes into your home and gives
away over $500 worth of merchandise for nothing. There has to be a
catch, right?

Well, Mr. & Mrs. _____, there is a catch. See, we realize the
value of word-of-mouth advertising, especially between friends and
neighbors. Therefore, as you use your library, you will be so impressed
that you will tell your neighbors and friends about it. This will increase sales. But equally as important, when our salesmen are out in
the field, they can use you as a testimonial for our set.

In order to accomplish this, we will require three things from you:

[1]Fictitious company name.

First: sixty to ninety days after you have received the library and had a fair chance to look it over, we ask you to write us a letter giving your frank and honest opinion of the library. A letter of testimony, so to speak.

Second: the company reserves the right to photostat this letter and use it as sales material. You see, they're going to send their regular professional sales staff into your community in three or four months, and experience tells them the first question asked is who actually owns a library of this type here in town. Now, if they can truthfully tell these people the Browns over here and the Jones over there already own a library of this kind and can show them a letter of recommendation—well, you can get the sales psychology behind this, I am sure.

And third: that you keep the set up-to-date with our yearbooks. Remember that your neighbors will be coming to see your set. We want them to see, and for you to have, an updated set. You understand. (EXPLAIN YEARBOOK & BRING OUT PICTURE.) After all, if we *gave* you a Cadillac, would it be too much to ask you to buy the gas from our station? (GET A VERBAL "NO" FROM BOTH.)

Exactly the way that we feel about it too. The yearbooks cost us fifty dollars a year, which is the cost of a daily newspaper, and that is all that we will charge you. All we ask is that you maintain your set for ten years. Isn't that fair? (DO NOT WAIT FOR AN ANSWER, CONTINUE . . .)

Needless to say, to do our work properly, we must make placements intelligently. We must place these libraries with families who have a genuine use and appreciation for material of this type in their home. After all, if we place these libraries with families who have accepted it only because it was something for nothing, and stored it in the attic or used it as a doorstop, it would defeat our advertising purpose completely.

So, I would have to ask another question: If we could extend to you the invitation, would you and your family appreciate material of this type in your home? In other words—if there were nothing else involved and we would send you a complete twenty-four volume library and even pay the shipping expenses to get it here, would you be willing to give us the advertising help we ask for by writing a letter of testimony? (GET COMMITMENT FROM BOTH.)

(IF ANSWER IS IN AFFIRMATIVE) . . . Well, is this something that you and your family would use and appreciate over the years as well as now if you had it in your home? (GET COMMITMENT FROM BOTH.)

In summary, then, folks, all that we ask in return for this magnificent free library is that you:

1) Send us a testimonial letter;

2) Give us permission to use and reproduce it;

3) Agree to keep your set current for the next ten years.

In order to help you with the yearbook, we will send you an Intercontinental Calendar Bank. (EXPLAIN BANK). By saving fifteen cents a day, the cost of a daily newspaper, you can keep your set up to date.

Quite frankly, though, Mr. & Mrs. _____, the only objection that we've run into is that nobody wants to fool with fifteen cents a day for ten years, not to mention the cost of bookkeeping and accounting that we would incur.

Therefore, we have another proposition that will benefit both of us. If instead of taking ten years, you would pay for the yearbooks in three years; you would not have anything to pay for the remaining seven years. Also, you would save us seven years of bookkeeping costs.

So—if you will do this—pay for the yearbooks in three years, we will pass on our accounting savings to you by way of extra merchandise.

If you agree, we will send to you, at no cost, the following:

1. a fifteen-volume Junior Set (EXPLAIN);

2. a ten-year Research Service (EXPLAIN);

3. a bookcase (SHOW PICTURE).

Thus, for your advertising cooperation and your agreement to pay for the yearbooks in three years rather than ten, you will receive:

1. a thirty-volume Intercontinental Encyclopedia.

2. a fifteen-volume Junior Set

3. a bookcase;

4. ten-year Research Service;

5. yearbooks for ten years.

Now if I can get some information from you, I will see if your family qualifies for this program. (FILL OUT AGREEMENT AND CREDIT APPLICATION).

Well, Mr. & Mrs. _____, from all the preliminary information, your family qualifies. If you will fill out this Registered Owner's Card, then OK the application here (PUT "X" ON SIGNATURE LINE OF AGREEMENT), I will submit it to the home office for final approval.

Now all I need is ten dollars to cover the shipping charge, and we will process your application.

(PACK UP MATERIALS WHILE THEY WRITE CHECK OUT. AFTER BEING HANDED THE CHECK, STAND UP . . . WALK TO DOOR . . . AND SAY:)

Congratulations and welcome to the Intercontinental Family of Library Excellence.

(WALK OUT OF DOOR.)

Appendix B
David Namer:
Encyclopedia Sales Scenario

Namer: OK, let me set it up this way. Take the Braswells, Joan and
Ted, who live in a lower middle class neighborhood, comprised
mainly of one-story, single-family dwellings. The homes
have wash on the line, automobiles and pickup trucks occupy
cluttered carports, and toys and young children fill most
front yards. Ted holds a decent job as day-shift foreman at
a local manufacturing plant, his salary covers month-to-month
expenses. Joan helps out with the monthly budget occasionally by taking in wash and working part-time for a caterer.
They have two children, Anne 10, and Ted, Jr. 8.

Several weeks earlier Ted noticed an appealing coupon
insert in a national magazine, filled it out, and mailed it. The
advertisement promised a free booklet entitled "Views of
Tomorrow," which offered hitherto unimagined worlds to its
recipient in print, in glorious color photographs, and in
illustrations.

The postage-free card arrives in the national sales headquarters of Intercontinental Encyclopedias, Inc. (IEI). We'll
use a phony company so we don't step on any toes. It is
catalogued and then sent to the regional sales director in
charge of the territory where the Braswells reside.

Mike McNamara, our fictitious salesman, receives the card
as a lead, after paying a modest service charge to the
company. Mike is an independent sales agent who contracts
with IEI to market their encyclopedias in his territory. Mike
telephones the Braswell home to make an appointment.

"Hello, Mrs. Braswell, my name is Mike McNamara. I'm
a representative of IEI. We received a request that you made
for some information regarding the special offer we have
on the Intercontinental Encyclopedia set. I'm calling to find
out the best time to get together with you and your husband
to show you the details of this special program. I was
wondering if perhaps you had time this evening, or possibly
Friday or the weekend would be better for you?"

At this point Mrs. Braswell replies that they wouldn't be
home that evening.

Mike continues, "I see, well how about Saturday, will
your husband be home then?"

Joan answers in the affirmative.

"Aha, great, how about if we make it this Saturday at eleven o'clock, or say between eleven or eleven-thirty? Is that OK?"

Joan agrees.

"Great I'll be looking forward to seeing you then, thank you."

Mike is punctual. At eleven on Saturday, he parks his car at the curb, walks to the front door, and rings the bell.

Ted Braswell answers the door, Mike takes two steps backward and introduces himself.

"Mr. Braswell? Hi, I'm Mike McNamara from IEI. I have come to deliver the booklet you requested several weeks back depicting the wealth of knowledge and pleasure available to you from Intercontinental."

Ted scowls and says that he didn't expect any salesman, only the booklet.

Mike continues, "Mr. Braswell, Intercontinental is so excited about their new edition that they asked me to bring you free and without obligation their sixty-page colorful and informative booklet called "Views of Tomorrow," and complete details . . ."

Ted interrupts, saying that he is not interested.

Undeterred, Mike goes on, "and complete details on how to receive this magnificent set direct from the publisher on the special monthly payment plan."

Ted asks if there is any way that Intercontinental could put the booklet in the mail.

Mike responds, "Yes sir, there is. In fact we do have a booklet that we can mail out to you. Unfortunately though, there is nothing contained in that book that will give you the specific information that you are looking for. In other words, information on the quality of the bindings, the prices, and so on and so forth. This is why the company has asked that I take about fifteen to twenty minutes of your time to give you a review of what we've come out with. I feel that this would be twenty minutes of your time well invested insofar as your future and the future of your family is concerned. Whether you buy the set or not, at least you would have a more enlightened view of the set; and in the future, when you do get ready to buy, you'll be in a better position to make a decision."

Ted indicates that he has no intention of buying a set at this particular time, and apologizes for causing bother and inconvenience to Mike.

"Well, Mr. Braswell, it is my job to show this set on a
public relations basis. Whether you buy it or not is up to you;
in other words, all I ask is that you look at it. If you like
it, you buy it; if not, I thank you for your time.

"I feel that by showing it to you, it will not only give you
an awareness of just what Intercontinental is but also will
help to dispel a lot of rumors which may or may not crop
up about Intercontinental. It will also make you a very good
representative of our company. When someone comes to
you and starts talking about encyclopedias, you will be able
to give them the benefits of your education in that field."

Ted raises no further objections and, still skeptical, grudg-
ingly allows Mike to enter the room. Mike requests that
Mrs. Braswell be present for the demonstration. Ted goes
toward the rear of the house to summon Joan.

The most outstanding features in the room are an imposing
leatherette bar grouping, a new twenty-five-inch color television set, and a huge leatherette lounge chair. The rest of
the furniture is old and scratched; both the sofa cover and
the curtains are tattered chintz.

Mike hears Ted Braswell's loud voice from the rear of the
house, which indicates that he is venting his frustrations on
Joan for arranging the interview in the first place. Shortly
thereafter, the Braswells enter the room.

Mike reintroduces himself to Joan, "Hi, Mrs. Braswell, I'm
Mike McNamara, I spoke to you on the phone the other
day."

Joan reacts pleasantly, noting that the soothing voice that
she recalled from the phone call is attached to a well-
dressed, handsome young man.

Ted mumbles that it is about time to get "this thing" over
with and sits down in the lounge chair. Joan follows suit
on the edge of the sofa. Mike kneels down and delves into
his presentation case.

First, he brings a sample volume of the encyclopedia out
of the presentation case and hands it to Joan Braswell. She
accepts the book with the rich, dark brown, leather binding
and gives it an admiring gaze. She starts thumbing through
the volume while paying close attention to Mike.

"Mr. and Mrs. Braswell, as I indicated earlier, the reason
I'm here is to talk about IEI's new edition, which we feel
is a real breakthrough in the field of encyclopedias. We
sincerely believe that no other reference set can touch this
new edition and Intercontinental is so excited about it that

they have decided to introduce the set, complete with convenient credit terms, so that everyone can take advantage of our offer."

Mike proceeds carefully, step by step in company-approved fashion. His pitch is intentionally slow and deliberate, eliciting favorable responses from Mrs. Braswell at the close of each train of thought. Ted Braswell occasionally nods or grunts, but remains generally silent.

Mike describes the bindings and paper as the finest available. Joan agrees and passes the sample volume to Ted, who glances at it, flips it over twice, and then tosses it on the table. Mike continues unperturbed. He then emphasizes the star-studded panel of contributors, scientists, professors, businessmen, etc. who have lent their expertise in preparing IEI's new edition. It is a lengthy and impressive list. Mike then goes on to describe the attention to detail in the set; the time it took to collect and assemble the data; and the cost to finally produce the new edition. The figure is staggering.

Mike then begins to explain some of the valuable services that IEI provides for owners of their reference sets. He decides that he will start to work on Ted Braswell.

"Perhaps some day, Mr. Braswell, you might want to go into business for yourself. The Intercontinental research staff is at your disposal to answer any questions that might come up, be they on engineering, management, merchandising, taxes, accounting, or any other subject. At any rate, any technical question you might have about your present job would gladly be handled by IEI, too. Don't you think this could be very helpful to you?

Ted replies that it might come in handy some time. Mike goes on, "Mrs. Braswell, we can help you in the home to save time, steps, and money—three things I'm sure you're very interested in. Also, we'll help you with your outside activities. For example, if you were on the entertainment committee of the PTA, write and tell us how big your group is, what kind of budget it has, what kind of things were done in the past, and we'll supply you with information on what other groups like yours have done in other parts of the country." Joan nods enthusiastically and adds that such a service could be "invaluable" to her. Ted maintains his silence.

Mike keeps the pitch moving, "Incidentally, are your schools crowded in this neighborhood like they are everywhere else?" Joan replies that they "sure are." Mike continues, "Then you know that the brighter child has just as much of a problem as the child who gets behind. It seems that our schools are geared only to the average. With our service, your children can use this excellent learning tool to pursue their own interests and to help them if they have difficulty with any particular subject. You know, the curiosity of our children is probably our nation's most important asset. If we don't help them to find out how to get the right answers and encourage them to keep their interests in things, how will our country ever get the doctors, scientists, and leaders that we so desperately need?"

Joan Braswell responds immediately, "I want the very best for my children and this encyclopedia set could be the key to their future. If Anne and Ted, Jr. could grow up to be rich and famous, I'd pay almost anything."

At this point, Mike briefly outlines the credit terms that IEI offers. Neither Ted nor Joan objects to the payment plan he presents. Mike now has qualified his clients, created a need for the product, and arranged reasonable financial terms, the three key elements of a successful close. He then makes his first move toward wrapping up the sale. "Let me ask you, can you folks see how our encyclopedia set and services could be a great benefit to the future of your family?"

Ted Braswell replies, after a slight pause, "Well, it looks like a pretty good deal, but I don't think I want to spend the money right now. Why don't you come back in a few months?"

Mike begins to push, "Mr. Braswell, let me ask you just three questions before I go. Do you think your family would use and enjoy our encyclopedia set?" Ted nods yes. "Do you feel that IEI's $600 selling price is fair?" "Yes, I guess so," Ted answers. Mike counters, "You guess so, sir. Do you feel we're being excessive with the charges?" "No, not really. It seems to be a fair price," Ted finally replies. Mike then pops the most crucial question, "Can you afford the set?" Ted, a bit indignant answers, "Yeah, we can afford it, but I just don't want to buy it."

Mike then thinks he has them and starts to push harder. "Mr. Braswell, you've just told me that you feel your family will use and enjoy the set, that the set is worth it to you, and that you can afford it. I really don't think it would be fair of you to deprive your wife and children of this educational opportunity any longer. The price is bound to increase if you delay because of inflation. Besides, we're both here now. You've given me your time; I've given you my time and knowledge." Mike then decides to use what he hopes will be the clincher. "Mr. Braswell, if I could bring into your home a magician who could given you access to 10,000 of the world's greatest minds, who could recreate 10,000 of the world's greatest historic moment—all at your personal request, would you want him? Ted says, "Sure, why not?" Mike quickly proceeds, "The magician has only one drawback, you must give him a pack of cigarettes once a day. Wouldn't it be worth it to you to be able to have this magician for only one pack of cigarettes?" "Yeah," Mike answers, "but it's not the same as a bunch of books sitting in a corner."

Joan Braswell suddenly blurts out, "Ted, you're being stubborn. You're hurting the future of this family. If you won't come up with the money for this, I don't know what I'll do!"

Mike glances around the living room, eyeing the new bar set and the big color TV. He is forced to play his ace-in-the-hole. "There are only two basic reasons that a person won't buy this encyclopedia set. One, that person is absolutely destitute, completely broke, but looking around this room, I'd have to say you're living pretty comfortably. I think you'll agree with me there. The second reason is that the person is plain ignorant! But, I don't think you're ignorant, either. In fact, I believe you're an intelligent man. I think this encyclopedia is something you want, something your family wants, and particularly something your wife wants. Now, you don't want her to cut you off, do you? You're the one that's got to live with her. I really believe you'd be helping your family by taking this reference set."

"I guess you're right," Ted eventually answers.

Mike brings out his order pad while Joan and Ted whisper to each other. The details of the credit terms are easily worked out within a few minutes. Mike feels that he has performed another mutually profitable transaction. As he gathers up his possessions, Mike thanks the Braswells for their courtesy and adds, "Thank you for the order, I'll be on my way to get things moving on it properly. You should have the complete set by dinner time tonight. Welcome to the IEI family!"

Case 29

Mermax Toy Company, Inc.

Thomas Smith, vice-president of marketing for Mermax Toy Company, sat at his desk contemplating the memorandum he had just received from William Jones, president of Mermax. The memorandum, as well as the request outlined therein, came as no surprise to Smith, as it was merely a follow-up to the conference held the previous day among the top executives of Mermax. Various problems that Mermax was presently experiencing has been examined and analyzed by the group during their meeting. Among those problems were such issues as: (1) decreasing sales; (2) a loss in market share; (3) declining profits; and (4) excess inventory—consisting, mainly, of several "fad" items which had been overproduced. The executives were particularly concerned, because, until recently, the company had experienced steady growth since its inception. However, that pattern of growth had been interrupted by what seemed, in hindsight, to be several ill-advised decisions.

It was now early February 1981, and the executives had decided that by early June a long-range plan for 1982–1987 should be completed. They agreed that the plan should outline steps designed to turn the company around. The executives felt that at least some of their bad decisions had been the result of a lack of long-range planning. Smith's particular role in the planning process involved his taking a hard

This case was developed by Professor Charles M. Futrell for Mermax Toy Company. The company name has been changed. Copyright 1980.

look at the results of several marketing research studies recently completed by his staff. He had been instructed to utilize the results of these studies to develop a revised, overall marketing strategy for the company. The company's existing marketing plan was sketchy, at best, and had not been updated in recent years to reflect the type of strategies needed to compete successfully in a dynamic, ever-changing industry such as the toy industry. Specifically, the memorandum stated that Smith should overhaul the marketing strategy for the company's present product line; propose alternatives for the elimination of excess inventory items; investigate the possibility of new target markets; propose new products to reach those target markets; outline procedures for the production and timely introduction of those products; and develop procedures to create a sales force.

Smith, who had only been with the company for two months, knew that his performance on this task was crucial to his future with the company. His predecessor had been asked to resign as a result of the predicament in which the company found itself. The previous vice-president of marketing had failed to utilize marketing studies routinely performed by the marketing staff. He preferred instead to make "seat of the pants" decisions based upon his "feel" for the market. This method had proven successful for him in several instances, and, consequently, his fellow executives had come to rely on his judgment quite heavily. However, several poor decisions he had made regarding the production of "fad" items, as well as his increasing emphasis upon the marketing of such items, had caused the company to sustain some very heavy losses in 1974 and 1975.

Background on the Company Mermax Toy Company was started in 1953 by William P. Jones, father of the present company president. During its first decade and a half, the company was a closely held corporation; all of its stock was held by members of the Jones family. In the late 1960s, the corporation went public in an effort to raise additional capital for expansion. During the first fifteen years of operation, Mermax manufactured toys and games for children in the five- to fourteen-year-old age bracket. Their product line consisted of "staple" items—cars, trucks, trains, dolls and traditional games. They manufactured high quality toys—a major objective of the company from its inception. The company's distribution channel was a manufacturer's agent, Glass and Associates, that sold directly to retailers—primarily exclusive toy stores and better department stores in large cities throughout the nation. Jones and Bob Glass, head of Glass and Associates, had been friends since high school. Glass handled non-competing lines of toys and had excellent relations with major department stores and toy stores in the fifteen largest cities in the United States.

As disposable income grew in the 1960s, the top executives of the corporation decided they must expand their product line if they were going to maintain their market share. The expansion monies were used to introduce a greater variety of staple products, as well as several "fad" items. The "fad" items proved successful for a few years, encouraging the company to venture even further into this area. As a result, more and more emphasis was placed upon the introduction of fad products. Such items have a short life cycle and are risky to manufacture. Most of the fad items introduced by the company in 1974 and 1975 had failed in the market place. This resulted in the profit loss with which the company was now faced.

The Toy Industry The toy industry is a highly competitive industry in the United States. As an industry, it has enjoyed steady growth since the early 1950s. In 1969 total industry sales were about $2.2 billion. By 1972 industry sales reached the $2.7 billion mark, an increase of 12.8 per cent over the previous year's $2.4 billion in sales, and reached $16.9 billion in 1979. Toy sales are highly sensitive to consumer spending patterns, i.e., they depend heavily upon disposable income. The product lines of toy companies are generally characterized as broad and constantly changing, and a company's success is largely dependent upon its ability to develop new products that respond to changing shifts in tastes and preferences. Furthermore, the toy industry has historically been considered highly seasonal in nature; it has been heavily dependent upon Christmas for the bulk of its sales. With the advent of television, promotion became a major component in the marketing mix, as companies came to rely more and more heavily on television commercials to promote their products.

The late 1960s and early 1970s brought changes to the industry as a whole. Costs rose as a result of several variables: (1) increasing costs of raw materials; (2) increasing costs of labor; and (3) increased emphasis upon toy/product safety. Toy companies also began to receive criticism from various consumer groups for deceptive packaging and advertising. Furthermore, the industry was faced with a declining birth rate, as well as shifting preferences, primarily in the ten- to fourteen-year-old age group. Moreover, distribution patterns were changing as discount stores entered the retail scene throughout the country. In order to combat the seasonal nature of their business, as well as the declining birth rate situation, many toy companies began to diversify. They entered related areas such as motion pictures, pet products, amusement parks, sporting goods, swimming pools, and beach products.

Mermax Marketing Studies Thomas Smith was well aware of the various shifts and movements in the industry as a whole. With hindsight he identified quite readily numerous opportunities that had been missed by Mermax. He believed that some of the strategies that had been implemented by various successful toy companies were worthy of consideration by Mermax. However, he was also aware that if Mermax was to regain and/or increase its market share, he must also anticipate future trends upon which Mermax could capitalize. For such projections, he turned to the recently completed marketing studies that had been done by the Mermax marketing staff. In these studies he noted a rising demand for: (1) preschool products; (2) toys that were educational in nature; (3) unisex toys; (4) games; (5) crafts; and (6) sporting goods. He noted also that there was a growing demand among adults for the last three product areas mentioned. Furthermore, one of his studies indicated an increasing demand in overseas markets. These markets had proven successful for some companies in the marketing of fad items whose life cycle had peaked in the United States. Yet, Smith felt he needed to be cautious. An article in *Standard & Poor's Industry Survey* reported that electronics had increased sales for the entire toy industry, but several of the large toy makers were experiencing profit losses.

With these variables in mind, he proceeded to sketch out the first draft of his new marketing proposal for Mermax Toy Company. Included in the plan would be the development of a sales organization. Smith would examine the total toy market; develop the organizational structure; establish geographical units; develop a job analysis, description, and specifications; recruit, select, and train salespeople; develop a compensation program; and establish an appraisal system for both individual salespeople and the sales organization.

Questions

1. Discuss and/or develop a marketing program for Mermax, including steps to take in creating a sales force for the firm.